'You **don**'t have to be able to hum M[...]
engro**ssing**. As a fan of both the fabl[...]
Glover, *Mozart in Italy* is a match ma[...]
down.'
Joanna Lumley

'An ac**c**ount of the teenage Mozart's operatic awakening is packed
with **hum**anising detail . . . [Glover] makes clear that Mozart lived
very **much** in the real eighteenth-century world of dirt, illness, bedbugs **and** discomfort, not permanently wrapped in some fuzzy
golden halo of brilliance.'
The Guardian

'*Mozart in Italy* is a fascinating account of classical music's greatest
failure – a story of promise unfulfilled, opportunities missed and
roads not taken.'
The Spectator

'A fine conductor, Glover is also an accomplished writer, displaying,
as in her earlier books, a nonchalant grace in marshalling her
sources, reading cannily between their lines and taking care to provide proper historical context as the Mozarts zigzag over the
chessboard of Italian princely states.'
Literary Review

'Glover's historical awareness of Italy's operatic legacy is profound,
like her expertise on things Mozartian . . . Glover is, rarer than a good
conductor, an enchanting explainer. Her literary approach resembles
her sometimes exceedingly subtle and decorous conducting.'
Opera Now

'Brimming with life, Glover's vibrant account of Mozart's unique
and absorbing adolescence is joyously rewarding.'   *Toronto Star*

MOZART
IN
ITALY

In Jane Glover's long and hugely successful career as a conductor, she has been Music Director of the Glyndebourne
Touring Opera, Artistic Director of The London Mozart
Players, and, since 2002, is Music Director of Chicago's
Music of the Baroque. She has conducted all the major
symphony and chamber orchestras in Britain, as well as many
in the United States of America and across the world. She
appears regularly at the BBC Proms and is a regular broad-
caster, with highlights including a television series on Mozart.
She is also the author of *Mozart's Women* and *Handel in
London*. *Mozart in Italy* is her third book. She lives in London.

Also by Jane Glover

Mozart's Women
Handel in London

MOZART
IN
ITALY

Coming of age in the land of opera

JANE GLOVER

PICADOR

First published 2023 by Picador

This paperback edition first published 2024 by Picador
an imprint of Pan Macmillan
The Smithson, 6 Briset Street, London EC1M 5NR
EU representative: Macmillan Publishers Ireland Ltd, 1st Floor,
The Liffey Trust Centre, 117–126 Sheriff Street Upper,
Dublin 1, D01 YC43
Associated companies throughout the world
www.panmacmillan.com

ISBN 978-1-5290-5990-8

1 3 5 7 9 8 6 4 2

A CIP catalogue record for this book is available from the British Library.

Map artwork by ML Design

Typeset in Ehrhardt by Jouve (UK), Milton Keynes
Printed and bound by CPI Group (UK) Ltd, Croydon, CR0 4YY

Visit www.picador.com to read more about all our books
and to buy them. You will also find features, author interviews and
news of any author events, and you can sign up for e-newsletters
so that you're always first to hear about our new releases.

for Kate and Richard

Contents

Mozart in Italy – First journey

HOLY ROMAN EMPIRE

SWISS CONFEDERATION

KINGDOM OF SARDINIA

MILAN

REP. OF GENOA

D. OF PARMA

D. OF MODENA

REP. OF LUCCA

Ligurian Sea

Corsica

KINGDOM OF SARDINIA

GRAND DUCHY OF TUSCANY

PAPAL STATES

REPUBLIC OF VENICE

Adriatic Sea

Tyrrhenian Sea

KINGDOMS OF NAPLES AND SICILY

Ionian Sea

Towns and cities visited by the Mozart family on their first journey to Italy

① Salzburg
② Innsbruck
③ Bressanone
④ Bolzano
⑤ Trento
⑥ Rovereto
⑦ Verona
⑧ Mantua
⑨ Cremona
⑩ Milan
⑪ Lodi
⑫ Parma
⑬ Bologna
⑭ Florence
⑮ Rome
⑯ Naples
⑰ Loreto
⑱ Rimini
⑲ Brescia
⑳ Turin
㉑ Vicenza
㉒ Padua
㉓ Venice

Mozart's first journey
→ December 1769 to March 1771

0   25   50   75   100 125 miles
0   50   100 150 200 kilometres

Mozart in Italy – Second and third journeys

HOLY ROMAN EMPIRE

SWISS CONFEDERATION

MILAN

KINGDOM OF SARDINIA

REPUBLIC OF VENICE

D. OF PARMA

D. OF MODENA

REP. OF GENOA

REP. OF LUCCA

Ligurian Sea

GRAND DUCHY OF TUSCANY

PAPAL STATES

Adriatic Sea

Corsica

KINGDOM OF SARDINIA

Tyrrhenian Sea

KINGDOMS OF NAPLES AND SICILY

Ionian Sea

MEDITERRANEAN SEA

Towns and cities visited by the Mozart family on their second and third journeys to Italy

① Salzburg
② Hall
③ Bressanone
④ Bolzano
⑤ Trento
⑥ Rovereto
⑦ Verona
⑧ Brescia
⑨ Milan

Mozart's second and third journeys
---⇄--- August to December 1771
···⇅··· October 1772 to March 1773

| 0 | 25 | 50 | 75 | 100 | 125 miles |
| 0 | 50 | 100 | 150 | 200 kilometres |

List of Illustrations

Author's Note

After I wrote *Mozart's Women*, nearly twenty years ago, I thought that I had said all I had to say about the composer whose music has most engrossed my life, joyously, challengingly, and with immeasurable spiritual reward. In that book, I told his story (which hardly needed telling, yet again) through the prism of the women in his life: his mother and sister, his wife and her sisters, and the remarkable women for whom he wrote. But I subsequently came to realize that I had largely skimmed over one part of his life, simply because none of those women was directly involved in it: the three extraordinarily important trips he made with his father Leopold to Italy, at the most impressionable of ages. I had reported on these only as he and his father had described them, in letters back to his mother and sister, and therefore as the women had received them. There was so much more to investigate, in their actual experience of travel, of social encounters, of hardships as well as delights, and of course of musical influence and then achievement – all in the context of a country which has beguiled and inspired its visitors since the days of its earliest civilization. As I performed the music that Mozart wrote in these crucial years, I became increasingly convinced that, at some point, I did need to repair my sins of omission.

Then, in 2020, the Covid catastrophe happened. The planet

screeched to a halt, and all our lives were changed: we found ourselves in social isolation, with bewilderingly empty diaries. So I revisited this subject, and began to formulate this book. My wonderful agent, Maggie Hanbury, supported the project, and our old friend and colleague Georgina (George) Morley, who has edited my last two books, accepted it. Between devastating waves of infection and lockdown, I did manage to travel to Austria and Italy, and follow the routes that Mozart and his father had taken – exactly two hundred and fifty years later, as it happened. (With one glorious piece of serendipity, I found myself in Bologna on the exact anniversary – to the day – of Mozart's taking the examination for membership of the august Accademia Filarmonica. I attended a conference there that evening, and sat in the very room where he had taken the test.) Despite lockdown restrictions and closures, I was able to access most of what I needed; and, everywhere I went, I met courtesy, assistance and encouragement.

My profound thanks therefore go first to Maggie and George, for their sharp eyes and sympathetic ears; and to George's formidable team at Picador (Rosie Shackles, Nicholas Blake, Penelope Price, Stuart Wilson, Lindsay Nash, Bryony Croft and Connor Hutchinson). Jonathan Keates, superb historian, writer and fount of all knowledge relating to Italy, read the book in typescript, and as always was generous with his time, and extremely perceptive with his comments. My brother-in-law John Price, antiquarian book dealer, has again been crucial to my locating eighteenth-century publications, especially during the months of restricted access to libraries. Nick Guthrie accompanied and supported me on the inter-lockdown journeys in Austria and Italy. I am constantly grateful to all the musicians with whom I continue to perform the music of Mozart, for the insights they bring to it, and for the discoveries that we make together. And my greatest gratitude, really, is to Mozart himself, for sustaining me, not just through a lifetime of collaborative performance, but through the solitude too of lockdown, from which I could escape into a past world of adventure and beauty.

'In no country have I received so many honours, nowhere have I been so esteemed as in Italy; and certainly it is a distinction to have written operas for Italy.'

Mozart to his father, 11 October 1777

'Nothing can be compared to the new life that the discovery of another country provides for a thoughtful person. Although I am still the same I believe to have changed to the bones.'

J. W. Goethe, *Italian Journey*

1

⟶ ◦⧫⧫⧫⧫◦ ⟶

CIRCUMSTANCE

'His father wishes to take him to Italy'

More than almost any other country, Italy has influenced the course of European, and often therefore world, development. Although it was not united until 1861, the peninsula as a whole has repeatedly been a pioneer in thought and, especially, culture. From the mighty stability of the Roman Empire, powerful and far-reaching for several hundred years from the third century BC, to the intellectual explosions of Renaissance Florence, Italian states have led and illuminated the civilized world with a matchless confidence. If the chaos and instability of Italy's political allegiances lend some confusion to the narrative of its history, the constant beacons of its artistic achievement – coupled with the staggering beauty of its many different terrains – have ensured that the peninsula has been an irresistible and beguiling magnet to those from other lands.

Throughout the eighteenth century, the geopolitical map of Italy was subject to much change. The basic components remained the same: at either end of the peninsula were the large kingdoms of Sardinia in the north and Sicily in the south; between them lay the all-important Papal States, the Grand Duchy of Tuscany and the smaller but impressive duchies of Milan, Parma and Modena; and then there were the independent republics of Venice in the east and Genoa in the west. But, as in the rest of Europe, there were kaleidoscopic shifts of territory and boundary, largely the consequence of long-standing hostilities between the (French) Bourbons and the (Austrian and Spanish) Habsburgs. Back in the sixteenth century Italy had been the main battleground between them, until France had renounced its territories in the peninsula in exchange for others, and in the seventeenth century the focus of their enmity had shifted to northern Europe. There, alliances became religion-based too, when the conflict between Catholics and Protestants resulted in the Thirty Years' War (1618–48). As Spain's power declined and the Habsburg regime weakened, France became predominant. The Spanish Habsburg Charles II died in 1700, at which point Louis XIV of France claimed his throne for his grandson Philip, giving rise to the War of the Spanish Succession (1701–14), won by France. As the eighteenth century progressed, there were further wars and skirmishes (the War of the Polish Succession, 1733–5, and especially the War of the Austrian Succession, 1740–8), all of which continued to alter the colours of the European map. In the north, Austria was threatened by Prussia, and France by Britain. But in 1756 – the year of Mozart's birth – the old alliances switched dramatically in the Diplomatic Revolution: Prussia joined Britain, and Austria joined France. For the first time in 200 years, the two opposing dynasties were finally standing together. The War of the Austrian Succession was the last major conflict before the French Revolution to involve all European powers, and the second half of the eighteenth century was to remain relatively stable.

In much of this European warfare the Italians had been somewhat peripheral participants, and as France withdrew its attention from the peninsula, Austria's interest was renewed. The key player in an energetic quest to secure Habsburg dominion there was that most important ruler in the age of enlightened absolutism, the Empress Maria Theresa. Her marriage at nineteen, in 1736, to Francis Stephen, Duke of Lorraine, would lead to her first encounter with Italy, when Francis became Grand Duke of Tuscany in 1737. Over the next nineteen years she bore him sixteen children: her last, Maximilian Franz, was born in the same year as Mozart. Ten of them survived into adulthood, and eight of them could, as soon as they reached their mid-teens, be coolly – ruthlessly, even – married off to spouses with territorial advantage. In a hectic decade of imperial matrimony between 1760 and 1771, Maria Theresa secured Habsburg tentacles in Spain, Bavaria, Saxony, France (with her youngest daughter Maria Antonia destined for her wretched guillotine), and especially Italy.

The first of the marriages with Italian reward was in 1760, when Maria Theresa's eldest son and heir, Joseph, later her co-regent and finally her successor, married Isabella of Parma. Isabella died only three years later, a bereavement from which Joseph never really recovered. Maria Theresa then arranged Joseph's second marriage, to Maria Josepha of Bavaria, daughter of Charles VII, the Holy Roman Emperor. This marriage too was brief, for Maria Josepha died of smallpox in 1767; Joseph never married again. Meanwhile the Empress had earmarked her daughter Johanna, ever since she was a child, for the Crown Prince Ferdinand of Naples. But Johanna had died of smallpox in 1762 at the age of twelve, so Maria Theresa's next daughter, another Maria Josepha, had been lined up instead. Then poor

Maria Josepha also died of smallpox in the same year as her identically named sister-in-law, so yet another daughter, Maria Karolina, was inserted as a swift replacement. That marriage duly took place in 1768; Maria Karolina became Maria Carolina, and spent the rest of her life in Italy. In the following year Maria Theresa moved in on Parma again, marrying her daughter Maria Amalia to its Duke Ferdinand. This was a joyless marriage (the bride had been happily expecting to marry a man she truly loved, Prince Charles of Zweibrücken, and never forgave her mother for destroying her plans), but Maria Amalia too spent the rest of her life in Italy. Nearby, in Modena, young Princess Maria Beatrice d'Este was marked as a bride for Maria Theresa's third surviving son, Ferdinand: they would marry in 1771, when he was seventeen. Her second son, Leopold, in addition to marrying the Infanta of Spain, had inherited the Duchy of Tuscany from his father on Francis' death in 1765. So Maria Theresa had strong family representation down the spine of Italy. For Austrians travelling there in the second half of the eighteenth century this was fertile ground: there were familiar and sympathetic links with those in charge, from one region to the next.

And there was indeed much travel in eighteenth-century Italy. In those reasonably tranquil decades between the end of the Seven Years' War in 1763 and the arrival of Napoleon's occupying forces in 1796, there was a flood of traffic from northern Europe. This was the age of the Grand Tour. Travellers were increasingly drawn to the peninsula by its history, antiquity and culture, its great natural beauty and gorgeous climate, its delicious and often exotic food and wines, and its vibrant festivities at regular points in the year; and their experiences broadened their minds. Many of them kept diaries and journals, copious in detail, and some of these were then turned into travel guides for the instruction of those who followed. In Britain, Thomas Nugent's mighty (four-volume) *The Grand Tour: Containing an Exact Description of most of the Cities, Towns, and Remarkable Places in Europe*, for instance, was published in 1743 and much reprinted, as young Englishmen (very rarely English women) encouraged each other to travel. Similarly, in Germany, Johann Georg Keyssler's immensely thorough *Neueste Reisen durch Deutschland, Böhmen, Ungarn, die Schweitz, Italien und Lothringen* was first published in 1740–1 (with an English translation appearing in 1760) and much reprinted and disseminated. Mozart's father Leopold acquired his own copies of Keyssler's four volumes after the 1751 reprinting; their richly informative pages were crucial to all the planning that he would deploy for himself and his family. Whenever and wherever the Mozarts travelled, Keyssler's relevant volumes came too.

For all those heading to Italy, the principal destinations were the same. The main focus was the Eternal City and capital of the Papal States, Rome. Its vibrant, multi-layered, ancient and modern history and the buildings, sculptures and artworks associated with it, and its position as the spiritual centre of the Christian world, gave it an overwhelming predominance in the planning schedule. Tourists would aim to arrive in Rome in time for Holy Week, when people flocked to St Peter's Square to receive a papal blessing. The guidebooks generally agreed that, with a daily dose of three hours' sightseeing, a visitor would need at least six weeks to experience the full glory and grandeur of Rome. Florence, the heartbeat of the Renaissance, with its somewhat slower pace and smaller scope, was nevertheless full of glorious palaces and churches, rich with paintings and sculpture; and the Uffizi Gallery, housing the many possessions of the Medici family, was opened to the public in 1743. (This was the last wish of Anna Maria de' Medici, defiantly retaining the family's treasures for Florence, as Maria Theresa and her Bourbon husband Francis brought the Grand Duchy into the Habsburg-Lorraine dynasty.) Venice, once the centre of a powerful republic with huge international trading powers, had by the eighteenth century lost its political and economic supremacy, but was still unique in its staggering aquatic beauty. Its reputation now was as a city of wonderful dissolution, and travellers would plan to be there especially for its Carnival season, which ran for several weeks. (In Rome, Carnival was over in twelve days.) Once there, they could revel in its extravagant pleasures of regattas, masquerades, street parties, gambling and courtesans. But again, its palaces and churches were ablaze with architectural, pictorial and sculptural evidence of the city's glorious past; and there was opera too, in the city which a century earlier had established the art form as an entertainment for all classes, and built or adapted theatre after theatre to accommodate it. And the fourth unmissable centre for any Italian visitor was Naples. Despite its huge and apparently uncouth population (one traveller, Leonardo di Mauro, described it as 'a paradise inhabited by devils'), its setting in its bay, with Vesuvius – preferably smoking – in the background, was breathtaking. For tourists seeking extreme adventure, there was the challenge of actually climbing the volcano, negotiating cinders and hot ash. Then the allure of the city's own rich heritage was, in the eighteenth century, more than doubled by the archaeological excavations in Herculaneum (begun in 1738) and Pompeii (1748). As fascination with these grew, and Naples's appeal superseded even that of Florence, the southern half of the peninsula began to open up. But it was still relatively barren of culture in comparison with the north, which also contained the smaller but dynamic centres of Milan, Parma, Mantua, Modena and Bologna, all densely packed with their own treasures.

Of especial interest to eighteenth-century travellers, even those with essentially philistine tendencies, was Italy's paramount place in the history of music. In all contexts, liturgical, instrumental or theatrical, its diverse artistic centres had been leading the way for centuries. From the early organization of plainchant, supervised by Pope Gregory in the seventh century, to the supreme polyphonic sophistication of Palestrina, or the rich polychoral contrasts of the Venetian school in the Renaissance, church music had thrived in Italy, with high standards of performance, and with the involvement too of instruments – not just organs, but consorts of cornetts or viols. In the seventeenth century, as instrument-makers in Cremona and other north Italian cities developed the brilliant new violin family, the writing of purely instrumental music surged too, and the concerto style of Corelli, for instance, was soon being imitated all over Europe. But Italy's main musical revolution before the eighteenth century was in theatrical music. The earnest invention of a 'reciting style', or *stile recitativo*, whereby dramas could be entirely sung rather than spoken, in music which followed the natural inflections of speech rhythm, led, around 1600, to the birth of opera. This dazzling new art form, combining as it did drama, music and spectacle, spread in the seventeenth century away from the privileged courts of Florence and Mantua into the public theatres, first in Venice, then across the whole of Italy, and subsequently throughout Europe. Different countries adapted opera to their own requirements, but Italy continued to build opera houses in all the major cities and towns (Venice alone built or adapted as many as sixteen of them between 1637 and 1700), and to produce the personnel – composers and singers – to execute it. Going to the opera in Italy was as natural and regular as going to church: it was a way of life.

Italian opera in the eighteenth century fell into two distinct categories: comic and serious. Comic opera, or *opera buffa*, had its roots in the *commedia dell'arte*, with uncomplicated vocal writing, and told lively stories in everyday contemporary settings, often incorporating local dialects. *Opera seria*, on the other hand, concentrated on ancient heroes in neoclassical settings, with a high moral tone, generally following the Aristotelian unities of drama. The operas were therefore designed to educate as well as entertain, although a tragic ending was usually replaced by a happy one, or *lieto fine*: virtue really should triumph. The singers who delivered these lofty roles were extremely competent, and with the development of the art form came the development of their vocal technique. As the eighteenth century progressed, from Caldara through Alessandro Scarlatti, Vivaldi, Handel and Hasse, individual arias depicting single emotions became very elaborate, and audiences were attracted to opera as much by the flamboyant display from its performers as by any dramatic content. In due course, some librettists and composers complained about this, deeply regretting the relegation of drama to a position of secondary importance. Gluck, in the preface to his opera *Alceste*, performed in Vienna in 1767, famously railed against the 'mistaken vanity of singers', which distorted any coherent storytelling; his own operas restored an essential balance between dramatic impetus and musical repose. But, while this revolution was stirring north of the Alps, Italians remained perfectly content with their familiar *opera buffa* and *opera seria*, and with the dazzling exponents of it that they continued to produce. For the greatest singers across Europe all came from Italy. They were treated like royalty and paid enormous sums of money, and were as responsible as the composers for attracting musically minded European travellers to eighteenth-century Italy, where unquestionably good opera was always and everywhere to be found.

Travel to and in Italy in the eighteenth century was, if not by sea, by carriage. Some travellers hired or even purchased private coaches, with two or four horses; others relied on post-coaches, which had regular timetables and carried both passengers and parcels from region to region, from country to country. Despite having very hard seats, giving general discomfort therefore on long journeys, the post-coaches were larger and quicker than the private conveyances, often being drawn by as many as eight horses. Depending on the prevailing terrain, a coach would travel at an average speed of four miles per hour, and horses would have to be changed and refreshed at staging posts, ranged approximately fifteen miles apart. The maximum distance a traveller could achieve in a day would therefore be in the region of fifty miles. But nothing was guaranteed: all travel was at the mercy of the weather. Heavy rain or snow, causing blocked passes or swollen rivers, could delay progress for hours if not days. In the winter months little travel continued after dark, particularly in temperatures of extreme cold. But in the summer, and especially in the south of Italy where the daytime heat was often insupportable, passengers preferred to rest during the daylight hours and continue their journeys through the night. Unless a carriage was privately owned or rented, which granted relative freedom in the making of decisions, seats on a post-coach had to be negotiated, and there was often a bewildering range of prices, depending on the number of passengers, the number of horses, even the number of wheels. All carriage travel came with risks and dangers. There were not infrequent accidents (overturning vehicles, broken axletrees, lame horses), and in remote rural regions there could be bandits, robbers and highwaymen.

Particularly in view of potential crime, it was inadvisable to carry much money on long journeys. Furthermore there was a wide range of currencies in different countries or regions, and exchanges at borders could involve pricey or even dodgy commissions. So travellers carried instead letters of credit from their banks, or from a private source, and these could be honoured by corresponding banks elsewhere. And just as currencies varied from region to region, so indeed did the very roads on which the tourists travelled. Throughout Europe, and especially in Italy, much of the road system was based on that created centuries earlier by the Romans; but surfaces were often poorly paved, if at all. Again, the weather affected the condition and maintenance of roads, especially on mountain passes where they could become insuperable by carriage. In that case passengers had to dismount and proceed on foot while their vehicle was dismantled, laboriously hauled over the summit, and reassembled on the other side. Travellers approaching the Alps from the northern countries of Britain or the Low Countries could be overwhelmed by their first sight of them, and utterly daunted by the feats they would have to endure to surmount them. But for Austrians, like the Salzburger Mozarts who had grown up among mountains, they held less terror, although no crossing of them, especially in winter, can have been without peril.

If there was great variety in the quality of roads, so there was in the provision and quality of accommodation. Even fundamental comforts were often at a premium. Generally there was decent lodging to be had in the main towns and cities, whether at inns or in rented rooms. Luckier travellers, with connections or letters of introduction to local family members or acquaintances, could recover from the rigours of a journey in some luxury. But in the long distances between major cities there was little if any comfort to be found. Roadside inns offered the most basic conditions, with terrible food and sanitation, little warmth (unglazed windows were separated from the elements by thin paper coverings), and a veritable menagerie of vermin, bugs and fleas. For gentlemen travellers these were challenging conditions indeed; for women they would have been almost unimaginable.

No eighteenth-century tourist travelled light. First, his luggage would have to include clothes for all seasons and for all occasions, from the most formal and grand (exotic and bejewelled) to the most basic (the very clothes in which indeed, often for days on end, he travelled). In wooden caskets he would carry his toiletries and everything needed for washing and shaving. Then he would need guidebooks and other books of instruction or language; maps, a compass and perhaps a telescope, together with tables for calculating distances, and lists of post-changes; writing tools, including paper, ink and sand; a medicine chest containing his own preferred remedies for any number of possible ailments or injuries; and then, probably, some kind of weapon for self-defence, whether a sword or a pistol. For travelling musicians like the Mozart family, there would also be instruments and scores. All this would be stowed in vast trunks, whose safe passage into the post-coaches also had to be negotiated and afforded.

When the thirteen-year-old Wolfgang Amadeus Mozart and his father Leopold set out for Italy in December 1769, they were already old hands at the whole business of travel. Leopold, a court composer in the service of the Prince-Archbishop of Salzburg, had an unusually broad background. His education and training had been in the classics, philosophy, law and music, first in his native Augsburg and then at the Benedictine University in Salzburg. After a brief period as a violinist in the service of Count Johann Baptist Thurn-Valsassina, he had joined the Archbishop's court as a fourth violinist, supplementing his lowly salary by teaching. It was this experience as a teacher, coupled with Leopold's profound if somewhat restless intellectual curiosity, which led him to write a teaching manual, *Versuch einer Grundlichen Violinschule* – of exceptional value to students and performers both then and ever since, and also, in its compulsive and authoritarian detail, indicative perhaps of an obsessive side to his nature. His *Violinschule* appeared in 1756, the same year that his wife Maria Anna gave birth to their son Wolfgang. He was the seventh and last child that she bore him, but one of only two survivors. Their daughter Maria Anna, always known by the diminutive Nannerl, was five years old when her baby brother was born.

From early infancy both children were discovered to have outstanding musical abilities. Leopold began to teach Nannerl the piano when she was seven years old, and was thrilled at her natural proficiency and rapid progress. In July 1759, just before her eighth birthday, he put together a collection of keyboard pieces for her. But then, in Nannerl's tenth year, Leopold became even more aware of her brother's gifts. Aged only four, Wolfgang too was working through Nannerl's music book, and quickly mastering its contents. By the time he was five he was also composing his own little pieces, and his astonished father was writing them down for him. As Leopold nurtured the burgeoning gifts of both his remarkable children, he began to formulate plans to display them to a wider world.

In 1792, the year after Wolfgang's tragically early death, it was Nannerl who told of the first occasion that the Mozart family had taken to the road. Compiling an invaluable set of childhood reminiscences for an article in an obituary collection, published by a young German scholar named Friedrich Schlichtegroll, she remembered their 'first journey . . . to Munich, where both children played before the Elector [Maximilian III]'.[1] This was in the early months of 1762, when she was eleven and Wolfgang had just turned six. Apart from the fact that they then remained in Munich for three weeks, there is no documentation of their stay. But this trip was the first time that Leopold had planned a route, selected and organized accommodations both on the journey and at the destination, and met head-on the whole paraphernalia of taking a family including two small children on the road. Munich is approximately ninety miles from Salzburg, so the journey alone would have taken at least two days, and most likely three. Together with the three weeks they actually spent in Munich, the family would have been absent from Salzburg for nearly a month. But clearly Leopold's planning and the children's performances were such a success that a longer and more ambitious journey was instantly devised. If they had so delighted the Elector of Bavaria, why not aim for the Empress Maria Theresa herself? Leopold set his sights on Vienna.

Since any journey to the capital, some 185 miles from Salzburg, would involve a considerably longer period than the Munich trip, Leopold had to establish a system of funding and cash flow. It was then that he initiated a routine that would endure for many years, involving the landlord of the Mozarts' small apartment on the third floor of Getreidegasse 9. Johann Lorenz Hagenauer was a spice merchant who operated his business out of the same building. In addition to being Leopold's landlord, he was also a close friend – his wife Maria Theresia and their eleven children were constantly around Nannerl and Wolfgang as they grew up – and now, effectively, Hagenauer became Leopold's banker. He provided him with letters to his business contacts in other towns and cities, and this mercantile credit network would allow Leopold to acquire cash wherever he went. When he returned to Salzburg, Leopold would have to repay all these sums, so it was imperative that the family should somehow acquire monies, whether rewards or gifts, while they were away. And Hagenauer had another function too. On their travels Leopold would write detailed letters to him describing their activities (challenges as well as triumphs), whose contents Hagenauer should then dispense widely among the Salzburg cognoscenti. If there was anything that Leopold did not wish to have broadcast, he would make this emphatically clear to Hagenauer.

The journey to Vienna in the autumn of 1762 took nearly three weeks in itself. The Mozarts did not take the most direct route, but first travelled north to Passau, where they spent five days. They then continued to Vienna by river transport, on the Danube (Europe's second-largest and most impressive river), certainly the fastest way to travel in that downstream direction. They stopped at Linz and remained there for another five days, as Leopold continued tirelessly to build important links in his network of people with influence who could blaze their trail. This was another technique of his which, honed here, would successfully be deployed for several years. As he wrote to Hagenauer from Linz on 3 October 1762:

my children, the boy especially, fill everyone with amazement. Count Herberstein has gone on to Vienna and will spread in advance a sensational report about them. And yesterday Count von Schlick, Captain-General of this district, left with his wife for Vienna. Both were uncommonly gracious towards us. They said that, as soon as we reached Vienna, we must go to see them; meanwhile they would speak to Count Durazzo and make our arrival generally known there. To judge by appearances, everything ought to go well.[2]

The family arrived in Vienna in reasonable health, considering what Leopold admitted was 'our irregular life, early rising, eating and drinking at all hours, and wind and rain', and instantly began to progress through the upper echelons of society.[3] Within a week of their arrival they were already at its pinnacle: they were received at the Palace of Schönbrunn by the Empress Maria Theresa herself, together with her husband and younger members of her family.

At this stage Maria Theresa was evidently very taken with the gifted and enchanting children. She listened to them playing; she let her daughters Johanna and Maria Antonia (at twelve and seven, both close in age to Nannerl) take them on a tour of the palace; and she arranged for them to spend time with her youngest sons Ferdinand (eight) and Maximilian (six – the same age as Wolfgang) three days later. The lives of some of these young archdukes and archduchesses would intersect again with Wolfgang's within a few years. Next, Maria Theresa sent the Mozarts suits of clothes – effectively hand-me-downs from her own children's wardrobes, but of a quality and finery beyond anything the Mozart family would have experienced. Nannerl and Wolfgang had their portraits painted in these clothes, and they also wore them to subsequent gala evenings at the Hofburg, which they all attended as spectators. And, best of all perhaps for Leopold, the Empress sent the family a gift of one hundred ducats, with indications that she would happily receive them all again. Leopold was heady with all this success. It was not just that one hundred ducats far exceeded his own annual salary in Salzburg. He began to envisage a future in which ready money could be acquired with relative ease. The world was opening up.

There were of course setbacks. Both Leopold and, more significantly, young Wolfgang had periods of illness. Wolfgang was out of action for ten days with what was deemed to be scarlet fever, so all performing appearances were suspended: if he could not play to admirers, then neither apparently could Nannerl. ('We had to send messages to all the nobles.'⁴) Then, while the Mozarts were on an excursion further downriver to Pressburg (now Bratislava), Leopold's own illness (actually little more than severe toothache) stalled them again. On their eventual return to Salzburg at the beginning of 1763, an exhausted Wolfgang, still not quite seven years old, took to his bed for a week. But ultimately this Vienna visit had been a triumph, and Leopold was completely addicted to the sequence of travel, exhibition and reward. Within six months of their return, the entire family were off again. This time they would be away for three and a half years.

∾

Leopold's plan was to travel through Germany to France, cross the sea to England, cross back again to visit the Low Countries, and return home. The main focal points were to be the sumptuous royal courts of Paris, London and The Hague, but en route they would take in many other cities, including Munich again (renewing their favour with Elector Maximilian), Mannheim, Frankfurt, Brussels, Amsterdam and Geneva, giving as many concerts as they could arrange, and receiving monies with which to finance their onward progress. Fortunately for Leopold, foreign travel for Salzburg musicians was much encouraged by his current employer, Prince-Archbishop Schrattenbach. Many of Leopold's court colleagues, both singers and instrumentalists, were going abroad to hone their skills, mainly in Italy, so it was by no means unusual for him to petition for a substantial leave of absence too. Remarkably, his salary would continue to be paid while he was away, and this essential sum, if not exactly copious, would be the bedrock of his travel budget. Again with Hagenauer's help, Leopold then set up his financial network with bankers and merchants in towns and cities on his route, and he simultaneously initiated his chain of influential contacts who would provide performing opportunities and introductions to the greatest salons. These contacts would be continually activated and renewed on their travels. Leopold acquired his detailed guidebooks and devoured their contents, working out routes between the main cities where the family would spend weeks if not months, and identifying possible stopping places to break up the long periods of travel between them. Inevitably his basic plan would again be subject to change, depending on any number of factors – the weather conditions (with which not surprisingly Leopold was constantly obsessed), the health of all four Mozarts, and the unexpected opening or indeed closing of doors in strange lands. He polished up his linguistic skills. In addition to his native German, fluent French and comfortable Italian, he would need to understand and speak English; and he had to initiate his young children too into all these languages' basic requirements. But having already sharpened his organizational abilities on his two previous expeditions, Leopold was now more than ready to embrace the foreign unknown.

The trials and tribulations, but ultimately the triumphs of the Mozarts' own Grand Tour are well known and documented. The family did indeed gain access to Europe's crowned heads (after the Elector Maximilian came Louis XV in Paris and George III in London), and its greatest salons. They made an enormous amount of money – much more than Leopold would ever divulge even to Hagenauer (perhaps least of all to Hagenauer) – and received a dazzling array of gifts including watches, jewellery, snuffboxes, fans, fine materials and lace, all of which had to be piled into their travelling trunks or somehow sent back to Salzburg. The children were constantly performing in public, whether in the gilded halls of Versailles or in the upstairs room of a London tavern (Leopold resorted to rather desperate measures when London emptied of society during the summer months, and his funds were running low), and were confident, exquisitely proficient and infinitely charming. Wolfgang could also sail with nonchalant perfection through any musical test or challenge that was put in front of him. Wherever they went, they met count-less musicians and heard their compositions, both at court and in public places like concert halls or pleasure gardens, and their musical palettes expanded beyond Leopold's wildest imaginings. Wolfgang continued to compose too, not just little pieces for him-self and his sister to play, but, in London at the age of only eight, his first symphonies – quite phenomenally assured and idiomatic works, after the manner of those by the London-based Germans Carl Friedrich Abel and Johann Christian Bach. Their visual experience of the world literally opened up before them: as they left their mountainous region of Austria, they travelled through lower-lying countries, and finally saw the sea for the first time when they crossed from Calais to Dover (with some discomfort – none of them, it turned out, was spared seasickness). They saw palaces, castles, cathedrals, fine parks, great paintings, impressive statuary. They learned much about European history through the exhilarating medium of experiencing its real consequences. They met people from a complete cross section of European society, and were comfortable with all of them. In a most spectacular way, the Mozart children were having a matchless education.

There were of course terrible times too, which certainly balanced the euphoria of achievement and reward. In these strange and literally foreign conditions, Nannerl and Wolfgang had to endure more childhood illnesses, and their mother, without recourse to familiar doctors or medicines, had to nurse them. In Holland, Nannerl was so ill with an intestinal typhoid that her parents truly feared they would lose her: on one grim night she was even given the last rites. But Nannerl pulled through, and in fact lived to the age of seventy-eight, displaying a sturdy resilience which was not shared with her brother. Wolfgang did recover from his many bouts of sickness, but was fundamentally debilitated by them: for the rest of his life he never truly enjoyed vibrant health. But he took his illnesses in his stride, as he did every other setback, disappointment or inconvenience. It is a tribute to Leopold, and perhaps especially to Maria Anna, that, through all the chaos and discomfort and disorientation of travel, their children felt secure, appreciated and loved.

༄

The Mozarts returned home at the end of November 1766, to the proudest welcome from the town, and a rather more impatient one from the court. Without doubt they had brought great credit to Salzburg, and had made sure that Hagenauer had dis-seminated widely every detail of their triumphant passage across Europe. But they had been absent for much longer than anyone had anticipated. Just before they left, in 1763, Leopold had been promoted to the position of Vice-Kapellmeister, when the Ital-ian tenor Giuseppe Francesco Lolli had become Kapellmeister. Leopold had accepted his post with no increase in salary, which was perhaps a fair arrangement since he had spent so little time at his court duties, and was about to absent himself again. The whole system of remuneration was bewilderingly arbitrary and inconsistent. Although the stipend of all court musicians com-prised a basic wage plus payment in kind (regular allowances of wine, salt, bread, grain, firewood), some appointments came with free lodging, but not others; some promotions involved salary increases, but not all. The ladder up which Leopold no doubt hoped safely to climb was in fact very rickety. And now, after his long absence, he will have been expected by his employer the Archbishop Schrattenbach – and no doubt his musical colleagues too – to exercise his duties. So while Leopold certainly received the admiring compliments of his friends and neighbours, and put all the glittering booty from their travels on display in Getreide-gasse (in a special cabinet he had asked Hagenauer to procure in advance of their return), he scuttled back to work with some trepidation, and resumed his position with – for the moment – an air of solemn obedience.

For the rest of the family it was perhaps just as well that Leopold was out of the house for most of the day. Even after the cramped conditions of their travel arrangements, to which they had all become completely accustomed, their third-floor apartment in Hagenauer's building on Getreidegasse must have felt claustrophobically small for a family of four. There was only one real bedroom, in which both children had been born, plus a living room, a study, a small storage room and a kitchen. In comparison with all they had seen and experienced, these were meagre spaces, especially as Nannerl was now fifteen and surely desirous of some privacy. But while Leopold was out at court, the rest of them resumed their normal activities. Maria Anna ran the house; Nannerl and Wolfgang continued their home-schooled studies and practised their instruments; the whole family picked up the parlour games and card games that they so enjoyed. And Wolfgang composed.

Since taking huge strides on his recent travels, writing music had become for the eleven-year-old not just an enjoyable thing to do, almost like a game, but a real passion. Leopold was undoubtedly guiding and overseeing his son's progress, and marvelling at the results, but he was by no means dictating or controlling them. He seized on opportunities for Wolfgang's music to be presented locally. In the course of 1767, the boy had several works performed in public, and three of them especially showed his phenomenally precocious development in new and complex directions. In March he wrote the first act of a Lenten sacred drama, *Die Schuldigkeit des ersten Gebots,* K.35. The other two acts were by Leopold's very adult colleagues, the composers Michael Haydn (younger brother of Joseph, and a colourful, if not entirely reliable, or indeed sober, member of the Archbishop's cohort) and Anton Cajetan Adlgasser. The text was supplied by a local textile merchant, Ignaz Anton von Weiser; the performers – both singers and instrumentalists – were also Leopold's colleagues on the court roster; and it was performed in the Archbishop's Residenz. This was followed by a passion cantata, *Grabmusik*, K.35a, presumably also performed in the Easter period. And in May Wolfgang wrote a short comic opera, to a Latin text no less (he surely had some help here from his father), *Apollo et Hyacinthus*, K.38, to be performed by students of the Benedictine University between the acts of a Latin tragedy, *Clementia Croesi*. All three works, written and performed within weeks of each other, are remarkable, whether setting German or Latin texts, whether for solo singers or duets, trios or choruses, and are refreshingly imaginative in their awareness of mood and gesture, and in their ability to be colourfully descriptive.

Yet even as these excitements occupied the thoughts and activities of the Mozart family through the spring and summer months of 1767, they will have speculated as to where they might travel next. For Leopold the obvious lure of Italy was becoming inevitable, and he was no doubt eagerly consulting his travel guides and history books. But then his attention was aroused and diverted. The much-heralded marriage between Crown Prince Ferdinand of Naples and Maria Theresa's twelfth child (and second choice), the Archduchess Maria Josepha, was due to be celebrated in Vienna in October 1767. As with all royal weddings, this would be a glittering and richly social occasion, attracting nobility from far and wide; and Leopold perceived a golden opportunity. He had glorious memories of the family's encounters with the Empress and her children back in 1762. Now that one of those archduchesses was to become prominent in Naples, which Leopold had every intention of visiting, he could not only impress the imperial family with the continued development of his prodigious children, but at the same time set up a powerful connection in southern Italy. In September 1767, after only ten months at home, he secured yet more paid leave, along with other colleagues including Michael Haydn (a Salzburg presence at these high-profile festivities would only reflect well on Schrattenbach's court), and set off for Vienna. If the wedding was taking place in October, the Salzburg musicians would surely be back by Christmas. But, unlike his colleagues, Leopold once more packed up his entire family.

This time, however, nothing went according to plan. First, the Empress herself was considerably changed. Her beloved husband Francis had died in 1765, and she felt his loss keenly. She had partially withdrawn from public life, and had promoted Joseph, her eldest son and successor, to act as co-regent with her. When, five years earlier, the Mozarts had first come to Vienna and petitioned to be heard by Maria Theresa, they were welcomed to the Palace of Schönbrunn within a week of their arrival. Now they met only deflections and polite refusals. Leopold, somewhat contrary to his nature, resolved to be patient. He settled the family into an apartment on Weihburggasse, worked on building his Viennese network of useful people, and sampled as much as he could of the city as it excitedly prepared for the big marriage ceremony. The Mozarts saw elaborate firework displays and illuminations, and attended plays and, most significantly, operas. Among the operas they heard, within two weeks of their arrival, was *Partenope*, commissioned for the wedding festivities from the veteran composer and master of the *opera seria*, Johann Adolph Hasse, to a text by the court poet and already legendary librettist Pietro Metastasio. Leopold pronounced in a letter to Hagenauer: 'Hasse's opera is beautiful, but the singers, be it noted, are nothing out of the ordinary for such a festive occasion'.[5] Nonetheless Hasse, whom the Mozarts came to know well in the ensuing weeks, and 'Signor [Venanzio] Rauzzini, from Munich, the leading castrato', at just twenty-one already enjoying an exciting career, would both within a few years become important to Wolfgang in Italy. And meanwhile the wide-eyed and open-eared eleven-year-old boy was absorbing and learning from the most distinguished opera composer of his day.

But then another drawback occurred. Vienna had earlier that year been hit by an epidemic of smallpox, which, as with all diseases, was no respecter of class. Maria Theresa herself had caught it and recovered; but her daughter-in-law, Josepha, Emperor Joseph's second wife, had died of it in May. Now the Archduchess Maria Josepha, the bride-to-be, visited the tombs of her father and her late sister-in-law in the week before her marriage, and suddenly fell ill too. She died on 15 October, the very day that she should have been married. A further wave of smallpox surged through the traumatized city, giving Leopold yet more anxiety, not just for the safety of his own family, but also for the state of their finances. He confessed in confidence to Hagenauer that he needed extra funds: 'Do not be surprised if we draw four hundred or even five hundred gulden . . . Perhaps in one single day I shall pay it all back. So far we have played nowhere, for we have not yet performed at court.'[6] Having drawn his extra cash, Leopold moved his family away from Vienna, travelling over a hundred miles north to Olmütz (now Olomouc) to try to escape smallpox. But it was too late: first Wolfgang and then Nannerl contracted it. Mercifully they both recovered, and the Mozarts took refuge for three weeks over the Christmas period in Brünn (now Brno) with Franz Anton Schrattenbach, brother of their Salzburg Archbishop. When they finally got back to Vienna in mid-January, they had already been away from Salzburg for four months, and had no intention yet of returning.

At last the Mozarts were received at court. On 19 January they played before the Empress Maria Theresa and several of her children, including the Emperor Joseph. And in the course of a pleasant afternoon of gracious small talk, the Emperor apparently made a casual remark about opera, asking young Wolfgang if he had ever thought of writing one. Leopold excitedly took this to be an invitation to do so, and put his son to work on composing his first full-scale dramatic work in Italian, *La finta semplice*, a comic opera to a libretto by the resident poet at the Burgtheater, Marco Coltellini. But the opera was never performed in Vienna. Leopold believed that there were hostile intrigues against the notion of a (now twelve-year-old) boy composing a whole opera, and that Wolfgang's deserved path was being blocked. For several months he made a nuisance of himself with the Burgtheater's exasperated manager Giuseppe Affligio, with any number of musical dignitaries whose support he attempted to reel in (including none other than Gluck, whose truly mould-breaking *Alceste* had just been premiered in December, while the Mozarts were in Brünn), and even writing querulous protestations and appeals to the Emperor Joseph himself. And meanwhile, as time continued to pass and still the Mozarts failed to return home, Leopold's Salzburg salary was stopped: he had far overrun his permitted leave of absence. For virtually the whole of 1768 the family remained in Vienna, with some benefits certainly, for Wolfgang continued both thoughtfully and instinctively to learn and compose, to attend as many opera performances as he could, and to give concerts of his own music. In a small indication that the imperial family could soften their attitude to the now tiresome Leopold, Wolfgang was invited to compose and conduct a concert of his own music, including a whole Mass, at the consecration of the orphanage church, in December. Maria Theresa herself attended this, together with her youngest sons, the Archdukes Ferdinand and Maximilian, Wolfgang's former playmates. But when at the end of the fallow year the Mozarts finally returned to Salzburg, the disasters of their sixteen-month absence far outweighed the advantages. They had lost money, had little exposure, and in fact had seriously damaged their own reputation: Leopold's badgering of both the theatrical authorities and the imperial family was to have long-term consequences. But Leopold himself seemed to be quite unaware of the profound havoc he had wrought.

One impressive ally, though, was Johann Adolph Hasse. The sixty-nine-year-old opera composer had come to know the Mozarts during their stay, and had observed and possibly even guided the keen interest and development of the young boy. (It is very tempting to speculate on how much the family were aware of the achievements of Hasse's wife, the retired Italian soprano Faustina Bordoni. Her own hugely successful career had taken her, some forty years earlier, to London for three seasons to work with none other than Handel; and her perceived rivalry there with fellow Italian Francesca Cuzzoni had been most passionately followed and colourfully chronicled. After she married Hasse in 1730, her career had run in parallel with his, in both Italy and Germany, and had been altogether more sedate and comfortable. They were much lauded as a partnership: Metastasio referred to them as 'a truly exquisite couple'. Faustina, as she was universally known, had retired from the stage in 1751.) Leopold had clearly appealed to Hasse for support, if not in the debacle of *La finta semplice*, then certainly – planning ahead – in contributing to his chain of influential people for the much-contemplated visit to Italy. Hasse's response was both generous and candid. On 30 September 1769 he wrote to a wealthy and well-connected Venetian friend and opera lover, Giovanni Maria Ortes, introducing the Mozarts and explaining their circumstances:

I have made the acquaintance here of a certain Sig. Mozard, *maestro di capella* to the Bishop of Salzburg, a refined man of spirit and of the world; and who, I believe, knows his business well, both in music and in other things. This man has a daughter and a son. The former plays the harpsichord very well, and the latter, who cannot be more than twelve or thirteen years of age, is already a composer and master of music. I have seen the compositions which must be his own, which certainly are not bad and in which I have found no trace of a boy of twelve; and I dare not doubt that they are by him, seeing that I took him through various tests on the harpsichord, on which he let me hear things that are prodigious for his age and would be admirable even for a mature man.

Hasse then arrived at the point of his letter, which he handled with considerable delicacy:

Now, his father wishing to take him to Italy to make him known there, therefore wrote to me asking me to give him . . . some letters of recommendation, and I shall take the liberty of sending him one for you. You see how much I presume to rely on your kindness. This letter shall, however, have no other aim than that you might permit him to make your acquaintance and that you will consent to give him your usual wise counsel, such as you may judge useful and necessary for him in your country; and if, apart from this, you should introduce him to and let him be heard by some lady of your acquaintance: that will be much more than I shall have led him to expect.

Following this careful request, Hasse concluded his letter with a summary of his own clear-eyed and actually quite prophetic response to the Mozarts:

The said Sig. Mozard is a very polished and civil man, and the children are very well brought up. The boy is moreover handsome, vivacious, graceful and full of good manners; and knowing him, it is difficult to avoid loving him. I am sure that if his development keeps due pace with his years, he will be a prodigy, provided that his father does not perhaps pamper him too much or spoil him by means of excessive eulogies; that is the only thing I fear.[7]

The Mozarts returned to Salzburg on 5 January, and again Leopold slotted back into the large team of instrumentalists and singers who supplied music at court. As Vice-Kapellmeister he would have had responsibility for teaching the boy choristers, as well as for playing in or directing ensembles for any number of formal or informal occasions; and sometimes Wolfgang was brought in too, generally as a supplementary violinist. But Leopold's salary, which had been suspended since the previous April, was still being withheld, and in early March he was compelled to write a formal petition, pleading not just for payment for the two months that he had actually just served, but also for the previous nine months in Vienna. During that time, he claimed, somewhat preposterously, 'I myself as well as my son have composed sundry things for the Church, and especially for the use of the archiepiscopal Cathedral Church'.[8] The court pay office would have none of this, but did reinstate Leopold's pay from the beginning of January, and thus his essential security was restored.

The family resumed its normal domestic life in the ever-cramped conditions of the Getreidegasse apartment – confines probably felt more keenly by Nannerl, now approaching her eighteenth birthday, than by her brother. And yet Wolfgang, for all his teenage exuberance, had no need of monastic silence for his own creative spirit to take flight. As he would repeatedly demonstrate throughout his life, he could compose music in any circumstances, no matter how crowded or noisy or uncomfortable. So now, as Nannerl practised her piano and began, like her father, to teach, Wolfgang continued to increase his portfolio of compositions. Inspired by the operas he had seen in Vienna, and especially following Hasse's example, he wrote several Italian arias, often settings of the mighty Metastasio. Instrumental chamber pieces for various combinations of instruments – constantly exploring and developing his palette – and more symphonies too all flowed from him, as he happily pursued his favourite pastime. His father's connection with the Benedictine University, and his own recent experience of writing *Apollo et Hyacinthus* for them, gave him another platform for supplying music for their end-of-year ceremonies. And he continued to write church music, following his Waisenhaus Mass, K.47a, for the orphanage in Vienna, and the new level of confidence he had attained there. One very special commission came from the family of the Mozarts' landlord and good friend, Lorenz Hagenauer. Hagenauer's son Kajetan had recently entered the priesthood at St Peter's and was due to celebrate his first Mass there, as Father Dominicus. For this occasion Wolfgang wrote his Dominicus Mass, K.66 – 'the most splendid and ingenious music', wrote St Peter's abbot, Beda Sauer, approvingly in his journal[9] – and after the service he improvised at the organ before a packed congregation. On the following day there was a celebratory lunch for fifty people at the Hagenauers' summer house in the outer district of Nonnthal, and again Wolfgang, together with Leopold and

Nannerl, entertained the guests with more music, 'to everyone's astonishment'.[10]

Meanwhile the Mozarts were still anxious to get some return from Wolfgang's unperformed Viennese opera, *La finta semplice*. To Wolfgang's profound and lasting frustration, there was no opera house, and therefore no opera company, in Salzburg. But they conceived a plan, borne on the success of Leopold's rehabilitation among his court colleagues, to perform the opera at court on 1 May 1769, the name-day of Archbishop Schrattenbach. Wolfgang felt reasonably confident that the roles he had written for the Italian singers he had so closely observed in Vienna could now be taken by the resident Salzburg singers, many of whom had trained in Italy. He did make some changes to the orchestration, adding extra wind instruments that were available to him among his father's colleagues and continuing to demonstrate his imaginative technical assurance. If the opera's arias are generally short, monothematic and lightly scored – as might well be expected from a boy of twelve in his first attempt at a full-length opera in Italian – it is the finales to each of the three acts which show startling precociousness. They are all multi-sectional, juxtaposing different gestures, moods and keys, and the sense of real narrative through musical and textural variety is remarkable. The young composer is in his element, and the promise of a miraculous future in this medium is palpable. A programme was printed for the planned day of the Salzburg performance of *La finta semplice*, which certainly implies that it took place; but the Archbishop was not actually present. But even allowing for the various disappointments of unfinished business, *La finta semplice* had provided the most perfect training for a fledgeling composer intent on visiting the country at the heart of the opera world.

For now it really was time for Leopold to pull together his

Italian plans. He meticulously assembled his portfolio of recommendation letters; again with Hagenauer's help, he arranged for
the availability of funds in Italian towns and cities; and – bravely,
perhaps, after only another ten months of Salzburg obedience – he
petitioned the Archbishop for further leave of absence. Schrattenbach actually complied with surprising munificence, granting
Leopold permission to go to Italy, again on full salary. Furthermore, knowing that titles were helpful as evidence of status, he
also appointed Wolfgang to the position of Konzertmeister. As yet
this would be unpaid, but he promised that Wolfgang would start
to receive a salary on his return. And lastly, for good measure,
the Archbishop gave the Mozarts 120 ducats. So, with financial
stability, archiepiscopal approval, promising connections in the
Habsburg dominions throughout the Italian peninsula, and his
copies of Keyssler's travel guides constantly before him, Leopold
was able to draw up a plan. Like most eighteenth-century travellers to Italy, he aimed to arrive in Rome for Holy Week, even if
this meant leaving Salzburg in the depths of winter. He fixed a
departure date in mid-December, and, in a now very familiar routine, prepared to pack his travelling trunks with everything they
could possibly need.

But this time there was to be one enormous change. Only
Leopold and Wolfgang would travel to Italy, and the women
would remain in Salzburg. For many reasons, this monumental decision – probably taken unilaterally by Leopold – was
extremely sensible. Travel and accommodation costs would be
halved, as would all risks to health, and risks therefore of delays
through illness to schedule and progress. (They had had much
experience of this.) He and his son would no doubt proceed more
quickly without having to be aware of feminine sensitivity and
sensibility: quite apart from the ever-present possibility of petty

or more serious crime on the road, coach journeys might have to be shared with rowdy and unmannered companions, and roadside inns were often barely adequate. Leopold's reasoning was very logical. But Maria Anna and Nannerl were devastated. The family had always done everything together. On all their previous journeys Nannerl's own not inconsiderable talent had been constantly displayed too; and although she had never drawn the same ecstatic appreciation and applause that her brother had, she had become perfectly accustomed to being part of his slipstream, and she had loved her experiences. Young women of her age, with musical talent probably not even as great as hers, but who were part of the Archbishop's musical establishment as singers, had had similar bursaries for travel to Italy, and had benefited enormously from the excellent training they had received there. Nannerl had almost certainly imagined herself pursuing a similar path, even if her brother's was to be at a higher level. Both she and her mother had been longing to visit Italy for years, sharing Leopold's histories and travel books (he had two copies of Keyssler's monumental guide, one of which he would take with him, leaving the other for the women), and poring over them knowledgeably. Like her brother – indeed, probably with her brother – Nannerl had been learning to read and speak Italian. The lure of Rome, Florence, Venice and Naples was immense for her and her mother, seasoned and appreciative travellers that they were. So to be excluded now was bitterly disappointing, and it was a shock for Nannerl to acknowledge that her own part of a glittering existence was essentially over. Life cannot have been easy for any of the four Mozarts, in their claustrophobic Getreidegasse apartment, as the final preparations were made for a departure that would split the precious family unit in two. One half would be left behind feeling anxious, abandoned and vulnerable, for months, if not years.

2

DEPARTURE AND ARRIVAL

'As he progresses through Italy, he will cause the same
astonishment wherever he goes'

On 13 December 1769, Wolfgang and Leopold bade farewell
to the miserable Maria Anna and Nannerl, and trundled away
from Getreidegasse in a hired coach, heading in a direction
entirely new to them, south-west towards Innsbruck. Despite
predictably cold temperatures and heavy snow, the terrain was
reasonably forgiving and the roads passable, and they were
warm and comfortable inside their coach. Both of them appreciated the competence of their driver – Wolfgang especially;
like most young boys, he enjoyed the occasional burst of speed.
Their progress was steady, following the valley of the Saalach
river between Alps. They lunched in Kaitl, and spent their first
night in the small market town of Lofer, some twenty-five miles
from Salzburg. There, demonstrating immediate evidence of
Leopold's efficiency in his corralling of influential and helpful
people, at whatever level, wherever they went, they received 'a
fine room and a good bed' from the local prefect, Johann von

Helmreichen.[1] Their second day on the road followed a similar pattern. Breaking the journey at midday at the charming baroque town of St Johann in Tirol, they continued on to Wörgl, where, after another thrifty evening with the local vicar, Padre Hermann Kellhammer, they wrote the first of many letters home. These letters would form a detailed journal and chronicle of their forth-coming adventure.

For now it was Maria Anna, and to a lesser extent Nannerl too, who was to be the main recipient of Leopold's epistolary dis-cipline. The function hitherto served by Lorenz Hagenauer, of editing and disseminating through Salzburg the comprehensive news reports of their travel, now fell to the immediate family, for whom there were also some, but not many, more personal touches. In that first letter, written late in the evening in Wörgl, only one day after leaving home, Leopold did include some detail of what they had consumed on the journey so far (bad veal, good beer in Kaitl; hot chocolate for breakfast for Wolfgang in Lofer, while he preferred a hearty soup). But if Maria Anna was hoping to be continually reassured of her family's good nutrition she would be disappointed: Leopold quickly tired of imparting such information. What was more firmly established in that first letter was that Wolfgang would add his own greetings. His excitement, and considerable enjoyment of travel, was palpable: 'My heart is completely enchanted with all these pleasures, because it is such fun on this journey, because it is so warm in the carriage, and because our coachman is a fine fellow who, when the road gives him the slightest chance, drives so fast.'[2] Wolfgang also added some lines for his sister – in Italian, clearly indicating that they had studied the language together – and this too would become a frequent feature of letters home, though not always in Ital-ian. In those early days of travel Leopold wrote profusely: there were four letters in the week between 14 and 22 December, after which there were quite long gaps. Later, he and Wolfgang would settle into a more regular routine of writing once a week.

On 15 December the Mozarts arrived in Innsbruck, where they remained for four days. This would be their final stop before turning south towards the Brenner Pass. As they arrived in the town, Leopold noted that the surrounding mountains were not unlike those of the Hallein district of Salzburg, with which Maria Anna and Nannerl would be familiar, and remarked on the fact in his next letter home – a rare example of any kind of topographical description. They took lodgings at the Weisses Kreuz inn in the centre of town, and immediately made contact with the Governor of Tyrol, Count Johann Nepomuk Spaur, whose brother served in the chapter of Salzburg Cathedral. Both the Count and his wife were exceptionally welcoming, and offered Leopold the use of their carriage, which Leopold readily accepted, using it to visit as many of the local counts and barons as he could, and enrol them into his network of helpful contacts. On 17 December Wolfgang took part in a concert given at the house of Count Leopold Künigl, acquitting himself with his customary brilliance and receiving 'all honour' from the Count's audience. He also received a gift of twelve ducats – a fact imparted to Maria Anna in code, for monetary details were certainly not to be divulged to the Salzburg admirers. The Innsbruck concert was both a comfortable resumption of the Mozarts' practice for many years on their travels, and also a prelude of what was surely to continue in Italy. On the following day the local newspaper, the *Innsbrucker Montägige ordinari Zeitung*, carried a short but enthusiastic account of it, and of Wolfgang's 'extraordinary' talents.[3] It referred to Leopold as 'Kapellmeister to the Prince of Salzburg', which was of course an exaggeration of his court position. But it

was one that Leopold did not hesitate to encourage – even bra-
zenly instructing his own wife to address her letters to him 'à Mr:
Mozart Maître de Chapelle de la Musique de S: A: S: Le Prince
Archevêque de Salzburg'.[4] A subtle alleged promotion would do
no harm at all as he and his son headed into Italy.

On the afternoon of 19 December the Mozarts' coach left
Innsbruck and began the steady climb through the Wipp valley
towards the Brenner Pass. As Goethe, who travelled the same
road in 1786, just sixteen years later, described it:

> After Innsbruck the landscape becomes increasingly beauti-
> ful. On the smoothest of roads we ascended a gorge which
> discharges its waters into the [river] Inn and offers the eye a
> great variety of scenery. The road skirts the steepest rock and
> in places is even hewn out of it. On the other side one could see
> gentle cultivated slopes. Villages, large and small houses, cha-
> lets, all of them white-washed, lay scattered among fields and
> hedges over a high, wide slope. Soon the whole scene changed:
> the arable land became pasture and then the pasture, too, fell
> away into a precipitous chasm.[5]

This majestic scenery cannot have been lost on the Mozarts,
familiar though they were with mountains. But neither of them
referred to it in their letters, and this reticence as to what they
actually saw (that earlier glancing comparison to the Hallein
district mountains was unique), and indeed how they felt about
it, was to continue, probably as frustrating to Maria Anna and
Nannerl as it is to posterity. The steepness of the climb and the
twisting roads meant that they now travelled slowly, and a shorter
distance therefore than normal; but by evening they had reached
Steinach, just sixteen miles south of Innsbruck, and on the

following morning they crossed through the Brenner Pass, one of the most important routes through the Alps, and also one of the oldest, having been established in Roman times. Thereafter their gradual descent took them through the autonomous region of Sud Tirol (or Alto Adige) – in the eighteenth century still very much part of Austria. The ever-winding roads followed the Isarco river for approximately fifty miles, bringing the Mozarts through Sterzing (now Vitipeno) to Brixen (Bressanone), and then through Atzwang (Campodazzo) to the ancient town of Bozen (Bolzano), where they arrived on 21 December. There they rested for two days, and Leopold briefly wrote home once more, not to describe those charming Alpine towns and villages, but to report their busy social connections with the local dignitaries and musicians. ('We arrived safely at Bozen yesterday evening. Today I took my two letters to the post and lunched with Herr Kurzweil [violinist]. Tomorrow at midday we are invited to Herr Stockhammer [silk merchant], to whom Herr Ranftl gave us an introduction, and this evening we are going to Herr Antoni Gummer [financier].') Leopold also instructed his wife to write to them next at Rovereto; and his claim that his name was as well known in all post offices as 'a bad penny' was probably not an exaggeration.[6] Wolfgang did not contribute at all to this letter.

After Bozen, the Mozarts continued their descent out of the Austrian region into Italy, and the dramatic mountains became gentler rolling hills. According to Goethe, 'one travels . . . through a country which grows ever more fertile. Everything which, higher in the mountains, must struggle to grow, flourishes here in vigour and health, the sun is bright and hot, and one can believe again in a God.'[7] They passed through Neumarkt (Egna) and Trento, and arrived on 24 December at the hilltop town of Rovereto. Goethe observed that it was here 'where the language changes abruptly. North of this point it had wavered between German and Italian. Now, for the first time, I had a pure-bred Italian as a postilion. The innkeeper speaks no German and I must put my linguistic talents to the test.' The Mozarts, who will also have relished the change of language, again had connections in Rovereto, for the local *maestro di cappélla* was Domenico Pasqui, who had studied in Salzburg; so Leopold decided he and Wolfgang should stay there for the Christmas period. And while there, he resumed – a little late, for they had already been away for nearly two weeks – his earlier custom of keeping lists of the people they encountered on their travels. He set Wolfgang to work to recall, in a significant hierarchical order, the nobility and dignitaries who welcomed them, the musicians with whom they performed, and their families; and Wolfgang obediently, if not altogether fully (he could not remember the dates of their arrivals in Innsbruck, Bozen and Rovereto), complied.

As soon as they had established themselves at the Zur Rose inn, a pleasing social round began. A former violin student of Leopold's, Nicolaus Christiani, was now 'the chief man in Rovereto and the whole district, that is, Lieutenant of the County representing Her Majesty the Empress',[8] and he and his brother issued invitations for both that day and the next (Christmas Day), when 'a jolly midday meal' was enjoyed.[9] Leopold and Wolfgang agreed to give an impromptu concert that evening at the house of Baron Giovanni Todeschi, whom they had previously met in Vienna, and on the following day, after a similarly enjoyable lunch with the Cosmi family, it was suggested that Wolfgang should play the organ at the church of San Marco, for 'six or eight of the leading people'.[10] When they arrived at the church, they found it packed with townspeople who had got wind of the presence of the young Salzburg genius and were anxious to hear him play, and then had to fight their way up to the organ loft 'as everyone wanted to get close to us'.[11] The Mozarts stayed in Rovereto for three and a half days, revelling in the rapturous attention from all levels of its society, and appreciating this small town whose once poor reputation, according to Leopold, had been rescued by its hard-working citizens in the silk and wine trades.[12] (The local wine was none other than Marzemino, later to appear very specifically in the final scene of *Don Giovanni*.) And Rovereto never forgot the significance of Mozart's presence that Christmas. In 1931, the 175th anniversary of his birth, they put up a plaque on the side of Baron Todeschi's house, proudly marking the fact that he had given his first Italian concert there, at the beginning of a 'triumphant journey through the country'.

There were no letters home at all over that Christmas period, and although the Mozarts travelled south to Verona on 27 December, it was still another ten days before Leopold thought to tell his family where and how they were. After the constant flurries of communication, however brief, at the start of the journey, such a long silence since Bozen on 22 December was probably alarming to Maria Anna and Nannerl; but when eventually Leopold did settle down to write his first letter in two and a half weeks, in his Verona inn on 7 January, he began not with apology or even much reassurance, but with admonition that Maria Anna had not let him know how many of his letters she had received. ('*Praise God, we are well*! It would have been helpful if you had told me how many letters you had received from me, for I sent you one from Wörgl, one by the hired coachman, one from Innsbruck by post and one from Bozen.'[13]) Turning defence into attack in this way was a technique to which Leopold would return.

The forty-three miles between Rovereto and the ancient Roman city of Verona were easily achieved in a single day of gradual descent and a levelling out of terrain. The Mozarts booked into a fourteenth-century inn, the Due Torri, in the centre of town, and for several days pursued their ever-growing portfolio of influential contacts with great energy. Principal among these were the officers of the Accademia Filarmonica. This society, the first of its kind, had been founded in 1543 as a forum for the discussion and performance of music; following its lead, several similarly motivated academies had sprung up in Italy throughout the Renaissance. In the early eighteenth century, Verona had built its magnificent opera house, the Teatro Filarmonico, which had opened in 1732 with Vivaldi's *La fida ninfa*. Its opera season had then become celebrated throughout Italy and beyond, attracting the best composers and singers of the day. The centre of musical activity in Verona, the Accademia Filarmonica was an obvious primary focus therefore for the Mozarts, to court its officers, to attend its operas, and preferably to perform there.

The Accademia welcomed the Mozarts with open arms. The Marchese Alessandro Carlotti and the Count Carlo Emilei, respectively its censore and secretary, both immediately issued lunch invitations and, in Carlotti's case, offered the use of a box at the opera. Similar hospitality came from Count Giusti, whose beautiful villa with celebrated gardens and a picture gallery had an impressive entry in Keyssler's *Neueste Reisen*, which in due course Leopold encouraged Maria Anna to read. Pietro Lugiati, from another prominent and wealthy Verona family, and a high official in service of the Venetian Republic (of which Verona was part), was especially welcoming, asking if Wolfgang might sit for a portrait, and producing a distant cousin, Saverio della Rosa, to paint it. And the merchant Michelangelo Locatelli (not actually related to the famous violinist Pietro, but a determined lover of music) offered to show the visitors Verona's many historical monuments, principally of course its Roman amphitheatre, which Leopold will certainly have been anxious to inspect, and its many Romanesque buildings too. So, in those hectic early days in what was truly their first Italian city of consequence, an enticing schedule was assembled. There were to be rehearsals with the best local musicians (all duly entered into Leopold's list) for a concert at the Accademia Filarmonica on 5 January; two sittings for the portrait at the house of Pietro Lugiati; at least one day of sightseeing with Locatelli; and several more lunches and dinners. But before any of that, there was an event which, although not unusual in the Mozarts' social activity, was even more significant than all that was to follow. They went to the opera, and for the first time heard an Italian work, written and performed by Italians, on Italian soil. Although they had attended many opera performances in Vienna, of the highest standards and with excellent singers, the experience now of doing so in, as it were, its own clothes, was one that made a profound impression on young Wolfgang.

The opera heard by the Mozarts in Verona on 3 January 1770 was *Ruggiero*, by the immensely prolific but now largely forgotten Pietro Alessandro Guglielmi. A young poet, Caterino Mazzolà, in his first attempt at writing for the stage, had adapted a familiar story from Ariosto's *Orlando furioso* and produced a libretto, and it had premiered at the Teatro San Salvatore in Venice in May 1769. It is unlikely that Mazzolà (or indeed Guglielmi) would have encountered Wolfgang at a performance of that early Verona revival, just six months later. But in twenty years' time their paths would indeed cross, when they collaborated on *La clemenza di Tito*, Mozart's last opera.

Schooled as he had been in Vienna, attending performances of *opera seria* under the watchful supervision of Hasse, Wolfgang now surveyed *Ruggiero* with an alert and critical eye, communicating his responses to Nannerl, as he, like his father, sat down to write home at last on 7 January. His portion of their joint letter adopts a tone that he was often to use with his sister – above all affectionate, but also teasing, playful, and studded with amusing anecdotes, challenging puzzles or riddles, and linguistic acrobatics (although he wrote most of it in German, some of it is again in Italian, and he signed off in French). But in reporting on the visit to *Ruggiero*, Wolfgang disclosed how he was processing the whole experience. He outlined the basics of the plot, with its confusing convention of certain characters having to be in disguise, and gave brief but surely astute comments on each of the performers (as well as some criticism of the audience):

Oronte, father of Bradamante, is a prince (and sung by Signor Afferi). He is a fine singer, a baritone, but forced when he sings falsetto, but not as much as Tibaldi in Vienna. Bradamante, daughter of Oronte, is in love with Ruggiero (she is to marry Leone, but she does not want him). Her part is sung by a poor Baroness, who has had a great misfortune, but I do not know what it was. She is singing under an assumed name, but I do not know it. Her voice is tolerably good and she has a not bad presence, but she sings devilishly out of tune. Ruggiero, a rich prince who is in love with Bradamante, is sung by a castrato, who sings rather in the manner of Manzuoli and has a very fine powerful voice and is already old: he is fifty-five and has a flexible throat. Leone, who is to marry Bradamante, is very rich, but whether he is very rich off the stage, I do not know. His part is sung by a woman, the wife of Afferi. She has a most beautiful voice, but there is so much whispering in the theatre that you cannot hear anything. Irene's part is sung by a sister of Lolli, the great violinist whom we heard in Vienna. She has a muffled voice and always sings a semiquaver too late or else too early. The part of Ganno is taken by someone whose name I do not know: this is his first time [singing] in an opera.[14]

Submerged in this slightly wild stream of consciousness, there is actually a stern critic here. Wolfgang is discussing with Nannerl the basic resources he might be given if he were to write an opera in Italy, as was fervently hoped, and the challenges therefore of a complex plot and quirky singers with dodgy rhythm or poor intonation. Although he added a comment on the ballets at the end of each act (which he liked), he wrote nothing at all about Guglielmi's actual music. In his assessment of the whole experience, he did not need to pay attention to the part that would be his own responsibility, and of which he was blithely confident.

Neither Wolfgang nor, more surprisingly, Leopold made any reference in their joint letter to the concert that Wolfgang had given two days earlier at the Accademia Filarmonica. Perhaps because the shape and content of the event was so familiar, both to them and also to Maria Anna and Nannerl, they felt it unnecessary to elaborate on it. But it was clearly a triumph, and the local press was ecstatic. The *Gazzetta di Mantova* described the proceedings:

On Friday, the 5th inst., this youth gave, at one of the halls of the noble Accademia Filarmonica, in the presence of the civic authorities and a crowded concourse of nobles of both sexes, such proofs of his expertise in [music] as to astonish everyone. In the company of a number of distinguished professors he was able to exhibit first a most beautiful overture of his own composition, which deserved all its applause. He then splendidly played a harpsichord concerto at sight, and afterwards sonatas that were entirely new to him. This was followed by four verses submitted to him, on which he composed on the spot an aria in the best of taste in the very act of singing it. A subject and a finale proposed to him, he marvellously improvised upon according to the best rules of the art. He also played a trio by Boccherini very well at sight, and a theme given to him on the violin by a professor he admirably composed in score. In short, on this and other occasions, subject to the most arduous trials, he overcame them all with an inexpressible skill, and thus to universal admiration, especially among the music-lovers . . . We have no doubt that, as he progresses on the journey he is now taking through Italy, he will cause the same astonishment wherever he will go, especially among the experts and the intelligentsia.[15]

For several years Wolfgang had repeatedly been put through these sorts of paces, and he had no trouble at all in breezing through them now; and Leopold felt no need to describe his son's reception in his first big Italian concert. His only comment, to Maria Anna in a subsequent letter, was that the review, which he enclosed, had got wrong both Wolfgang's age and his own Salzburg position ('for it says "the present Kapellmeister" ') – despite the fact that he himself was encouraging his wife to address her letters to him in precisely that way. It seems he was exonerating himself ('you know how it is: journalists write as it occurs to them and whatever comes into their minds') from any official fallout once this Mantua review was circulating in Salzburg.[16]

Wolfgang duly had two sittings for his portrait, seated beside a 1583 Celestinus harpsichord, with a piece of his own music on the stand, at Lugiati's house on 6 and 7 January. After the second one he was taken to the church of San Tomaso to play its two organs. As had been the case in Rovereto, a snap decision to play to a handful of friends nevertheless resulted in the gathering of an unruly throng eager to see and hear the young genius:

> ... such a crowd had assembled that we hardly had room to get out of the coach. The crush was so great that we were obliged to go in through the monastery. But in a moment so many people had rushed up to us that we should not have been able to proceed at all, if the Fathers, who were already waiting for us at the monastery doors, had not taken us into their midst. When the performance was over, the throng was even greater, for everyone wanted to see the little organist.[17]

The Mozarts spent the next day exploring Verona's historical buildings with Michelangelo Locatelli – an exhilarating preparation, surely, for what they would in due course see in Rome. ('The amphitheatre is the first great monument of the ancient world I have seen,' wrote Goethe in 1786, 'and how well preserved it is!'[18]) Then there was another round of social calls, taking leave of all their Veronese hosts. Among the farewell gifts they received were two laudatory tributes from Verona's foremost poets: one, a sonnet by Zaccaria Betti, addressed to the 'Giovanetto ammirabile', and the other, an ode in Latin, to the 'Dulcissimo Puero et elegantissimo Lyristae' by Antonio Maria Meschi. (In due course this Latin poem would be made more accessible to the people of Salzburg, in a German paraphrase by Frau Hagenauer's half-brother, Ignaz Anton von Weiser.) Leopold was certainly impressed with these poems, as he reported to Maria Anna ('in Verona the poets vied with one another in composing verses for [Wolfgang]'),[19] and he enjoyed recounting too the various tales

45

of their impressive social whirl – even an embarrassing clash of priorities when an invitation from the Bishop coincided with Wolfgang's second sitting for the portrait. He was curiously off-hand about their day of sightseeing; but he grumbled a lot about the cold, complaining that their hands were 'black-blue-red', that Verona's freezing dining rooms had no stoves or fireplaces, and that he would prefer to eat in a tavern.[20] The Mozarts had perhaps been expecting greater warmth and sunnier climes as they headed south, and had therefore been unprepared for the kind of persistent damp chill that descends on the North Italian Plain in mid-winter. But it is also possible that, in exaggerating the discomforts they had to endure, Leopold was trying to give Maria Anna a balanced picture of their existence, reminding her that triumph and excitement were always tempered with hard-ship and inconvenience, and that it was therefore probably just as well that she and Nannerl had remained in Salzburg.

At the end of their triumphant fortnight in Verona, a city domi-nated by its ancient Roman heritage, Leopold and Wolfgang moved on to Mantua, whose own prominence had peaked in the Renaissance with the truly splendid Gonzaga court. Almost an island city, in that it was surrounded by four (now three) artificial lakes built in the twelfth century as a defence system, its enclosing walls were renovated in the fourteenth century by the Gonzagas, and within these, throughout the fifteenth, sixteenth and seven-teenth centuries, Mantua had become a thriving centre of art, of humanism and of music. Its substantial cohort of musicians included, from 1591 to 1613, none other than Claudio Monte-verdi; and it was there, in 1607, that Monteverdi had produced opera's first unquestionable masterpiece, *L'Orfeo* – barely a decade after the revolutionary notion of through-composed *dramma in musica* had tentatively been explored in Florence. (Would the name, let alone the achievement, of Monteverdi have been familiar to the Mozarts? Were they aware that Mantua's appropriation of the new art form, with which Wolfgang was now so fascinated, did so much to anchor it into Italian and therefore European culture?) Although, by the time of the Mozarts' arrival in 1770, the direct line of the Gonzaga family had ceased and Maria Theresa's Habsburgs were now in charge, the glories of its past were still evident in its buildings (Giulio Romano) and on its walls (Mantegna, Perugino). The Habsburgs themselves had undertaken a new building programme of many palaces and especially their own Reale Accademia di Scienze, Lettere e Arti (Royal Academy of Science, Letters and Arts). Its magnificent theatre, the Teatro Scientifico, designed by Antonio Galli Bibiena from Parma, had only recently been completed and had opened on 3 December 1769, just six weeks before the Mozarts crossed the causeway and entered the imposing gates of the city.

Mantua is only twenty-seven miles from Verona, but the Mozarts' journey had taken them most of a day ('although it is near, [it] is almost a winter day's journey on account of the filthy road', wrote Leopold gloomily before they left[21]). But as soon as they had arrived in the late afternoon, and established themselves at their inn, the Ancora Verde, they again went straight to the opera. They saw *Demetrio*, a celebrated libretto by Metastasio, probably in its most recent setting by Niccolò Piccinni, which had been premiered in Naples in the previous May. (Among the forty-three settings thus far of the text – and sixteen more were to follow – was one by Hasse from 1732, often assumed to have been the one that the Mozarts saw that night; but it is highly unlikely that this thirty-eight-year-old score would have been presented in Mantua in 1770.) While Leopold divulged no opinion of it, Wolfgang was again absorbed by the experience, and over two weeks later reported on it fully in his letter to his sister. Once more, while applying his customary veneer of sibling levity to his tone, his memory of the opera's individual performers, of their strengths and their weaknesses, was comprehensive:

> The opera at Mantua was charming. They played 'Demetrio'. The prima donna sings well, but very softly; and when you do not see her acting, but only singing, you would think she is not singing at all. For she cannot open her mouth, but whines out everything. However, we are accustomed to that now. The seconda donna looks like a grenadier and has a powerful voice too, and I must say does not sing badly, seeing that she is acting for the first time. The primo uomo, il musico, sings beautifully, though his voice is uneven. His name is Caselli. The secondo uomo is already old and I do not like him . . . As for the tenors, one is called Otini. He does not sing badly, but rather heavily like all Italian tenors, and he is a great friend of ours. I do not know the name of the other one. He is still young, but not particularly good. Primo ballerino – good. Prima ballerina – good, and it is said that she is not hideous, but I have not seen her close to. The rest are quite ordinary. A grotesco was there who jumps well, but cannot write as I do, I mean, as sows piddle. The orchestra was not bad.[22]

Wolfgang also revealed to Nannerl that he had been setting an aria from *Demetrio*, 'Misera tu non sei'. The whole process of opera, its creation and execution, was becoming something of a preoccupation for him.

As ever, Leopold busied himself with delivering his letters of recommendation, and opening up his conduits of support and hospitality in the city. His first lead was an excellent one. The Salzburg chamberlain, Count Johann Georg d'Arco, had written an enthusiastic letter to a Mantuan cousin, Count Francesco Eugenio d'Arco, who duly received the Mozarts into his family with warm cordiality. He proffered lunch invitations and onward connections to Mantua's patrician society. (He was certainly more sympathetic to Wolfgang than Count Joseph d'Arco, son of Johann Georg, who much later, in 1779, would follow his father into the Salzburg chamberlain's office and deliver the celebrated 'kick on my backside' which marked Wolfgang's welcome dismissal from the Archbishop's service.[23]) But not all of Leopold's connections worked out well. Prince Michael Thurn und Taxis was a member of a large family, for a branch of whom Leopold had worked very early in his career; among other things, they had been responsible, since the thirteenth century, for operating the postal services between Italian city states. When the Mozarts called at the Thurn und Taxis palace in Mantua, they were turned away. But Leopold persisted, even going to the ignominious lengths of pursuing the Prince's carriage after attending a church service, all the way back to the palace – in effect stalking his prey. Again he was informed by an embarrassed servant that the Prince had no desire to see him, and that he should never call again. Leopold might have recognized such haughty aristocratic indifference from some of his unfortunate experiences in Vienna, just over a year earlier, and learned perhaps to try to temper his behaviour. But little would distract him from his dogged mission to line up the best people to further their cause. And, in the main, his complex network was working well. The secretary of Verona's Accademia Filarmonica, Count Carlo Emilei, who had just supported the Mozarts so generously, had written a recommendation to his counterpart in Mantua, and as a result Wolfgang was introduced to several 'Masters and Professors of music' who subjected him to a number of tests in their private homes. And then, for public consumption, a concert in the Mantuan Accademia's brand-new Teatro Scientifico was swiftly organized for 16 January: they actually brought forward the date of their monthly event, so keen were they to present him. Like the concert eleven days earlier in Verona, the programme also involved local musicians, both singers and instrumentalists, but largely consisted of more challenging trials for Wolfgang, from sight reading to improvisation to transposition to instant composition in various styles (contrapuntal, operatic, symphonic). Again Wolfgang brilliantly and no doubt enjoyably accomplished all this: he unquestionably thrived on being put to the test by distinguished senior musicians. And although he never made any reference to the concert in his subsequent letter to Nannerl (for surely she would have been familiar with these sorts of occasions), this one was a step up from the Verona event, and the *Gazzetta di Mantova* was again effusive, both in its elaborate description of the proceedings and then in its praise of Wolfgang's 'amazing talents and extraordinary mastery':

... this youth appears to [the Masters and Professors of music] to be born to vanquish all the experts in the art; and this view accords well with that of a noted literary man of Verona, written to the Secretary of our Accademia Filarmonica in recommendation of Sig. Wolfgango; namely that he is a miracle in music, and one of those freaks Nature causes to be born ... Meanwhile he now tours Italy with Sig. Leopoldo, his Father, who is also a man of talent and a Kapellmeister of repute; and

they both have that which will cause wonder on Italian soil . . .
The concert was thus a most brilliant success and altogether
satisfactory . . . of great exquisiteness and perfection.[24]

Leopold will have been gratified that he too was praised in the
Gazzetta. But what impressed him most, quite understandably,
was the very beauty of the new theatre, and he communicated
this to Maria Anna in his next letter home: 'I wish you could
see the hall where the concert took place, the so-called Teatrino
della Accademia Filarmonica. In all my life I have never seen
anything more beautiful of its kind . . . It is not a theatre, but a
hall built with boxes like an opera house. Where the stage ought
to be, there is a raised platform for the orchestra and behind the
orchestra another gallery built with boxes for the audience.' And
he continued by giving his wife a hint of the excitement he had
felt at the ecstatic reaction of the audience: 'The crowds, the
general shouting, clapping, noisy enthusiasm and "Bravo" and,
in a word, the admiration displayed by the listeners, I cannot
adequately describe to you.'[25] The general adulation of Wolfgang
continued in their social rounds, before and after the triumphant
concert; and again a poet was quick to produce an encomium.
A Signora Sartoretti wrote a thirteen-verse Anacreontic poem
(lines of eight syllables) and presented it to him along with a
probably even more welcome gift of money. She also took a rather
motherly interest in young Wolfgang, observing how, as Leopold
had reported to Maria Anna, his hands and face were chapped
and red, and supplying him with a soothing emollient cream.

For without doubt it was still miserably cold for the travellers. Leopold again listed their discomforts in a postscript to his
wife, and it is clear that, after only a month away, he was feeling
the strain: '. . . I am hustled to death. Nothing but dressing and

undressing, packing and unpacking, and with no warm room, so that one freezes like a dog. Everything I touch is as cold as ice. And if you were to see the doors and locks in the rooms! Just like prisons!'[26] Having spent nine days in Mantua, which he eventually found to be too cut off from the mainstream ('It is very quiet here and one never hears a word about anything. It is just like being in Germany'), he was ready to move on, and head for their first major destination, Milan. There, if everything went as he hoped, they could stay for several weeks, and find some stability at last after their gruelling time on the road.

There were two possible routes to Milan. The travellers were now long past the hazards of mountainous terrain, but their passage in mid-winter across the frigid and extremely flat North Italian Plain held its own challenges. As Leopold explained to Maria Anna, 'if the weather is cold and the roads are frozen, we shall travel through Cremona. If it is mild and the roads in consequence bad, we must go through Brescia.'[27] So although Leopold hated the persistently cold temperatures, anything warmer would mean sodden and impassable roads, and necessitate a detour to the north of the more direct route. In the event, the continuing freeze ensured that they could travel through Cremona. But before they left, Leopold bought two footbags lined with wolf's fur, which would give them 'excellent service . . . in the Italian sedia'.[28]

Leaving Mantua on 19 January and heading west, the Mozarts stopped for a night at the small town of Bozzolo. News of their travels, however, had spread, and on arrival they were immediately waylaid and swept off for an evening of more musical display before a gathering of inquisitive admirers. The *Gazzetta di Mantova* reported a week later:

> They write from Bozolo that . . . the celebrated boy Sig. Wolfgango Amadeo Mozart arrived here, who had no sooner alighted at the coaching inn of the town than he was most courteously received by the Archpriest Don Carlo Saragozzi, Professor of Music, and then taken by the same in a carriage to his house; and that the said famous little boy in the course of some two hours gave proofs of his amazing talent . . . giving unspeakable pleasure and satisfaction to both the Political and the Military authorities there, and many other Gentlemen who happened to be present.[29]

Wolfgang had to continue this very familiar exhibition on the following morning, before Bozzolo's excited citizens would let him continue on his journey.

Later that day the Mozarts reached Cremona, the city renowned for producing not only Monteverdi, but the greatest violin makers in history (Amati, Stradivarius, Guarneri); and they found themselves in the former Duchy of Milan, now the Austrian Imperial province of Lombardy, and therefore under Austrian hegemony once more. Again they went straight to the opera, where they saw *La clemenza di Tito*, by Valentini. Wolfgang's next letter gave Nannerl another little review of it, with more pithy thumbnail sketches summarizing each performer. While he was only moderately enthusiastic about the singers ('The prima donna is not bad; she is quite old, I should say, and not good-looking'),[30] he praised the orchestra, implying that it was better than that at Mantua, and even, rarely, naming its leader: 'the first violin is called Spangnoletto [sic]'. Spagnoletto was the nickname for Francesco Diana, whose distinguished family was very much following Cremona's speciality of violin making and playing.[31] While Wolfgang rightly acknowledged the quality of Spagnoletto's playing, it is barely credible that Leopold, for whom the violin and its execution had been his own complete preoccupation until 1756 and the birth of his son, registered no interest, let alone joy, in at last being in the city at the centre of the violin world. Perhaps he did visit some luthier's workshop and attend to the state of their own violins, which were surely travelling with them; but there is no evidence that he did. He was possibly influenced by Keyssler's dismissal of Cremona as being in poor condition, with insignificant walls and buildings. Certainly his desire to get to Milan as quickly as possible, and stop his constant 'packing and unpacking' (a completely recognizable complaint among musicians on tour), was uppermost in his mind.

On 23 January, almost exactly six weeks since they had left Salzburg, the Mozarts arrived in Milan, the magnificent city at the heart of Lombardy. In its own rich history, Milan had become a duchy in 1395, when Wenceslaus IV had ennobled the ruling Visconti family. From 1535 to 1700 it had been under Spanish Habsburg rule, and had transferred to Austria after the War of Spanish Succession and the Treaty of Utrecht in 1713. Now it was governed by Maria Theresa's representative Count Karl Joseph Firmian, who had profound connections with Salzburg: he was a nephew of Leopold Anton Firmian, a former archbishop, and Leopold's first employer at court; and his brother Franz Lactantius Firmian was currently its high steward, and had been fundamental to the establishment of Leopold's Italian network, writing many letters of support. Count Karl Joseph was a civilized and generous patron of the arts, whose own broad education had been in Bavaria, Innsbruck and Salzburg. Subsequently he had travelled widely through the Netherlands, France and Italy, and in 1745, at the age of twenty-nine, he had become a counsellor to Maria Theresa's husband, Francis. Eight years later he was appointed ambassador to Naples, and then, in 1758, as Austrian minister plenipotentiary in Milan. Economy and culture thrived as never before under his governorship. He himself was an avid collector of books (his library contained over 40,000 of them) and paintings, and he was an elegant and distinguished host. The English historian Dr Charles Burney, also travelling throughout Italy at this time, referred to him as 'a sort of King of Milan, being prime minister there of the Empress Queen'.[32] A few months after this first visit of the Mozarts, Burney dined with Firmian, and was warm in his approbation: 'He seemed to me eternally to possess all the attributes of an illustrious character. There is great dignity in his appearance. And his address is full of graceful ease.'[33] Count Firmian would unquestionably become one of the Mozarts' most important supporters in Italy.

Immediate contact with the Count would be through his secretary Leopold Troger, who also came from Salzburg, and to whom therefore Leopold had recently been instructing Maria Anna to address her letters. Troger was not merely useful to Leopold, but in due course he and his family would become close friends. It was he who arranged the Mozarts' accommodation in Milan, at the Augustinian monastery of San Marco, very close to Count Firmian's residence at the Palazzo Melzi. Leopold and Wolfgang were delighted with their billet: they had three rooms between them, a young monk to look after them, and at last they were warm. With undisguised relief at finally being comfortable, Leopold described their conditions to Maria Anna:

We have three large guest rooms. In the first we have a fire, take our meals and give audiences; in the second I sleep and we have put our trunk there; in the third room Wolfgang sleeps and there we keep our other small luggage. We each sleep on four good mattresses and every night the bed is warmed, so that Wolfgang, when he goes to bed, is always quite happy. We have a brother, Frater Alfonso, especially for our service and we are very well looked after.[34]

As it happened, Count Firmian was unwell when the Mozarts arrived in Milan. Since nothing could proceed until they had first paid their respects to him, they settled quietly into their temporary home and took stock. After three days they got round to writing to Maria Anna and Nannerl again – over two weeks since Leopold's last letter from Mantua. They had heard from Maria Anna that she was alarmed by their silence, but again Leopold's response was unapologetic and defensive: 'You complain that for three weeks you have had no word from me. But I wrote to you from Verona and from Mantua. You ought to have received my first letter from Verona, as I posted it there on January 7th. The second letter cannot have reached Salzburg yet, for I only posted it in Mantua on the 15th.'[35] But he proceeded to give a lengthy description then of their time in Mantua, even telling the full story of how he had been so brutally snubbed by Prince Thurn und Taxis, from which he was clearly still smarting. (He did stress that this part of the letter was for Maria Anna's eyes only, as he would not have wanted it known around Salzburg that he had been refused an audience with the Prince.[36]) He balanced this unfortunate anecdote with glowing accounts of the people who had been 'charming' to them everywhere, enclosing Signora Sartoretti's poem and listing those who had entertained them so generously. (Maria Anna will perhaps have reacted with pain as well as relief when she read that Signore Bettinelli's sister-in-law had been 'truly like a mother to Wolfgang'.) He continued to elaborate on his financial anxieties, explaining that in Verona and Mantua their concerts had been free for the audience, and that everything in Italy was very expensive. But Leopold reassured his wife that, even as they waited in a sort of limbo for Count Firmian to recover and receive them, he and Wolfgang were both well. And he handed the letter over to his son, to add his own messages for Nannerl.

As always, Wolfgang seemed in a much sunnier mood than his father. He teased his sister about her male admirers, launched then into his detailed reviews of the operas they had seen in Mantua and Cremona, and added that they had not yet been to any opera in Milan, but that he had heard a lot about it. He already knew the opera schedule ('The opera is called: "Didone abbandonata". This opera will soon come to an end and Signor Piccinni, who is writing the next one, is here. I have heard that his is called: "Cesare in Egitto".')[37] and was manifestly impatient to continue indulging his current fascination. Meanwhile the Trogers were very attentive, and Frau Troger had addressed the persistent problem of Wolfgang's chapped hands, making up a special skin cream for him according to a formula sent by Maria Anna herself. And another member of Firmian's household, his steward Fernando Germani, was equally hospitable: 'The wife of Count von Firmian's steward is a Viennese. Last Friday we dined there and we are dining again next Sunday'.

Apart from these pleasant domestic evenings, Firmian's continuing indisposition meant that the Mozarts were still effectively grounded in their monastic environment, unable to launch their passage through the upper echelons of Milanese society. But they did have one important encounter. No doubt to Wolfgang's delight at last, they attended the dress rehearsal of Piccinni's *Cesare in Egitto* (which Leopold pronounced 'excellent'[38]), and introduced themselves to its enormously experienced composer. *Cesare in Egitto* was already Piccinni's sixty-seventh opera (he was forty-two years old), and forty-seven more would follow. Still not at the peak of his career, he was working in all the illustrious opera centres of Italy – Naples, Rome, Venice, Bologna – and would soon be invited by Maria Theresa's youngest daughter, Queen Marie Antoinette, to Paris, where he would be drawn into an unseemly rivalry with Gluck. Piccinni's strength was in *opera buffa* (comic opera), so his output represented the antithesis to the type of *opera seria* produced with such distinction by Wolfgang's earlier operatic mentor, Hasse. And the meeting here in Milan with Piccinni was as instructive for Wolfgang as that with Hasse had been in Vienna. Quite apart from observing the craft in Piccinni's perfectly delightful if unremarkable music, Wolfgang will have learned much from hearing how he wrote for individual singers, accompanying and exploiting their ranges, techniques and general strengths and weaknesses. (Significantly, Piccinni, like Hasse, was married to a singer.) Wolfgang listened, and absorbed. In the coming weeks he would return regularly to the opera (on 3 March, one month after this initial visit to a dress rehearsal, he told Nannerl that they had 'been to the opera six or seven times'[39]). The Italian speciality continued to increase its grip on him.

And there were other pleasurable encounters for Wolfgang. He was accustomed to moving almost exclusively in an adult world, which, though he was entirely comfortable with it, did deprive him of forming friendships with people of his own age. In Milan, possibly even in the context of the monastery where they were living, he met two excellent young castrato singers. As friendship developed, Wolfgang cemented it by writing for them. Leopold reported in his next letter: 'Wolfgang . . . is composing two Latin motets for two castrati, one of whom is fifteen and the other sixteen years old, who asked him to compose them, and to whom, as they are his friends and sing beautifully, he could not refuse anything'.[40] (These motets have not survived.) Leopold also wrote with some relief that the weather was now 'beautiful', but that the absence of Count Firmian was continuing to hold back their schedule, and that they might have to stay longer in Milan than they had planned. (Six months later, Charles Burney would suffer similar frustration there: 'The three principal personages here to whom I had letters were still out of town, and my time begins to hang a little on my hands.'[41])

On 7 February, fully two weeks after their arrival in Milan, the Mozarts were finally received by the recuperated Count Firmian – and they were not disappointed. The great man entertained them to lunch, along with several other impressive guests including the local *maestro di cappella* and prolific composer (pre-Haydn, even) of symphonies, Giovanni Battista Sammartini. Wolfgang went through his familiar routine of playing, improvising and passing tests; and Firmian presented him with the complete works of Metastasio ('nine volumes . . . the Turin edition, one of the most beautiful, and very handsomely bound', wrote Leopold approvingly)[42] – a gift of generous and thoughtful prescience. Firmian, in his turn, much as he will have been primed by his brother as to the extraordinary quality of his Salzburg guests, was greatly impressed by their meeting. He instantly set up other occasions when Wolfgang should come and demonstrate his talent, before more carefully selected influential guests. Perhaps already he was entertaining a notion that this phenomenal fourteen-year-old boy might actually write an opera for Milan, and suggested to him that he set some of Metastasio's aria texts for his next appearance in his palace. And on that same evening the Mozarts went again to the opera, to hear *Didone abbandonata* by Celoniati, in the magnificent Teatro Regio Ducale. (That opera house would actually burn to the ground five years later – a not uncommon occurrence for theatres where lighting effects were entirely achieved by oil lamps, tallow candles and reflectors. Two years after that, it would be replaced by the opera house which remains the most celebrated in the world, the Teatro alla Scala.)

After that first meeting with Count Firmian, everything accelerated. Wolfgang's second appearance at the Palazzo Melzi, on 18 February, was an even more glittering occasion than the first. Among the guests were Prince Francesco d'Este of Modena and his granddaughter Maria Beatrice. Since 1763, when she was thirteen years old, Maria Beatrice had been engaged to marry Maria Theresa's youngest son (and Wolfgang's sometime boyhood companion), Ferdinand, four years her junior. The Mozarts would have been intrigued to meet her, knowing that as soon as Ferdinand reached the age of sixteen there would be a mighty Habsburg wedding, such as they had hoped to witness in Vienna in 1767. Wolfgang acquitted himself with his customary aplomb, as he did again a week later in a public concert which, as Leopold reported vaguely, 'went off in the same way as our concerts have done everywhere, and therefore no further description is necessary'.[43] By then Wolfgang was also composing his Metastasio arias for their third concert at Firmian's palace. And as Lent approached, and Milan entered Carnival, he and Leopold became caught up in its elaborate festivities, and he did at one point seem somewhat overwhelmed by it all, writing to his sister: 'I am utterly confused with all the things I have to do. It is impossible for me to write more.'[44] The Carnival proceedings required the visitors to wear elaborate costumes and masks, and observe magnificent street processions. These absolutely delighted Wolfgang:

We have seen the facchinata and the chiccherata. The facchinata is a mascherata, a beautiful sight, so called because people dress up as facchini or valets. There was a barca with a number of people in it, and many persons went on foot, and there were four to six bands of trumpeters and drummers and a few companies of fiddlers and of players of other instruments. The chiccherata which we saw today is also a mascherata. *Chiccheri* is the Milanese word for the people we call petits-maîtres or, let us say, coxcombs. They all rode on horseback and it was a charming affair.[45]

Even Leopold was impressed ('It was not at all a bad show'),[46] but he deeply resented having to spend money on Carnival clothes, which he considered to be inessential trivialities: 'The tailor has just called with the cloaks and cowls we had to order. I looked at myself in the mirror as we were trying them on, and thought of how *in my old age I too have had to take part in this tomfoolery* . . . After having had to make this foolish expenditure, my only consolation is that one can use these costumes again for all sorts of things and can make linings, kitchen cloths and so forth, out of them.'[47]

Leopold's ill humour was rather exacerbated by his intense disapproval of what was going on in church services. He and Wolfgang attended a funeral Mass at the duomo and, on the following day, a vespers service. Leopold was, if not merely bored by the length of these, actually dismayed by their content:

> We have had the opportunity of hearing various kinds of church music and yesterday we listened to the High Mass or Requiem for old Marchese Litta . . . The Dies Irae of this Requiem lasted about three quarters of an hour. You must not expect me to give you a description of the church services here. I am far too irritated to do so. They merely consist of music and of church adornment. Apart from these the most disgusting licentiousness prevails. This very moment I have come in from a vesper service, which lasted over two hours . . .[48]

By Shrove Tuesday, 27 February, he was appalled that Italy's Catholic traditions permitted the delay of Lenten discipline until the first Sunday, rather than Ash Wednesday, and that even the monastic brothers surreptitiously went along with it:

> Here the inhabitants will still be eating meat tomorrow and on Thursday; every day operas and balls will still take place; and on Saturday the last ball will be held. This is according to the Use of St Ambrose, which the whole town follows. In the monasteries however, they observe the Roman customs and begin Lent on Ash Wednesday. But on that day and on Thursday all the priests run out of the monasteries to their acquaintances in the town and invite themselves to eat meat. What do you think of that?[49]

But he assured Maria Anna that he and Wolfgang were eating sensibly and in good health: 'Wolfgang will not spoil his health by eating and drinking. You know how he controls himself; and I can assure you that I have never seen him take such good care of himself as he does in this country. Whatever does not seem right to him he leaves and often he eats very little, yet nonetheless he is fat and cheerful and gay and jolly all day long.'[50]

When Carnival was at last over, the Mozarts could fully concentrate on preparing for the third and final concert at Count Firmian's palace, on 12 March. Wolfgang finished composing his arias, and Leopold busied himself with the preparation of the orchestral material ('I had to copy the violin parts myself and then have them duplicated so that they should not be stolen').[51] Wolfgang's new arias would be performed by the foremost singers from the opera (the soprano Antonia Bernasconi, the castrato Giuseppe Aprile and the tenor Guglielmo d'Ettore), and he himself will have rehearsed them and their instrumental colleagues who made up the small orchestra. Again the audience for the concert was stellar: 'Over one hundred and fifty members of the leading nobility were present, the most important of them being the Duke, the Princess and the Cardinal.' And the result of what surely had been an elaborate audition was the best possible news. As Leopold reported almost casually to Maria Anna, 'Wolfgang has been asked to write the first opera here for next Christmas.'[52]

This was an astonishing honour for a fourteen-year-old boy from Austria, to be invited to open the season in one of the most important opera houses in Italy, the country which had invented the art form. Clearly, Count Firmian, who was not just extremely impressed by Wolfgang but had also become very fond of him, was the prime mover in securing the commission. The contract was drawn up on the very next day, again in his Palazzo Melzi. Wolfgang would be paid one hundred ducats – the equivalent of Leopold's annual Salzburg salary – for the opera, and he and his father would receive free lodging for the weeks they would be required in Milan. He should write the recitatives in advance of his return and send them to the singers by the beginning of October. The Mozarts themselves should be back by 1 November, when Wolfgang would meet the cast and write their arias. Three possible singers were named.[53] While nothing could be finalized until Leopold had secured permission from his own employers in Salzburg to extend his absence, this was a formality: with both sympathetic Firmian brothers, Karl Joseph in Milan and Franz Lactantius in Salzburg, operating in parallel, there was no danger of permission not being granted. And the munificent Milanese Firmian, at a farewell dinner for Wolfgang and Leopold on 14 March, cemented their warm relationship by presenting Wolfgang with a gold-inlaid snuffbox and twenty very welcome ducats.

How Wolfgang himself felt about all this he did not reveal in his letters home. He did subsequently tell his sister that he knew he had had to go through some process of audition, and compose his arias 'in order that the Milanese . . . should see that I am capable of writing an opera', but that was all.[54] And Leopold seemed unable to express any delight in Wolfgang's achievement, merely complaining that this mighty news complicated his organizational responsibilities, as indeed it did: they would have to recalibrate their plans, making sure they were back in Milan by the autumn. But this, surely, was the best prize for which they could possibly have hoped. As they packed up all their possessions and prepared to leave Milan, it must have been with an enormous sense of accomplishment: the first important Italian city, and Habsburg hub, had been conquered, and an incredible commission achieved. Leopold and Wolfgang would head south towards Rome, and towards gentler, balmy spring weather, in the highest of spirits.

3

TO THE SOUTH

*'At his tender age he not only equals masters
of the art, but exceeds them'*

It was still Leopold's intention, like that of so many travellers in Italy, to arrive in Rome in time for Easter, which in 1770 would fall on 15 April. Leaving Milan on 15 March, the Mozarts had just a month in which to cover over 400 miles, and although initially the going would be fast through the Po valley, there would be more challenging territories ahead, with the Apennine Mountains to cross. But the days were lengthening as the weather warmed. Seasoned traveller that he was, Leopold will have taken advice and made his detailed calculations. Even allowing time to spend several days in Bologna and Florence, both major cities with formidable musical traditions, they should be safely in Rome before Maundy Thursday.

The first part of the journey, the 135 miles between Milan and Bologna, took the Mozarts nine days; they stopped en route in Lodi, Piacenza, Parma and Modena. How did they pass their time in the coach, through relentlessly flat countryside? With little or no visual distraction from the fundamental discomfort and ennui of coach travel, these will have been curiously arduous conditions. Leopold no doubt had many organizational tasks to fulfil, as he always had, one of the most immediate being to draft his letter to Salzburg requesting leave of absence for the period of Wolfgang's opera in Milan. But for Wolfgang, whose journeys in his infancy with the whole family had been constantly enlivened by the presence of his sister, with whom all manner of games and puzzles had been enjoyed, the boredom now could potentially have been mind-numbing. His solution, it seems, was to compose – in his head. Years later, after his death, his widow Constanze described his compositional process to Vincent and Mary Novello, as they noted in their travel diaries:

> When some grand conception was working in his brain he was purely abstracted, walking about the apartment and knew not what was passing around, but when once arranged in his mind, he needed no Piano Forte but would take music paper and whilst he wrote would say to her, 'Now, my dear wife, have the goodness to repeat what has been talked of', and her conversation never interrupted him, he wrote on, 'which is more', she added, 'than I can do with the commonest letter.'[1]

This ability to retreat into another mental environment was surely honed here on these dullest of travel days. Certainly when the Mozarts arrived in Lodi after twenty-five tedious miles, Wolfgang wrote out three movements of his string quartet no. 1 in G, K.80/73f. (He added a fourth movement three years later.) That first day had been profitable after all.

Lodi's chief claim to fame in the eighteenth century would come in 1796, when the young Napoleon Bonaparte would win his first major battle against the Habsburgs there. It was a small city of just 10,000 inhabitants, and there was no opera house. But Piacenza and Parma both had one, and the Mozarts inevitably lingered longer in each of these cities as they continued in their south-easterly direction towards Bologna. As Keyssler had no doubt informed Leopold, Piacenza had earlier presented some of the greatest Italian opera singers from the first half of the century: Carlo Boschi, known as Farinelli, had sung there, as had two of Handel's greatest interpreters in London, Giovanni Carestini and Francesca Cuzzoni (she being the other half of the 'Rival Divas' feud with Hasse's wife, Faustina Bordoni). In Parma the Mozarts befriended its current diva, Lucrezia Aguiari, who invited them to dinner. She was known to all, in a perfectly matter-of-fact way, as La Bastardella. Her vocal skills were formidable. As Wolfgang wrote to Nannerl, she had '(1) a beautiful voice, (2) a marvellous throat [technique], (3) an incredible range.'[2] Wolfgang then transcribed for Nannerl, with great excitement, precise examples of that technique and that range, demonstrating how she could sing, in tune and extremely fast, up to 'C in alt' – three octaves above middle C. (Brilliance in such stratospheric vocal heights never failed to thrill Wolfgang, as he would demonstrate even in the last weeks of his life, when he wrote the role of the Queen of the Night for his extraordinary sister-in-law Josefa Hofer.) Again he was agog to share with Nannerl his discovery of such a sensational singer, as he described the experience of meeting and hearing her. And even Leopold was impressed: 'In Parma Signora Guari, who is also called Bastardina or Bastardella, invited us to dinner and sang three arias for us. I could not believe that she was able to reach C sopra acuto, but my ears convinced me. The passages which Wolfgang has written down occurred in her arias and these she sang, it is true, more softly than her lower notes, but as beautifully as an octave stop on an organ.'[3]

Having dinner with the local star singer was unquestionably the highlight of the Mozarts' time in Parma. Other encounters were less fruitful. Their supportive patron Count Firmian, on the night before they left Milan, had supplied Leopold with several warm letters of introduction to potential supporters in many of the cities they were to visit. One was to the French politician Guillaume du Tillot, whose Enlightenment ideals had guided him in his post as ducal minister in Parma, where he had recently transformed its fortunes. He duly received the Mozarts with polite civility, but did not offer any further assistance or opportunity, and his supercilious dismissal would have infuriated Leopold, increasing his impatience to move on. Before he left, he sent off to the Chief Steward in Salzburg his request for further leave of absence, for their stay in Milan later in the year. His next letter on the subject would be to the Archbishop himself. He did not write home at all: again Maria Anna will have been growing anxious at such a long silence. But it is to be hoped that Leopold and Wolfgang will have satisfied their gastronomic appetites too in Parma, and enjoyed its renowned (then as now) cheeses and cured hams.

Travelling through Modena, the Mozarts finally arrived in Bologna, with its alluring towers, porticos and churches, on 24 March, and based themselves in the centre at the Pellegrino inn. Leopold was acutely aware of the importance of the city, founded in the Etruscan period in fertile land well served with rivers, and the centre therefore for a thriving economy built on agriculture. Since 1088, Bologna had also been the seat of the oldest university in the world (ahead of Oxford by just eight years). Currently under Papal rule, its supreme prosperity in the sixteenth century had somewhat declined after a series of plagues in the seven-teenth century, and now in the eighteenth century its economy was stagnant, giving rise to some startlingly high prices which disconcerted Leopold ('This place is the most expensive which we have so far struck in Italy').[4] But he was most keen to make an impression on this 'centre and dwelling-place of many mas-ters, artists and scholars', among whom was a legendary teacher, Padre Giovanni Battista Martini, whom he hoped to consult on Wolfgang's behalf. Among his many activities, Padre Martini was also instructing at Bologna's Accademia Filarmonica, founded in 1666 and probably the most distinguished of all such Italian academies. And Wolfgang, for his part, will have been most inter-ested in exploring the repertoire at Bologna's new opera house, built just a decade earlier, in 1760.

Still determined to reach Rome by Holy Week, the Mozarts could not linger in Bologna. They spent just five days there, but these were of the greatest intensity. Count Firmian had written to the Bologna-based Governor General of Lombardy, Count Gian Luca Pallavicini:

I take the liberty of recommending [the Mozarts] warmly to Your Excellency, moved by the assurance I have of your well-known generosity and kindness, and by the thought that perhaps you will not be displeased to find in young Mozart one of those musical talents but rarely produced by nature, inas-much that at his tender age he not only equals the Masters of the art, but even exceeds them, I believe, in readiness of inven-tion. I hope therefore that Your Excellency will be pleased to honour them with your protection during their stay there and to find them means of appearing in public.[5]

When the Mozarts presented this letter, Count Pallavicini responded instantly, organizing a concert in his palace just two days later. Like others before him, he could not have done more for the Mozarts, welcoming them into his family and his home, putting his carriage at their disposal, assembling '150 members of the leading nobility' to attend the concert, and no doubt interceding too with the musicians and singers who should come to rehearse and perform it.[6] Wolfgang had already heard the two singers. One of them, Giuseppe Cicognini, had been in Valentini's *La clemenza di Tito* in Cremona when the Mozarts had passed through there at the end of January: Wolfgang had reported approvingly to Nannerl that he had 'a delightful voice and a beautiful cantabile'. The other, Giuseppe Aprile, had also met with his approval ('sings well and has a beautiful even voice') when he heard him in a Milan church.[7] So he will have been delighted to collaborate with both of them now in Bologna, and to rehearse with them for a day as he and Leopold rapidly assembled their programme. The concert itself was a predictable triumph, lasting from 7.30 until 11.30 'because the nobles refused to break up the party'.[8] And both Leopold and Wolfgang received gifts of money (respectively twenty zecchini and 205 lire). Count Pallavicini himself was thrilled, and wrote an ecstatic report of the evening back to Count Firmian in Milan:

I immediately hastened to give effect to your justified desire that this city should know and admire young Mozart's rare talent. To this end a conversazione was held in my house on Monday evening, at which 70 ladies were present as well as the Cardinal-Legate, the Princes of Holstein and almost all the nobility, and the young professor gave such admirable proofs there of his knowledge, as would at his tender age seem incredible to anyone who had not witnessed them; they were all surprised and took infinite pleasure in knowing a boy of such singular merit.[9]

Among the august audience that night was none other than the sixty-four-year-old Franciscan friar, Padre Martini. A native of Bologna, he had taken holy orders at the age of sixteen, and when only nineteen had become *maestro di cappella* of the Basilica of San Francesco, where he remained for the rest of his life, composing much sacred music (most of it unpublished) and becoming such a formidable theorist, and teacher of contrapuntal skills and disciplines, that young composers from all over Europe came to study with him. Among his students had been Gluck, Johann Christian Bach (who knew the Mozarts in London and would have spoken to them of his former mentor in Bologna) and the prominent opera composers Nicolò Jommelli and the Frenchman André Grétry. Martini was currently engaged on two monumental writing projects, his multi-volume history of music, *Storia di musica*, of which to date only one volume had appeared, and his treatise on counterpoint, *Esemplare . . . di contrappunto*. Charles Burney would meet Martini later that year. He was planning his own *General History of Music* (which, unlike Martini's, would be completed), so he was especially anxious to engage with Martini and to exchange views. He was rather daunted by the contents of Martini's first volume, recently purchased and instantly devoured, which he found to be dealing with 'only the driest and most abstruse part of the subject'. But he was deeply impressed, not just by Martini's library of 17,000 books, but by the man himself. He described 'the excellence of his character, which is such as inspires not only respect but kindness. He joins to innocence of life, and simplicity of manners, a native cheerfulness, softness, and philanthropy . . . I never liked any man more'.[10]

Leopold was most gratified when Martini turned up at Count Pallavicini's palace to hear Wolfgang: 'The famous Padre Martini was also invited and, although he never goes to concerts, he came nevertheless to this one'.[11] And Martini too liked what he saw and heard, and invited Wolfgang to visit him at the Basilica of San Francesco. Over the next two days he twice tested the boy with contrapuntal challenges, and proffered advice and direction. He would remain an important figure in Wolfgang's life throughout these Italian travels, and beyond. And, even as Leopold kept an eye on his strict schedule, the Mozarts still had time to pay homage to those in the opera world. They visited the great Farinelli, who, after his triumphant career throughout Italy, then in Vienna, London and, for over twenty years, Madrid, had recently retired to the outskirts of Bologna, where he was building himself a lavish mansion. The Mozarts drove out there to see him. They also met the singers currently working at the opera, and the composers too, including the Bohemian Josef Mysliveček, whose life would occasionally intersect with Wolfgang's. And they had time for some sightseeing, as they had had in Verona, visiting museums and exhibitions, and admiring 'the churches, the paintings, the fine architecture and the furnishings of the various palaces', as Leopold reported to Maria Anna. 'What I have seen in Bologna', he concluded, 'surpasses the British Museum.'[12]

For, at last, Leopold did find time to write home again, and even managed two letters in those five days. He was particularly enthusiastic about Count Pallavicini, who had organized their activities with such generosity, diplomacy, sensitivity and extreme efficiency: 'I have already introduced you to Count Carl von Firmian; and now I should like you to know Count Palla-vicini too. They are two gentlemen who in all respects have the same outlook, friendliness, magnanimity, placidity and a special love for and insight into all branches of knowledge.'[13] Count Pal-lavicini had become a close friend of the Mozarts. Like Firmian, he wrote several important letters of recommendation, espe-cially to Rome, where one of his distant cousins was a cardinal and might even be instrumental in gaining access to the Pope ('I flatter myself he [Wolfgang] will meet with His Holiness's entire satisfaction', he added).[14] And he offered hospitality to the Mozarts when they passed through Bologna again on their way back to Milan, towards the end of the year.

Wolfgang could only add his contribution to one of Leopold's Bologna letters, so worn out was he by the end of their five days in the city, and he was possibly sickening too. Constant activity at the highest level, together with his continuing excited anticipa-tion of his Milan opera (he and Leopold were forever speculating about possible singers, noting where they were currently working and what the likelihood was of their being available to him), must have been exhausting for an adolescent, even one with an ability to meet all challenges with remarkable equanimity. And in truth, father and son were both weary: at the end of the fourth day, Leo-pold reported that 'Wolfgang has been snoring for a long time, and I fall asleep as I write'. As, yet again, he packed everything up for their onward travel, he did admit to being somewhat over-whelmed by all his responsibilities. 'We send our greetings to all our good friends . . . and I beg [them] . . . not to take it amiss that I do not reply. I hope they will bear in mind how much a traveller has to do, especially as I am single-handed. *Kommabit aliquando zeitus bequemus schreibendi. Nunc kopfus meus semper vollus est multis gedankibus.* [Sometime there will come a convenient time for writing. Now my head is full of many thoughts.]'[15] But Leopold and Wolfgang had nonetheless loved their time in Bologna, and must surely have continued on their journey with the same sense of satisfied achievement that they had enjoyed in Milan.

༄

The Mozarts' next destination was Florence, a powerful financial hub since the Middle Ages, whose wealth, especially under the mighty Medici dynasty, had supported the explosion of art, music, literature and science in the Renaissance: the city of Dante and Petrarch, of Michelangelo and Leonardo, of Galileo and of Machiavelli. Since the extinction of the Medici line and the accession of Maria Theresa's husband, Francis, as Grand Duke of Tuscany in 1737, it had been under Austrian rule, and at Francis's recent death in 1765, their son Leopold had succeeded him, aged only eighteen. The Grand Duke Leopold's own enlightened reforms would continue to give Tuscany stability, prosperity and progress, and in the second half of the eighteenth century Grand Tourists were flocking to Florence to admire its art and architecture. Keyssler approvingly noted that there were over 150 churches, 87 convents and 22 hospices in this relatively small city (with approximately 74,000 inhabitants, it was half the size of Milan, Rome or Venice, and merely a quarter that of Naples). It was well run, elegant and clean, with a greater degree of comfort than was to be found elsewhere. The few women travellers in Italy felt perfectly at ease in the city. In 1785, Hester Piozzi, for example, wrote lovingly of 'beautiful Florence, where the streets are kept so clean one is afraid to dirty them . . . by walking in them.'[16]

The journey from Bologna to Florence, some sixty-seven miles in a southerly direction through the Apennines, took the Mozarts two days. The conditions were not good. Leopold wrote of the 'rain and violent wind through which we drove in the mountains', and at night the temperatures dropped dramatically.[17] Burney, covering the same route some six months later, at the height of summer, wrote that 'the morning had been so cold on these mountains, that I was forced to walk several miles to warm myself'. And perhaps sustenance was difficult to acquire too. Burney also reported that he was 'so hungry that I was ready to eat the horses; but alas! There was nothing else to be had', although, on his second day, 'eggs, mushrooms, boiled rice, and bad fish, were welcome cates [delicacies] to a hungry traveller'.[18] It was the same story for Goethe in 1786: 'The inns were so bad that I could not find room even to spread out a sheet of paper.'[19] Leopold and Wolfgang had to endure these conditions in a much colder season, and by the time they arrived in Florence, on 30 March, Wolfgang, who had probably left Bologna in a state of some fragility, was decidedly unwell. Normally, when the Mozarts arrived in a new city, they strode out immediately to deliver letters of introduction, to visit a church or to go to the opera. But here in Florence they did nothing at all for a day and a half: they remained quietly in their room at the Aquila Nera inn. Leopold gave his wife a surely incomplete account of Wolfgang's symptoms, as he tried to reassure her that all was well: 'we spent the whole day indoors and Wolfgang stayed in bed until lunch, as he had caught a slight cold . . . I made him take tea and violet juice and he perspired a little.'[20] They had to decline an invitation to a musical soirée at the home of Lord Cowper, an English music lover who had come to Florence on his Grand Tour in 1759, and never left. (He entertained ambitions to be the British Resident in Florence, but these were thwarted by the long-standing incumbent, Horace Mann, who had been in post since 1737.) But by the following day the patient had recovered his energy, and the Mozarts spent the next five days, as they had in Bologna, executing another ferocious but fascinating schedule.

Armed with another of Count Firmian's letters, their first visit was to Count Franz Xavier Wolf Orsini-Rosenberg, the Austrian diplomat currently serving as high chamberlain at the court of Grand Duke Leopold. In fact, word of their arrival had already reached Rosenberg, as his house guest, the Imperial Ambassador Count Kaunitz, had very recently dined with the Mozarts at Count Pallavicini's palace in Bologna, and was now enthusing about Wolfgang. Rosenberg immediately arranged for the Mozarts to be presented to the Grand Duke at the Palazzo Pitti that very afternoon. (And later, in the 1780s, when he had become high chancellor and director of court theatres in Vienna, Rosenberg would again be helpful to Wolfgang, as he struggled to make a freelance living there.) The Grand Duke remembered meeting the Mozart family in Vienna, back in 1762, when Wolfgang was only six – and he himself merely fifteen. According to Leopold, he was 'uncommonly gracious, asked at once after Nannerl, said that his wife [the Spanish Infanta Maria Luisa] was very anxious to hear Wolfgang play, and spoke to us for a full quarter of an hour'.[21] So, on the next day, the Mozarts were driven out to the Grand Duke's summer palace, the Villa Medicea di Poggio Imperiale, where Wolfgang was put through his usual paces. The director of music at court, Marchese Eugenio Ligniville, whom Leopold (with a short memory, perhaps) claimed to be 'the finest expert in counterpoint in the whole of Italy', gave Wolfgang difficult fugue subjects to work, which he did 'as easily as one eats a piece of bread'. And he performed alongside a celebrated violinist and composer, Pietro Nardini, whom the Mozarts had first

1. Wolfgang was thirteen when this was painted in Verona, early in 1770.

2. Leopold Mozart.

3. Coach travel in the
   eighteenth century.

138

4. Plaque commemorating Wolfgang's stay in Rovereto, at the start of his 'triumphant journey across the country'.

IN·QVESTA·CASA·PATRIZIA
DALLE·GRAZIE·DEL·SETTECENTO·ARRISA
VOLFANGO·MOZART
IL·SVO·PRIMO·CONCERTO·ITALIANO
NEL·NATALE·1769·TENEVA
E·ROVERETO·NEL·SVO·VNANIME·PLAVSO
FAVSTO·PRELVDIO
AL·SVO·TRIONFALE·VIAGGIO
NEL·BEL·PAESE
IL·PRIMO·SALVTO·D'ITALIA
LIETA·ED·ORGOGLIOSA·OLI·PORGEVA
✦
NEL·CLXXV·ANNIVERSARIO·DELLA·NASCITA·1931

5. Gaspare Vanvitelli's view of eighteenth-century Verona, as the Mozarts would have seen it.

6. The interior of the Teatro Bibiena in Mantua, where Wolfgang played in 1770. Leopold wrote of it: 'In all my life I have never seen anything more beautiful of its kind.'

7. Canaletto's Milan, as the Mozarts would have seen it.

8. Count Firmian, Wolfgang's passionate supporter, and promoter of all his Milan operas.

9. Count Pallavicini, Wolfgang's passionate supporter, patron and host in Bologna.

10. This delightful group, painted in Florence, apparently depicts Wolfgang and his coeval English friend Thomas Linley.

11. Pio Panfili's view of eighteenth-century Bologna, as the Mozarts would have seen it.

12. Eighteenth-century Rome, as the Mozarts would have seen it: Forum, Campo Vacino, church of Santa Francesca Romana, and the Colosseum.

13. Pope Clement XIV, who bestowed on
Wolfgang the Order of the Golden Spur.

met in Augsburg in 1763. On that occasion, Leopold, the great violin authority, declared 'it would be impossible to hear a finer player for beauty, purity, evenness of tone and singing quality'.[22] He would have been gratified now to find him collaborating with his son.

Nardini too would have been intrigued to encounter the Mozarts again, not least because he currently had as a student another prodigious talent of exactly the same age as Wolfgang: an English boy called Thomas Linley. If Wolfgang had not been unwell, both boys would have played at Lord Cowper's musical soirée on the previous evening. But on the day after the encounter with Nardini at the Villa Medicea, they met at the home of the court's official poetess, Madalena Morelli-Fernandez, known as Corilla Olimpica. According to Burney, she too was a 'scholar of Nardini, on the Violin, which she plays on her lap, and looks like a tenth Muse, which she has often been called'.[23] She hosted regular musical evenings in her house, which was 'much frequented by foreigners, and men of letters'. And so it was she who brought together these two foreign fourteen-year-old boys, who instantly found rapport.

Thomas Linley came from a talented artistic family in Bath: his father, also Thomas, was a composer, and his elder sister Elizabeth Ann was a singer, and a girl of great beauty who was painted by, among others, Gainsborough and Reynolds. In due course she would marry the playwright Richard Brinsley Sheridan. Young Thomas's musical abilities, like Wolfgang's, had been acknowledged in his infancy, and since the age of seven he had been performing in public. As a child he was taught in London by William Boyce, Master of the King's Music, and also appeared on stage with his sister at the Covent Garden opera house. In 1768, aged twelve, he had come to Florence to study with Nardini.

Burney too would meet him on his visit to Florence later in 1770, and, like everyone else, make instant comparisons with Wolfgang: 'little Linley came to see me, he has been two years under Nardini, and is universally admired. The Tommasino, as he is called, and the little Mozart, are talked of all over Italy, as the most promising geniuses of this age.'[24] Like Wolfgang, Thomas had had little contact with other teenagers, and for both of them the discovery now of someone with similar experience and ability was profoundly important and moving. According to Leopold, 'the two boys performed one after the other throughout the whole evening, constantly embracing each other'.[25] They spent all the next day, 4 April, together at the Mozarts' inn, each enjoying not just the companionship of a like-minded contemporary, but the ecstasy too of musical collaboration at the very highest level. Then, on 5 April, at the home of the court finance minister, Giuseppe Maria Gavard des Pivets, they performed together 'not like boys, but like men!' Knowing the Mozarts had to leave on the following day, Thomas tearfully accompanied them back to their inn, and plans were discussed for a reunion, if the Mozarts were to return to Florence after their travels south to Rome and Naples. Thomas had asked Corilla Olimpica to write a poem as a parting gift for his new friend. And when their carriage left Florence on the following morning, Thomas went with them as far as the city gate. Sadly, that was in fact the last time the boys saw each other. The Mozarts had to change their autumn plans, and never made it back to Florence. And, eight years later, Thomas was tragically drowned, at the age of twenty-two, in a boating accident in Lincolnshire.

It was again with a gratifying sense of achievement that Leopold and Wolfgang left Florence on 6 April. They had loved the city and their welcoming, appreciative hosts. Leopold truly regretted that they had had only one week in which to 'see all that there is to be seen', professing to Maria Anna, somewhat insensitively, his sadness that she too could not see 'Florence itself and the surrounding countryside and the situation of the town, for you would say that one should live and die here.'[26] But in order to arrive in Rome in Holy Week, the Mozarts were facing a five-day journey of 185 miles (twenty staging posts), at some speed. Although their route to the Eternal City, largely down the Via Cassia, an old Roman road, took them through some glorious scenery and important Tuscan and Umbrian towns (Siena, Orvieto, Viterbo) with much to offer tourists, they determinedly kept going, their only swift nod to sightseeing being a visit to the preserved body of Santa Rosa in Viterbo. There, it seems, they did at least welcome a 'good supper' and a decent night's sleep, for again their travel conditions were lamentable and the weather persistently awful. Leopold confessed he 'could have been more easily persuaded to return to Salzburg than to proceed to Rome, for we had to travel for five days . . . in the most horrible rain and cold wind', and he described 'a more or less uncultivated countryside and the most horrible, filthy inns, where we got nothing to eat save occasional eggs and broccoli'.[27] (Five months later, Dr Charles Burney travelled the same route, and equally bemoaned its 'wretched villages', a 'desolate barren country' and the apparent availability only of 'two or three eggs tolerably fresh', concluding that he too had 'never travelled in greater misery'.[28]) Leopold was right, it seems, to be 'glad that neither of you undertook this journey with us'.

At midday on Wednesday, 11 April, the Mozarts arrived at

last in Rome. The city of emperors and popes, of barbarians and plunderers, effortlessly intertwines the richest threads of European civilization. The imperial splendour of the Colosseum is neighbour to Renaissance churches, baroque palaces and everything in between; no traveller, in any era, fails to find it uplifting. The Mozarts too were immediately energized by the city, despite the rigours of the journey and appalling weather conditions (they arrived in the middle of a violent thunderstorm). With the help of their good friend Leopold Troger in Milan, and his Roman acquaintance the Abate Francesco Antonio Marcobruni, whom as it happens the Mozarts had known when he was a student in Salzburg, they had already arranged some modest accommodation. They changed their clothes and set off straight away for Vatican City, where they attended Mass in the Sistine Chapel. The service included the special setting by Gregorio Allegri of Psalm 51, 'Miserere mei, Deus', written in the 1630s during the reign of Pope Urban VIII for the sole use of the Vatican in Holy Week. So protected was this exclusive setting that there were at the time only three authorized copies of it beyond the walls of the Vatican. One was in the possession of the King of Portugal, another with the Grand Duke of Tuscany, in his role as Holy Roman Emperor, and the third with none other than Padre Martini in Bologna. Wolfgang and Leopold had recently spent time with the last two of these, either of whom could have engaged the interest of the fourteen-year-old boy, who loved secrets and codes and intrigues, in this rare treasure, the unique and jealously guarded property of the Holy See. Wolfgang heard the work that afternoon after his long journey, returned to his lodging, and famously wrote it down from memory. Allegri's 'Miserere' is for two choirs in dialogue, and helpfully repetitive; but it culminates in nine-part polyphony, and it was no mean feat for Wolfgang, treating this perhaps as he did all the tests and challenges to which he was constantly being subjected by learned professors, to make his transcription. Leopold proudly told Maria Anna and Nannerl what Wolfgang had done:

> You have often heard of the famous Miserere in Rome, which is so greatly prized that the performers in the chapel are forbidden on pain of excommunication to take away a single part of it, to copy it or to give it to anyone. *But we have it already.* Wolfgang has written it down and we would have sent it to Salzburg in this letter, if it were not necessary for us to be there to perform it. But the manner of performance contributes more to its effect than the composition itself. So we shall bring it home with us. Moreover, as it is one of the secrets of Rome, we do not wish to let it fall into other hands.[29]

And twenty-three years later Nannerl, who had become a passionate hoarder of detail as she received news of her brother's exploits, charmingly recalled that Wolfgang 'the next day . . . went back again, holding his copy in his hat, to see whether he had got it right or not.'[30] In fact, for all the Mozarts' attempts at secrecy, confessing Wolfgang's act of larceny only privately to Maria Anna and Nannerl, intelligence of this extraordinary feat did spread swiftly through Rome, and even reached the Pope himself. But, far from causing outrage and the inflicting of punishment, the news only enhanced Wolfgang's reputation. Maria Anna panicked when she heard that disclosures of her son's achievement had gone public, and feared that some dreadful retribution would be handed down to him. A month after the event, Leopold cheerfully reassured her: 'On reading the article about the Miserere, we simply burst out laughing. There is not the slightest cause for anxiety. Everywhere else far more fuss is being made about Wolfgang's feat. All Rome knows and even the Pope himself that he wrote it down. There is nothing whatever to fear; on the contrary the achievement has done him great credit.'[31]

The Mozarts' acts of subterfuge continued on the day after their arrival, Maundy Thursday. In accordance with tradition, the Pope (Clement XIV) was to serve the poor in a public ceremony. So again the Mozarts dressed in smart clothes, joined the crowd, and pushed their way to the front, as Leopold shamelessly recounted in his letter home: '. . . we had to pass through two doors guarded by Swiss guards in armour and make our way through hundreds of people . . . But our fine clothes, the German tongue, and my usual freedom of manner . . . soon helped us through everywhere. They took Wolfgang for some German courtier, while some even thought he was a prince . . . I myself was taken for his tutor. Thus we made our way to the Cardinals' table.'[32]

Not only did they therefore witness His Holiness's humble rituals at the closest possible quarters ('we were standing beside him at the top of the table'), they also – somewhat serendipitously – succeeded in meeting a man high on their list of people to contact in Rome, the Cardinal Pallavicini, cousin of their recent generous host in Bologna. Again, Leopold described the encounter:

Wolfgang happened to be standing between the chairs of two Cardinals, one of whom was Cardinal Pallavicini, who made a sign to him and said: '*Will you be so good as to tell me in confidence who you are?*' And Wolfgang told him. The Cardinal showed the greatest astonishment and said: '*Ah, you are the famous boy, about whom so many things have been written to me*'. Whereupon Wolfgang asked him: '*Are you not Cardinal*

Pallavicini?' The Cardinal replied: '*Yes, I am, but why?'* Then
Wolfgang told him *that we had letters to deliver to His Eminence
and that we were going to pay him our respects.* The Cardinal
appeared to be delighted, remarked that Wolfgang spoke Italian very well and among other things added: '*Ik kann auck ein
benig deutsch sprecken'.* When we were leaving, Wolfgang kissed
his hand and the Cardinal took off his berretta and bowed very
politely.[33]

Wolfgang was perhaps disappointed not to hear the Allegri 'Miserere' again, to check his memorized transcription. (A different
setting was sung, and he would have to return on Good Friday
for the next performance of the Allegri.) But he and his father
would have been more than satisfied with the success of the day.

After these initial Roman excitements, the Mozarts were a little
quieter over the Easter weekend. Leopold himself professed to be
under the weather ('I have been a bit of an invalid').[34] And they
did have to address the matter of their accommodation, for the
single-room lodging with only one bed was clearly not going to
be acceptable for a lengthy stay ('Mamma can well imagine that I
get no sleep with Papa', complained Wolfgang).[35] So, again with
the help of the Abate Marcobruni, they moved into a spacious
and comfortable set of rooms on the second floor of Palazzo Sca-
tizzi, overlooking the river Tiber. Its owner, Stefano Uslenghi,
was a papal courier, and at the time travelling in Portugal. But
his wife and daughter Margherita, who was learning to play the
harpsichord, treated their new house guests as if they were family
members, feeding them regularly and giving them full run of the
house. Leopold and Wolfgang were there for nearly four weeks,
and so charmed their hostess that they had difficulty in paying
her any rent: Leopold made arrangements through Marcobruni

that Signora Uslenghi would be reimbursed on their return, later in the year.[36] From this new-found and spacious comfort, the Mozarts attended services at St Peter's Basilica over Easter, and also managed to explore it very thoroughly. (To his teenage embarrassment, the diminutive Wolfgang 'had to be lifted up' to kiss the foot of St Peter's statue.[37]) Leopold continued, after his disgruntled observations in Milan, to nurture his contempt for the Italian clergy, whom he judged to be self-important and pompous: 'You cannot conceive how conceited the clergy are here. Any priest who has the slightest association with a Cardinal, when on business connected with His Holiness, drives with a cortège of three or four carriages, each of which is filled with his chaplains, secretaries and valets.'[38] But this first letter from Rome back to Maria Anna and Nannerl also contained a new contredanse (K.123) written by Wolfgang, with detailed instructions for how it should be played and danced. It seems likely that this composition too was the product of those five uncomfortable travel days, as Wolfgang had distracted himself from their gruelling conditions.

On Easter Monday, Leopold and Wolfgang began to deliver their twenty letters of introduction, most of them generating from Count Pallavicini, and almost immediately they bore fruit. In two and a half weeks, between 19 April and 7 May, Wolfgang, together with his father, performed eight times, in some of the most exalted palaces in Rome, and before an impressive assembly of princes and princesses, dukes and barons, ambassadors, and of course the lofty clergy, headed by Cardinal Pallavicini. Since the early stages of this Italian journey, Leopold had followed his usual custom of compiling lists of people they met at each stop on their travels. These lists had begun quite modestly, with small-town mayors and priests, and had gradually grown in status as well as volume, especially through Verona, Milan and Bologna. Now, surely, his list hit its zenith. The Roman roll-call is headed (not entirely truthfully, for they had not actually met him yet) by none other than 'Il Papa Clemente 14e', followed by three of his cardinals. After them come all the Mozarts' royal and patrician hosts, including the Prince St Angelo of Naples, the Prince and Princess Chigi, the Princess Barberini, and their various distinguished guests; and finally the musicians with whom the Mozarts engaged.[39] Among those whom Leopold forgot to list in his journal, but certainly met on two of these august occasions, was Charles Stuart, 'the Pretender or so-called King of England', as he reported to Maria Anna.[40] (Bonnie Prince Charlie, after his defeat at Culloden in 1746 and subsequent failures in all further attempts to invade Britain, had settled back into his life in Rome, where under the name of the Duke of Albany he was a regular ornament in princely salons.) Beneath the admiring gaze of all these variously assembled dignitaries, Wolfgang – as ever – performed with effortless distinction and received his customary plaudits.

Several of the Mozarts' hosts, the original recipients of epistolary encomia from Count Pallavicini, wrote back to him to express their delight and astonishment at Wolfgang's talents, and their gratitude for having been introduced to him. The Count's cousin, Cardinal Pallavicini, who would similarly become a pivotal supporter of the Mozarts, wrote: 'The testimonial which your most sensitive discernment procured me about [Wolfgang's] extraordinary talent for Music only enhanced the interest I shall take on all occasions in everything that is of advantage to you'.[41] Prince Andrea Doria Pamphili likewise described his 'most intense pleasure' at the connection with the Mozarts, and expressed his desire to 'seek ways and means to oblige them apart from what I am able to do myself'.[42] And Baron Saint-Odile became another link in Leopold's chain, for he too wrote introductory letters to friends and colleagues in Naples, where the Mozarts were heading next. Again, it seems that, while Wolfgang was sailing through all his Roman exhibitions, Leopold was tying together the threads of his connective influential fabric, with the greatest efficiency and satisfaction.

In one significant respect, this first visit of Wolfgang and Leopold to Rome, in that Easter period of 1770, differed from any other prolonged stay thus far in an Italian city. They saw no opera at all, for, between seasons, none was presented. But Wolfgang was still utterly preoccupied with this essential Italian art form, and especially with his own upcoming commission for Milan. In their letters home, while Leopold described conditions and connections and strategic plans, Wolfgang, writing expressly to his sister, and now almost always in Italian, in addition to describing games and puzzles, and continuing to tease her about her male admirers, shared with her his thoughts about his opera. He was primarily concerned about the choice of libretto ('The libretto has not yet been chosen. I recommended to Don Ferdinando and Herr von Troger a text by Metastasio'),[43] and was also curious about his potential cast. Knowing that Nannerl would remember (for she forgot little) all the singers they had met together on their earlier travels, he reported on the possibility of the celebrated castrato Giovanni Manzuoli being part of his team. Manzuoli had been in London when the Mozart family were there, in the 1764–5 season. They had got to know him a little, and Nannerl and Wolfgang had possibly even taken singing lessons from him. Now, in 1770, just before Wolfgang and his father had left Florence, they had met him by chance in the street, and it seems that Manzuoli himself, having heard of the

Milan project, was keen to be part of it: 'Manzuoli is negotiating with the Milanese to sing in my opera'. Wolfgang shared other considerations too with Nannerl: 'It is not known for certain whether Gabrielli will come. Some say De Amicis will sing. We are to meet her in Naples. I should like her and Manzuoli to take the parts.'[44] In the meantime, as he waited for news of his libretto and cast, he was continuing to set aria texts from his collected edition of Metastasio: 'At the moment I am working at the aria: Se ardire, e speranza' (K.82/73, from Metastasio's *Demofoonte*). And he was writing other music too, including at least two four-movement symphonies (K.97 and K.95), which his father then copied for him.

In amongst all this musical activity, there must have been sightseeing. Although in their letters both father and son were tantalizingly reticent about the great attractions of ancient Rome, and its many museums and palaces, it is clear that they did indeed have several outings ('During the last few days we have . . . seen several fine things', Wolfgang wrote vaguely to Nannerl),[45] and also made social calls to acquaintances old and new. On one occasion they ran into a man named Porta, whom they had met in Paris in 1764 and engaged as a servant to accompany them to London. Back then, Leopold had approved of his skills ('he arranged everything well and did all the bargaining'),[46] but now, for some reason, he felt only deep suspicion, and 'refused to have anything to do with him'.[47] Others were more warmly greeted. One of Salzburg's more celebrated court singers, Joseph Meissner, was also now travelling in Italy, and joined Wolfgang therefore for his concert at the Collegio Germanico in Rome on 2 May. And there were 'a great many Englishmen' too, with whom the Mozarts 'walked for a couple of hours . . . in the garden of the Villa Medici'.[48] Both father and son were in good spirits and good health, as Leopold reassured his anxious wife: '[Wolfgang] has grown a little. I am neither fatter nor thinner; and we have got accustomed to Italian food.'[49]

What certainly preoccupied Leopold as always, especially in the latter days in Rome, was the daunting prospect of their moving on to Naples, a distance of approximately 155 miles. This at least was shorter than the journey between Florence and Rome, which had been so disagreeable. But these southern roads, now following the ancient Roman Via Appia, were known to be the territory of bandits and robbers, and therefore extremely dangerous. Leopold wrote anxiously to Maria Anna:

For the last fortnight the roads have been very unsafe and a merchant has been killed. But the sbirri [police] and the blood-thirsty Papal soldiers were immediately sent out from Rome and we hear that a skirmish has already taken place in which five sbirri and three robbers were killed, four robbers taken prisoner and the rest dispersed. But now they have drawn nearer the Neapolitan borders and, if it is true that they have killed a Neapolitan courier on his way to Spain, every effort will be made from Naples to clear up the roads. I shall not leave here until I know they are safe[50]

Leopold's solution to these perils was to turn to the Church, and specifically to Augustinian priests. By attaching themselves to them, he and Wolfgang would not only acquire responsible travelling companions, but assistance too with accommodation on the road. And so, somewhat earlier than planned, the Mozarts headed south from Rome on 8 May. And in fact, with the now gloriously warm weather, the serious respectability of their fellow passengers, and the monasteries in which they therefore ate and

slept, their progress was certainly not dangerous, nor even par-
ticularly unpleasant, although its early stages passed through the
Paludi Pontini, the swampy marshland graphically described by
Burney later that year:

> the first thing we were able to see was the famous, or rather
> infamous, Palus Pontina, or Pontine Marsh . . . which has never
> yet been drained, notwithstanding the repeated attempts made
> by both the ancients and the moderns. It is to this stagnant
> water, and uncultivated land, that the 'Mall'Aria' on this side
> of the Campagna of Rome is attributed; and I shuddered with
> horror at the sight of this bog, and the sickly and putrid hue of
> its inhabitants . . . Here, Buffalos and black pigs abound – both
> the colour and ugliness of the D—l.[51]

Emerging from these dismal marshes at Terracina, the road then
followed the coastline, which the habitually landlocked Salzburg-
ers could well have found to be as dramatic as Burney did: 'the
sea foamed and beat against the rocks which are very high, in a
grand and terrible manner – I had never seen it so enraged'.[52]
Once they were in Neapolitan territory the roads improved,
for they had been newly made just two years earlier, in 1768, in
honour of Naples's new queen, Maria Carolina. The Mozarts
lingered only in Capua, just twenty-seven miles and therefore an
easy day's journey from Naples. One of their travelling companions had previously been employed at the Augustinian monastery
there, and persuaded Leopold to stay long enough to witness
the veiling of a young nun: 'Padre Segarelli . . . was to be present at this veiling and begged us to remain there too. Thus we
saw the ceremony, which was very magnificent and for which a
Kapellmeister with three or four carriages of virtuosi arrived on

the evening of the 12th and began the proceedings with symphonies and a Salve Regina. They all stayed in the Augustinian monastery, so you can imagine that on that evening we went to bed very late.'[53] Perhaps this welcome and jolly communion with fellow musicians gave the Mozarts renewed cheer. Certainly their final approach to Naples was through what Burney described as 'the richest [landscape] that can be imagined, truly abounding with corn, wine and oil; all of which are produced by the same land at the same time . . . a rich and most beautiful appearance';[54] and they still arrived two days earlier than they had originally planned. They took temporary accommodation with the Augustinians at their monastery of San Giovanni in Carbonara, before finally moving into their pre-booked lodgings, a private apartment run by a Signora Angiola. They would remain there for six delightful weeks.

The Mozarts probably had high hopes for continued social success in Naples, not least because of its Habsburg protection. Already in their southerly progress through Italy they had connected with two of Maria Theresa's useful children. In Milan, through their encounters with his future bride, Princess Maria Beatrice d'Este, they were beginning to forge a new link to the sixteen-year-old Ferdinand. Perhaps they had been hoping also to meet, though had not done so, his older sister Maria Amalia (aged twenty-four and uncomfortably married to Duke Ferdinand of Parma) when they had passed through that engaging city. They had certainly been charmingly received in Florence by the twenty-three-year-old Leopold, Grand Duke of Tuscany. Now they were hoping to obtain entry to the court of King

Ferdinand of Naples, and to meet again his bride of two years, Maria Theresa's thirteenth child, Maria Carolina. King Ferdinand himself had inherited his throne in 1759, when his father Carlo III abdicated in order to become King of Spain. Ferdinand was only eight years old at the time, and could not reign until he reached the age of majority. So the Marchese Barnard Tanucci, a powerful Tuscan lawyer and minister of justice for Carlo III, was appointed regent. Tanucci remained the power behind the throne even after Ferdinand turned sixteen, for he relished his position and rather wilfully neglected the training of the young king for his regal responsibilities. Ferdinand, for his part, was happy to devote himself to idle pleasure, and was energetic only in the cause of hunting, to which he was addicted. His marriage in 1768 did nevertheless alter the dynamic between Tanucci and the throne, for Maria Carolina had unquestionably inherited her mother's determination and political acumen, and enjoyed wielding influence in the council of state. In 1770, when the Mozarts arrived in Naples, the King and Queen were still only nineteen and eighteen years old, respectively, but already their behavioural patterns were established.

Naples itself, one of the oldest continually inhabited cities of the world, was also, in the eighteenth century, Italy's largest. Its population of over 350,000 was twice that of Rome, and its spectacular setting beneath Mount Vesuvius, in a plain rich with volcanic soil and with an abundance of fish in its adjacent seas, gave it a prosperity which encouraged constant artistic creativity. Originally settled by the Greeks and then conquered by the Romans, its connection to the ancient world too was profound; and now, in the eighteenth century, the excavations of nearby Pompeii and Herculaneum (in which Tanucci himself was passionately involved) generated considerable excitement. As with all large conurbations, there was inevitably a dark underbelly of poverty, hardship and deprivation, a high level of criminality, and a rough crudity therefore among a considerable proportion of the city's population. But art, culture and learning thrived. Naples's university was founded in 1224; its churches, palaces and castles proliferated in the medieval, Renaissance and baroque periods, and, following the arrival of Caravaggio in 1606, a school of painting was established. Similarly, Naples was an important centre for music, and especially for opera. The so-called 'Neapolitan school' had produced or attracted in the seventeenth and eighteenth centuries composers of the calibre of Alessandro Scarlatti, Porpora, Pergolesi, Jommelli, Paisiello and Cimarosa. When the Mozarts arrived in the city in 1770, there were three functioning opera houses, the most recent (built in 1737, and renovated already in 1768) being the magnificent Teatro San Carlo, attached to the Palazzo Reale, and in constant operation to this day.

Just as the Mozarts were leaving Rome to travel to Naples, one of their new-found Roman admirers, Baron Saint-Odile, was writing on their behalf to Giuseppe Bonecchi, secretary to the Imperial Ambassador at Naples, Count Ernst Kaunitz: 'I beg you, Sir, to make some special effort on behalf of my little Mozart, who is full of the best qualities. He well deserves to become known in the house of Tanucci'.[55] And it was indeed to Tanucci that Leopold turned his immediate attention as he began to distribute his letters of recommendation on his usual social round ('this Prime Minister is really a king and has enormous influence', he explained to Maria Anna).[56] The court had moved from the centre of Naples to the summer palace at Portici, and on three consecutive days Leopold and Wolfgang doggedly travelled out there to try to gain access to Tanucci. When they were finally received, it was with warmth. Meanwhile the Imperial Ambassador Count Kaunitz, who had already encountered and admired Wolfgang in Bologna and Florence, welcomed them again. Both Tanucci and Kaunitz involved their wives in setting up a concert for the Mozarts, which duly took place in Kaunitz's official residence on 28 May. 'On Monday we are giving a concert, which the Countess von Kaunitz, the Imperial Ambassador's wife, Lady Hamilton, Principessa Belmonte, Principessa Francavilla, Duchess Calabritta are organising and which, I think, will bring us in at least one hundred and fifty zecchini'.[57] So again Wolfgang's audience consisted of the cream of Neapolitan society, including, besides those proudly listed by Leopold, Count Kraft, who did indeed give them a generous gift of 150 zecchini, matched perhaps by the 'handsome present' that the Princess Francavilla produced on the next day.[58] Also at the concert were several English visitors, whose company the Mozarts had been enjoying. The British minister was Sir William Hamilton, whom they had met in London in 1764; his frail wife Catherine was not merely a passionate music lover who assisted with the organization of the concert, but also an excellent harpsichordist herself, as Leopold reported: 'we called on the English ambassador, Hamilton . . . whose wife plays the clavier with unusual feeling and is a very pleasant person. She trembled at having to play before Wolfgang.'[59] (After Catherine died in 1782, Sir William Hamilton married Emma, later the mistress of Admiral Horatio Nelson.) The Mozarts perhaps enjoyed exercising their linguistic skills again, as they mixed not just with the Hamiltons' English circle, but also that of the French ambassador, who sent them tickets for a ball in his residence on 3 June, in honour of the marriage between Louis XVI and Queen Maria Carolina's younger sister, the Archduchess Maria Antonia, now to be known as Marie

Antoinette. Every day, Leopold and Wolfgang were guests of different noblemen, who invited them to attend the 'passaggio', which Leopold described for Maria Anna:

> One of the finest sights is the daily passeggio, when in a few hundred carriages the nobles go out driving in the afternoon until Ave Maria to the Strada Nuova and the Molo. The Queen too goes out driving very often, always on Sundays and on holidays. As she drives along the sea coast, guns are fired off on the ships, and on the right and on the left the carriages stop and their occupants salute her as she passes them. As soon as it is twilight, the flambeaux are lighted on all the carriages and produce a sort of illumination. Since we drive there daily and always in a carriage belonging to some lord, I have two flambeaux, that is the servant of the lord who has sent his carriage has one and our servant has the other.[60]

From her own carriage, Queen Maria Carolina regularly recognized and acknowledged the Mozarts ('Her Majesty the Queen always greets us with quite exceptional friendliness'), but the King resolutely snubbed them. Nevertheless, even without regal approbation or support, the Mozarts were relishing the vibrancy of Neapolitan society. Wolfgang's performance calendar was nothing like as frenzied as it had been in Bologna, Florence or Rome, and they were able, quite simply, to relax and enjoy themselves.

And once more Wolfgang could indulge his current passion for opera, and here in Naples another encounter with a senior practitioner of it was crucial to his burgeoning development. Soon after their arrival, Wolfgang of course acquired the schedule for the upcoming opera season, and as usual shared it with

Nannerl: 'The opera, which Jommelli is composing, will begin on the 30th . . . Cafaro is composing the second opera, and Ciccio di Majo the third. It is not yet known who is composing the fourth.'[61] Niccolò Jommelli, aged forty-six, was another immensely prolific opera composer who, like Hasse (seventy-one) and Piccinni (forty-two) before him, took the young Wolfgang somewhat under his wing. A local man who had studied at two of Naples' fine conservatories, he had already travelled widely in his career, and recently had lengthy engagements in Rome (at St Peter's), Vienna and Stuttgart, as well as much operatic success in Bologna, Venice, Ferrara and Padua. Jommelli shared links with two of Wolfgang's own mentors. He had studied with Padre Martini in Bologna; and, in Venice, he had been recommended by Hasse for a post at the Ospedale degli Incurabili. Later, in 1763, Jommelli had met the Mozart family at Ludwigsburg, one of the residences of his Stuttgart employer, Duke Karl Eugen of Wurttemberg; and on that occasion Leopold, displaying a fundamental disdain for Italians which he never truly overcame, was critical of Jommelli's employing Italian rather than German musicians, and then sneeringly triumphant when: 'Jommelli . . . and some of his compatriots, who are ever swarming at his house to pay their respects, were heard to say that it was amazing and hardly believable that a child of German birth could have such unusual genius and so much understanding and passion'.[62] But now, as Jommelli's *Armida abbandonata* was to open the opera season at the Teatro San Carlo on the King's name-day, the Mozarts went to a rehearsal of it, and renewed their acquaintance. Wolfgang wrote to Nannerl: 'we were at the rehearsal of Signor Jommelli's opera, which is well composed and which I really like. He himself spoke to us and was very polite.'[63] He and Leopold subsequently attended the glittering premiere, and then Jommelli invited them to his home and introduced them to the impresario from San Carlo, who invited Wolfgang to write for them too. (Wolfgang could not accept the invitation, as it would have clashed with his Milan opera.) Like Hasse and Piccinni, Jommelli seems to have combined the warmest hospitality with generous support. Far from feeling threatened by the phenomenal talent of a teenage composer, he actively tried to assist him.

As usual, Wolfgang wanted to share with his sister his (candid) opinions of *Armida abbandonata*. 'The opera . . . is beautiful, but too serious and old-fashioned for the theatre. De Amicis sings amazingly well and so does Aprile, who sang in Milan. The dances are wretchedly pompous. The theatre is beautiful.'[64] Anna De Amicis was another singer whom Wolfgang knew Nannerl would remember, for she too had met the Mozart family, in Mainz, in 1763, on their major tour through Europe. A Neapolitan herself, she had already, in her mid-thirties, had a brilliant career singing throughout Italy, and in Paris, Dublin, Brussels and London. Burney had heard her at the King's Theatre in London in 1762, and never forgot his first impression. In his subsequent *General History of Music*, published in 1789, he wrote that she 'captivated the public in various ways. Her figures and gestures were in the highest degree elegant and graceful; her countenance, though not perfectly beautiful, was extremely well-bred and interesting; and her voice and manner of singing, exquisitely polished and sweet. She had not a motion that did not charm the eye, or a tone but what delighted the ear.'[65] Wolfgang too, at fourteen, was captivated by her, perhaps even starrily reading too much into her polite interest in him. When he wrote to Nannerl, 'We have been to see her and she recognised us at once', he thought better of it and crossed out the second half of his sentence.[66] But he was clearly hoping she would sing in his Milan opera; and although she was not available to him that year, her path would indeed intersect with his in a future season.

Aside from visits to the opera – of the *buffa* type as well as Jommelli's *seria* – the Mozarts spent their easy Naples days in the company of friends old and new. Among their old acquaintances now in the rich melting-pot of Neapolitan society were Baron Fridolin Tschudi, known from Salzburg; Jean-Georges Meuricoffre, a French banker whom they had met in Lyons; and a Dutch merchant, 'our good friend Mr. Donker, tall, handsome Donker of Amsterdam, who for the last three years has been living here with the French consul'.[67] Leopold gave up any hope of being received by the King ('You ask whether we played before the King of Naples? No, indeed! . . . what sort of a fellow the King is it is perhaps wiser to speak of than write about', he moaned to Maria Anna).[68] But they engaged as always with several musicians, all of high quality. And meanwhile Leopold was busy plotting the route of his return journey north. He was keen to maintain his link with the Imperial Ambassador, and possibly even to travel with him ('I am still determined to leave for Rome on the 16th with the procaccio, or possibly on the 20th, if I secure a private sedia in which I shall travel with the Imperial Ambassador Count Kaunitz').[69] But while they waited for some confirmation from the Count, Tanucci's wife sent the Mozarts a steward to show them 'all the rare sights of Naples'.[70] And so, in the third week of June, they had exhilarating excursions:

We drove in a carriage to Pozzuoli, and then took ship to Baia, where we saw the baths of Nero, the subterranean grotto of Sybilla Cumana, Lago d'Averno, Tempio di Venere, Tempio di Diana, Sepolcro d'Agrippina, the Elysian Fields, the Dead Sea, where Charon was the ferryman, la Piscina Mirabile, the

Centro Camerelle, and so forth. On the return journey we
visited many old baths, temples, underground rooms, Monte
Nuovo, Monte Guaro, Molo di Pozzuoli, Colosseo, Solfatara,
Astroni, Grotta del Cane, Lago d'Agnano, but especially the
Grotto di Pozzuoli and Virgil's grave . . . On Monday and
Tuesday we are going to Vesuvius, the two buried cities [Pom-
peii and Herculaneum] where entire rooms from classical
antiquity are currently being excavated, then Caserta and Capo
di Monte.[71]

This was total immersion in the region's incomparable history
and legend. And although the excavations of Pompeii and Herculaneum were still very much in their earliest stages, the gradual
uncovering there of remote civilizations, from the grandest architectural design to their smallest domestic receptacle or ornament,
would unquestionably have stimulated a teenage genius who was
about to engage, through the act of writing *opera seria*, with the
ancient world. For Wolfgang, following his experience among the
monuments of Verona and Rome, walking now into rooms where
lives had once been lived and seeing tangible artefacts which
had been held or worn by their long-dead owners, the classical
heroes whose stories he knew and who were the subjects of his
Metastasio texts all now assumed a human dimension. The realization and depiction of this would become an absolute hallmark
of Wolfgang's operas over the ensuing years.

So the relatively relaxed weeks in Naples were of great benefit
to both father and son. Although Leopold was never uncritical of
any environment he visited, and much of Naples duly earned his
fierce disapproval ('the filth, the crowds of beggars, the hateful
and godless populace, the disgraceful way in which children are
brought up, the incredible frivolity even in the churches'),[72] they

had enjoyed the food, the climate and – for the most part – the people. They had been received with kindness and generosity, and were in good health. Eventually Leopold decided to return to Rome not in ambassadorial splendour with Kaunitz (perhaps that had never formally been an option), but by the fastest possible means, the mail-coach. Thus they would avoid four and a half days' travel and 'most abominable inns', and arrive back in Rome in just over twenty-four hours.[73] Wolfgang was in the highest of spirits as he embarked on the return journey that would eventually lead to his new opera for Milan. 'I too am still alive and always merry as usual', he wrote to Nannerl, 'and I simply love travelling.'[74]

4

~~~~~

RECOGNITION AND TRIUMPH

'There is no musical excellence which I do not expect,
from his extraordinary quickness and talents'

Wolfgang might perhaps have revised his merry verdict on travelling after the return journey to Rome, which the Mozarts did
indeed achieve in a single, and very long (twenty-seven-hour),
day. It began well enough, with 'good horses and a quick service',
because Leopold, in another of his bold fabrications, 'announced
everywhere that I was the steward of the Imperial Ambassador,
as in these parts the stewards of such personages are very highly
respected'.[1] And indeed this deception ensured that the arrival
in Rome too was satisfactory: 'it was not necessary for me to go
to the Customs Office for the usual examination. For at the gate
I was received with a deep bow, and was simply told to drive on
to my destination, at which I was so pleased that I threw a few
paoli in their faces.' Their old friend Signora Uslenghi welcomed
them back to their familiar rooms. But those twenty-seven hours
on the road had nonetheless taken their toll, in both the short and
the long term. When they staggered off the carriage, having eaten

little and barely slept, they were in a state of complete exhaustion, from which Wolfgang in particular took at least a disorientated day to recover: 'As soon as we got to our bedroom, Wolfgang sat down on a chair and at once began to snore and sleep so soundly that I completely undressed him and put him to bed . . . When he awoke after nine o'clock in the morning, he did not know where he was or how he had got to bed. Almost all the night through he had lain in the same place.' But, even more seriously, there had been an accident on the final stage of the journey, and Leopold had sustained a nasty injury to his leg:

> . . . the postillion kept on lashing the horse which was between the shafts and therefore supporting the sedia. Eventually the horse reared, stuck fast in the sand and dirt which was more than half a foot deep, and fell heavily on one side, pulling down with him the front of the two-wheeled sedia. I held Wolfgang back with one hand, so that he should not be hurled out; but the plunge forward pulled my right foot so violently to the centre bar of the falling dashboard that half the shin-bone of my right leg was gashed to the width of a finger.[2]

Although Leopold refrained from telling Maria Anna about this for nearly a week, and even then tried to make light of it, his injury would cause him considerable discomfort for several months.

The Mozarts stayed in Rome for two weeks, which, in complete contrast to the time they had just spent in Naples, resumed high levels of excitement and activity. In their absence Cardinal Pallavicini had been lobbying the Pope for some recognition of Wolfgang's remarkable talent, and on 26 June, just as the Mozarts entered the city, the papal secretary of state resolved 'that His Holiness has deigned to confer the Cross of the Golden Spur on

Giovanni Amadeo Wolfgango Mozart of Strasbourg'.[3] Despite the almost comical confusions of Wolfgang's name and home town, which in fact persisted through later papal announcements, though not into the final patent, this was the most enormous honour. Originating in the fourteenth century, the Order of the Golden Spur was in the gift of the Holy See, and was conferred either on distinguished propagators of Christian faith, or on those who had contributed to the glory of the Church through illustrious achievement. Previous recipients in the latter category included Titian, Vasari and, curiously, Casanova, and a handful of musicians, among them the sixteenth-century composer Orlando di Lassus, and more recently (in a slightly lower category) Dittersdorf and Gluck. Wolfgang was surely the youngest person to be thus honoured. Even Leopold professed astonishment to learn of the news, which, as he wrote to Maria Anna, 'will fill you both with amazement. For Cardinal Pallavicini is said to have been commanded by the Pope to hand Wolfgang the cross and diploma of an order . . . When we were at the Cardinal's house a few days ago he once or twice called Wolfgang "Signor Cavaliere". We thought he was joking, but now I hear that it is true'.[4]

And so, on 5 July, at the Palazzo Quirinale, Cardinal Pallavicini solemnly presented Wolfgang with his red sash, sword and spurs; and three days later, in a ceremony at the temporary papal residence, the Palazzo Santa Maria Maggiore, the Mozarts were received by the Pope himself. In their letters home, neither Leopold nor Wolfgang was at all forthcoming in reporting this event – the pinnacle of all formal acknowledgements of Wolfgang's talent, and no doubt conducted with the sort of majestic pageantry that they both loved, and about which Maria Anna and Nannerl would have been longing to hear. But Leopold's genuine pride was barely disguised, even as he tried to make light of the achievement ('Wolfgang has to wear a beautiful cross which he has received. You can imagine how I laugh when I hear people calling him "Signor Cavaliere" all the time.').[5] And he had two copies made of the papal patent, sending one to his employer Archbishop Schrattenbach in Salzburg, and the other to Padre Martini in Bologna. Wolfgang himself, in a hastily scrawled, trilingual note to his sister, airily signed off 'Chevalier de Mozart', but gave no further insight as to what had happened or how he felt about it. He was actually more keen to praise Nannerl herself for a song she had written and sent to him: 'I am amazed to find how well you can compose. In a word, the song is beautiful. Try this more often.'[6] But perhaps his high spirits are in fact detectable in his breezily scatological addendum ('Keep well, and shit in your bed and make a mess of it.'), which, though written here in Italian, would become a not infrequent feature of his family letters for several years.

The monumental papal accolade was certainly the main event of the Mozarts' second, shorter stay in Rome; but they busied themselves with nurturing their important supportive friendships, visiting Baron Saint-Odile, and the Salzburg representative in Rome, Abbate Crivelli; and they spent time too with their delightful hostess, Signora Uslenghi. They observed and attended processions and fireworks on public holidays, and might perhaps have considered exploring more sights of ancient Rome, stimulated as their senses now were by their recent experiences in Naples. But there is absolutely no evidence that they did so. Rather, two matters continued to concern them. There was still no news of the subject matter, let alone a libretto, for Wolfgang's forthcoming Milan opera. In Salzburg, Maria Anna was clearly anxious about this too, for Leopold wrote to her on 30 June: 'You ask whether Wolfgang has begun his opera? Why, he is not even thinking of it. You should ask us again when we have reached Milan on November 1st. So far we know nothing either about the cast or about the libretto.'[7] They were however receiving rumours of possible singers, and it seems that Wolfgang and his father were eagerly discussing these, even as Leopold tried to convince them all that there was no hurry: 'Basta! We still have plenty of time.' Meanwhile the other matter of concern was the injury to Leopold's leg, which, contrary to the impression he was bravely trying to give his wife ('thank God, my foot is well'), was simply not healing. As he attempted to make decisions about how to spend the next three months before their return to Milan, Leopold was subdued and reticent. On 7 July he outlined a vague plan to visit Loreto and then return to Bologna. But his normal obsessive and verbose preoccupation with the detail of travel had deserted him. After that letter of 7 July he did not communicate again with Salzburg for two weeks. He was clearly far from well.

But Leopold was also increasingly alarmed now by Rome's 'dangerous heat and bad air', and felt they really had to leave the city.[8] On 10 July, healthy or not, the Mozarts bade farewell to Signora Uslenghi, who thoughtfully gave Wolfgang a copy of *Mille e una notte* (the Italian translation of the *Arabian Nights*), and set off on the night mail-coach. This was indeed the hottest time of the year, and it was essential to avoid travelling in the middle of the day. Over the next ten days, in what Leopold eventually described as 'the worst journey so far', the Mozarts laboriously pursued a north-easterly direction, eventually to arrive back in Bologna.[9] Their route took them via Civita Castellani, Terni, Spoleto, Foligno and Loreto to Ancona on the Adriatic coast, and then northwards through Pesaro, Rimini, Forlì and Imola. Far from inspecting any of these towns, they barely did more than try to snatch some unsettled sleep and refreshment.

They would start each day at three or four in the morning, travel for about five hours, and try to shelter from the heat until four in the afternoon. They would then set off again for another five hours. They found it difficult to sleep at any hour of day or night, not just because of the heat, but also because of an 'incredible number of insects, fleas and bedbugs'. Poor Leopold suffered horribly from the incessant shaking of the carriage, which re-opened the wound in his foot and caused his leg to swell so much that his 'calf and ankle were of equal size'. In considerable pain, he could barely move and went straight to lie down whenever they stopped. Occasionally Wolfgang could visit some local sights. He played the organ in Civita Castellani, visited the popular Catholic pilgrimage site of Santa Casa in Loreto (this probably bore fruit in his *Litaniae Lauretanae*, K.109, composed in Salzburg a few months later), and observed a fair in Senigallia. There was some excitement between Loreto and Rimini, over the constant pres-ence of soldiers policing the coastline for offshore pirates. But with Leopold in such distress, and a distance of some 190 miles to be covered in challenging conditions, the aim was clearly to get through this journey to Bologna as quickly as possible. The triumph of Wolfgang's honour and distinction in Rome had evap-orated completely: the peak of their Italian experience had been succeeded by its deepest and most miserable trough.

At last they arrived back in Bologna on 20 July, and checked in to the San Marco inn. Immediately Leopold took to his bed, and remained there for three weeks in a state of discomfort and depression, which he only confessed to Maria Anna much later ('it is no fun being ill in an inn';[10] 'When I was laid up with my foot, my old melancholy thoughts came back to me very often'[11]). But on the day after their arrival he did finally write home at some length, having been completely non–communicative throughout their harrowing journey, and having thus also missed the name-day of both Maria Anna and Nannerl. Bravely attempting to sound cheerful, he described some details of their travels, but reassured his wife that, here in Bologna, the typically generous Count Pallavicini, having heard of their woes, had offered doctors (which he foolishly refused – 'not necessary') and the use of a carriage.[12] Some visitors were received, including the composer Josef Mysliveček, and the Manfredini brothers, Giuseppe and Vincenzo, all friends from their recent earlier stay. Wolfgang managed to attend some events on his own: 'More than six times at least I have had the honour of going alone to a church and to some magnificent function', he boasted to his sister.[13] (If he was at all concerned about his father's health, he did not show it.) But there were certainly no opportunities for him to display his wares: most of Bologna society had fled to the country from the heat of the city. So the Mozarts lay low, confined to their room at the sweltering inn.

What Wolfgang certainly did, in his days of enforced stasis, was compose. Once more, he could remove himself from uncomfortable or even harsh reality, and escape to another realm in his imagination, where his creativity blossomed and bore fruit. By 4 August, two weeks after their arrival in Bologna, he told Nannerl that he had produced 'four Italian symphonies, to say nothing of arias, of which I must have composed at least five or six, and also a motet'.[14] If it is hard to determine precisely which of Wolfgang's early symphonies date from this Bolognese surge of activity, there are several (K.81, 84, 95, 97) written after the manner of the opera overtures of Piccinni or Paisiello, so many of which Wolfgang had recently been experiencing. (But, as always, he managed even in these early works brilliantly to outshine his models.) More relevant to his current preoccupation was his continuing to write arias, sharpening his tools for the great task ahead of him. For at last he received, on 27 July, the longed-for details of the opera he was to write for Milan. This would be an *opera seria* set in the first century BC (a period in which the Mozarts were currently steeped), *Mitridate, Rè di Ponto*, with a libretto by the Turin poet Vittorio Amedeo Cigna-Santi. Whoever chose this as an opera for Milan in the autumn of 1770 could well have seen the original setting of it, by Gasparini, in Turin in 1767. Along with the text, Wolfgang was also given the names of his cast, four of whom were already familiar to the Mozarts, as Leopold explained to Maria Anna:

We received yesterday the libretto and the list of the singers. The title of the opera is *Mitridate, Rè di Ponto* . . . The characters are:

Mitridate, Rè di Ponto	Il Signor Guglielmo d'Ettore
Aspasia, promessa sposa di Mitridate	Signora Antonia Bernasconi, prima donna
Sifare, figlio di Mitridate, amante d'Aspasia	Signor Santorini, soprano, primo uomo
Farnace, primo figlio di Mitridate . . .	Signor Cicognani, contra alto
Ismene, figlia del Rè dei Parti, amante di Farnace	Signora Varese, seconda donna, soprano
Arbate, governatore di Ninfea	soprano
Marzio, tribuno romano	tenore

We knew Signora Bernasconi already. Signor Santorini sang for us in Rome. Cicognani is here and is a good friend of ours. Ettore is also here.[15]

The arrival of the libretto of *Mitridate* certainly seemed to cheer both father and son, even as they remained incarcerated at their inn. Although there was some slow improvement to Leopold's injury, he was now suffering also from gout in his other leg, and therefore still unable to leave his bed. (He signed his letter of 4 August, 'I am at the moment your old impatient, gouty, bedridden MZT'.[16]) But shortly after this their luck at last changed, and dramatically. It seems that the estimable Count Pallavicini and his wife, perhaps noting that the proffered carriage had not been used at all, took matters into their own hands. On 10 August they brought the Mozarts out to their country house, 'Alla Croce del Biacco', approximately five miles from the centre of Bologna. And suddenly, after a whole month of overwhelming heat, excruciating pain and relentless misery, Leopold and Wolfgang found themselves in the lap of luxury. Leopold, describing it all to Maria Anna, could not contain his joyful relief:

... we arrived yesterday about noon at this country house ... At last we have now slept our fill. I need not send you a description of all the fine things here, for you can picture to yourself the rooms and the beds. Our sheets are of finer linen than many a nobleman's shirt, everything is of silver, even the bedroom sets, and the nightlights and so forth ... We have two servants to wait on us, a footman and a valet. The former sleeps in our anteroom in order to be at hand in case of necessity. The latter has to dress Wolfgang's hair. His Excellency has put us into the first rooms, which in Salzburg we would call the ground floor. Since in summer the upper rooms get all the heat, these are the best rooms, we do not feel the slightest heat the whole day long nor particularly during the night. In addition to our rooms we have the *sala terrena* where we take our meals and where everything is fresh, cool and pleasant.[17]

The Mozarts remained in this pastoral paradise for seven weeks, as the oppressive heat of August retreated ('The weather is very mild and the great heat is over'),[18] and they relished the comfort of their billet and its delicious local produce ('the finest figs, melons and peaches').[19] The infinitely kind Pallavicinis were at all times thoughtful and solicitous: 'My host and hostess never let me stand, but insist on my remaining seated with my foot propped up on another chair. Why, even at Mass today two chairs were put ready for me in the chapel.' They clearly knew when to leave their guests alone, and when to involve them in their own activities: they celebrated Mass with them every day, and the Countess would frequently take Wolfgang out driving in her carriage. And Wolfgang was again enjoying the company of someone his own age, as Leopold reported approvingly: 'The young Count, who is about Wolfgang's age and is sole heir to the property, is very talented, plays the clavier, speaks German, Italian and French and has five or six masters every day for lessons in various sciences and accomplishments. He is already Imperial Chamberlain. You can well believe that this young lord and Wolfgang are the best of friends.'[20] At last Leopold could recuperate, loving the temporary release from his responsibilities. 'I have no news whatever', he wrote cheerfully after two weeks.[21] He mused idly on local and wider politics, commenting both on the rising cost of living in Salzburg and on a current threat to suppress the Jesuits; and he weighed up his various options for future travel. But essentially he allowed himself to convalesce and unwind, free of obligations.

And Wolfgang too relaxed completely in his precious and

tranquil weeks in the country. He had not yet begun composing his *Mitridate*, as the recitatives were not due to be delivered
until the end of October, and he would write the arias after he
had met the singers during the month of November. He seemed
to rely on his father to oversee and determine that schedule. But
almost certainly they would together have spent time familiariz-
ing themselves with the libretto's dramatic structure, its energies
and reposes, its characters, and the overriding gesture and affect
of each aria text. Meanwhile, Wolfgang was changing physically.
He remained short of stature, but his limbs were filling out, and
his voice was just breaking – to his apparent vexation, according
to Leopold: 'He has neither a deep nor a high voice, not even
five pure notes. He is most annoyed, for he can no longer sing
his own compositions, which he would sometimes like to do.'[22]
Although most of Wolfgang's letters to Nannerl in these weeks
generally retain a tone of playful teasing, and delight in recounting hilarious anecdotes, a new, more mature seriousness enters
them too. He and Leopold had learned about the severe illness
of a Salzburg child, and as her condition deteriorated he was
solemn and concerned: 'I am sincerely sorry to hear of the long
illness which poor Jungfrau Martha has to bear with patience,
and I hope that with God's help she will recover. But, if she does
not, we must not be unduly distressed, for God's will is always
best, and He certainly knows best whether it is better for us to
be in this world or the next. She should console herself, however,
with the thought that after the rain she may enjoy the sunshine.'[23]
(This confidence in the sublime certainty of an afterlife never left
him.) He also wrote to his friend Thomas Linley in Florence,
breaking the news that he and his father would not now be able
to return there; and his beautifully composed letter, in excellent
Italian, again reveals a new maturity. (It is possible that this letter

was drafted for him by his father, or at least that Leopold – who certainly added his own one-line postscript of greeting – had had some hand in its content; but the tone, like the handwriting, is very much Wolfgang's own.) These seven weeks with the Pallavicini family were a period of immense importance for both father and, especially, son, as he too unwound from the rigours of the past nine months, and gently regenerated his strength for the excitements that lay ahead.

There were very occasional outings, beyond the daily drives with the Countess. On 30 August the Mozarts were taken back into Bologna to attend a concert in the church of San Giovanni in Monte, given by ten composers, all members of the illustrious Accademia Filarmonica. Each of them contributed a movement to a Mass or psalm setting, and directed its performance. The forces were enormous, with a hundred musicians in the choir and orchestra; the church's two large organs, on either side of the sanctuary, were both deployed, and there was a smaller organ brought in too, to support the choirs in the centre. The Mozarts had not heard any live music, beyond what they had made themselves for their own entertainment and that of their generous hosts, for several weeks, and would have been considerably refreshed by experiencing once more the power and immediacy of fine music in a mighty acoustic. But they were interested too in assessing the quality of the Accademia's composers, all of them past or present students of its greatest luminary, Padre Martini, whom no doubt they were hoping to meet again. Martini did not attend the concert; but the Mozarts did now meet, for their respective Italian journeys collided here, the English music historian Dr Charles Burney – who indeed claimed to have been sent there by Martini, as he 'wished to have the opinion of an unprejudiced professor, an utter stranger to [all the composers]'.[24] Burney had first encountered the Mozart family in London when Wolfgang was just ten; and now throughout his own Italian travels he was hearing reports of the boy's burgeoning talents. So he was intrigued to come upon him here in Bologna:

> who should I meet but the celebrated little German, Mozart, who in 1766 astonished all hearers in London by his premature musical talent. I had a long conversation with his father. I find they are inmates at the Palace of Prince Palavicini. The little man is grown considerably but is still a little man. He has been in Rome and Naples, where he was much admired. At Rome, the Pope has conferred on him the Order of the *Speron d'Oro*, or gold spur, the only civil or military order in the gift of his Holiness. He astonished the Italian Musicians wherever he stopt.

Learning too of Wolfgang's obligation to write an opera for Milan, Burney somewhat astutely declared himself 'curious to know how this extraordinary boy acquits himself in setting words in a language not his own. But there is no musical excellence which I do not expect from his extraordinary quickness and talents, under the guidance of so able a musician and intelligent a man as his father, who, I was informed, had been ill five or six weeks in Bologna.'[25] (Leopold himself, describing the concert to Maria Anna in his next letter, made no reference to this encounter with the learned Englishman.)

Eventually, on 1 October, the Mozarts returned from the country to the centre of Bologna, along with the rest of its society. They went to another huge concert, celebrating the patronal festival of the Basilica of San Petronio, one of the largest churches in the world. Wolfgang was impressed by the scale of the concert, but not by its execution, as he told Nannerl: 'I have heard and seen the great festival of St. Petronius in Bologna. It was beautiful, but very long. They had to fetch trumpets from Lucca for the fanfare, but they played abominably.'[26] Meanwhile the re-energized Leopold finalized his travel plans, scrapping any thoughts other than of arriving in Milan by the most direct route possible. But they did linger in Bologna for a few more days, as they had now renewed contact with Padre Martini. Leopold had arranged for a copy of his own treatise, the *Violinschule*, to be sent from Salzburg to Martini, whose own second volume of musical history had just been published; and a courteous exchange was effected: 'We are the best of friends . . . We are at his house every day and have long discussions on the history of music.'[27] But of greater importance than these scholarly interlocutions was Martini's daily contact with Wolfgang, whom the great teacher was mentoring. And there was perhaps an immediate reason for his attention, as Leopold hinted to Maria Anna: 'We intended to leave for Milan on Monday or Tuesday. But something is keeping us here until Thursday, *something* which, if it really happens, will do Wolfgang extraordinary honour.'[28] Sure enough, on 9 October Wolfgang went to the headquarters of the Accademia Filarmonica, and took its demanding entrance examination. He was handed a line of plainchant and given three hours, in a locked room, in which to rework it in strict four-part counterpoint. According to Leopold, Wolfgang completed the task in 'less than half an hour',[29] which, while this may be a not uncharacteristic parental exaggeration, is probably not far from the truth: the register of the Accademia Filarmonica itself states that Wolfgang took 'less than an hour'.[30] Leopold described for his wife and daughter what happened next: 'When Wolfgang had finished it, it was examined by the Censores and all the Kapellmeisters and

Compositores. Then a vote was taken, which was done by means of white and black balls. As all the balls were white, Wolfgang was called in and all the members clapped their hands as he entered and congratulated him, and the Princeps Accademiae informed him, on behalf of the company, that he had passed the examination.'[31] Wolfgang's resulting antiphon, 'Querite primum regnum Dei', K.86/73v, survives in two versions, and in one of them the hand of Padre Martini also appears, implying therefore that Wolfgang had indeed, before he took his test, had some specific instruction. In a testimonial written three days later, Martini confirmed that he had been assessing all Wolfgang's musical attributes:

I, the undersigned, attest that, having seen some Musical Compositions in various styles, and having several times heard [him play] the Harpsichord, the Violin, and sing, Sig. Cav. Giov. Amadeo Wolfgango Mozart of Salzburg, Master Chamber Musician to His Highness the eminent Prince Archbishop of Salzburg, aged 14 years, to my particular admiration, was found by me most highly versed in all the musical qualities indicated, he having passed every test whatever, above all in playing on the Harpsichord various subjects given to him to improvise, which with great mastery he carried out according to all the conditions demanded by Art.[32]

So, with the formidable support of Bologna's most distinguished living musician, yet another honour was bestowed upon the fourteen-year-old boy, for whom the Accademia's minimum age requirement (twenty) was waived, and whose admission fee was paid by Padre Martini himself. Again, Leopold's pride was boundless: 'This distinction does Wolfgang all the more credit for the Accademia Bonnoniensis is more than a hundred years old and, apart from Padre Martini and other eminent Italians, only the most distinguished citizens of other countries are members of it.'[33]

Four days later, on 13 October, the Mozarts finally left Bologna and headed in a north-westerly direction back to Milan, arriving on 18 October. They were familiar with the road, having travelled it in the other direction over nine days in March; but on this occasion they aimed to accomplish its 150 miles in perhaps four days. In fact they were delayed, as so often, by tiresome weather: swollen rivers and impassable roads meant that they had to spend an extra night in Parma, and driving rain accompanied them all the way into Milan. They took lodgings not, as before, near their great supporter Count Firmian, but close to the theatre, for the focus of this stay was to be entirely on the opera. Their accommodation consisted of two large rooms with big windows: a sitting room with a balcony and a fireplace, and a bedroom with just one bed – albeit a large one, 'about nine feet wide' – but no fireplace. 'So,' wrote Leopold, 'provided we do not freeze to death, we shall be sure not to smell, for we have enough air.'[34] Their landlord's son was profoundly deaf, incidentally giving Wolfgang the opportunity to learn a very special new language: 'at the moment I am talking in signs, as the son of the house has been without speech or hearing from birth.'[35] For the next twelve weeks, this convenient, reasonably spacious apartment would be the Mozarts' home, and the centre for all aspects – the composition, preparation and performance – of the opera *Mitridate, Rè di Ponto*.

∽

Mithridates VI, King of Pontus, ascended his throne around 115 BC. His tyrannical conquests gave him power in Asia, Greece and Macedonia, and he was a constant enemy of Rome. Eventually he was defeated and driven out of his territories, first by Lucullus and then by Pompey. He was conceiving a plan to invade Italy when his son Pharnaces revolted against him. Mithridates preferred death to captivity, and took his own life.

In 1673, Racine wrote his tragedy *Mithridate*, which was in the 1760s translated into Italian by the most distinguished living poet in Milan, Giuseppe Parini. This translation was then made into the excellent libretto by Vittorio Cigna–Santi that Gasparini had set for Turin in 1767, and was now the basis for Wolfgang's opera. Set in the Macedonian port of Ninfea, the libretto's main events centre around Mitridate, engaged in his wars against the Romans, and his betrothed queen Aspasia. His two sons, Farnace and Sifare, are also in love with Aspasia, and rivals therefore not merely with their father and each other for her, but with each other for their father's throne. She herself is dismayed by the advances of Farnace, for she loves the younger son, Sifare, and is torn between her feelings for him and her duty to Mitridate. Mitridate discovers Aspasia's love for Sifare and condemns her to death; she resolves to take her proffered poison, but is prevented from doing so by Sifare. Farnace, who has been plotting with the Romans against his father, repents his treachery and burns the Roman fleet, uniting with Sifare to try to save their father's kingdom. In the ensuing battle, Mitridate inflicts on himself a mortal wound; but before he dies he forgives Farnace and unites Aspasia and Sifare. In addition to the four main characters, there are three smaller roles: Ismene, daughter of the King of Parti, in love with Farnace; Marzio, a Roman tribune, with whom Farnace conspires; and Arbate, the Governor of Ninfea.

This true *opera seria* was a world away from the comic format and gestures of *La finta semplice* and Wolfgang's other previous operas, as both father and son knew. Embracing now the sombre subjects of honour, loyalty, fidelity and noble passion, and indeed serious considerations of suicide, it was an altogether adult project, which could so easily have presented challenges beyond the capabilities of a fourteen-year-old. But Wolfgang was now steeped in *opera seria*: he had minutely observed Hasse's craft in Vienna; in the last nine months in Italy he had seen and assessed many such operas, and spent time among their practitioners; and he had been given his collected edition of the works of Metastasio by Count Firmian, and flexed his muscles by setting many aria texts. Daunting though his task was, he felt he was ready for it.

As stated in Wolfgang's contract, drawn up back in March, and reiterated by Leopold in his letters home, the schedule for producing *Mitridate* was that 'the recitatives must be sent to Milan in October and we must be there by November 1st so that Wolfgang may write the arias.'[36] So, in mid-October, just before they left Bologna, Wolfgang had begun writing the recitatives, and now in Milan he addressed this essential first stage of his composition in earnest: 'I cannot write much, for my fingers are aching from composing so many recitatives', he wrote to his mother, two days after their arrival.[37] In his later operas, Wolfgang's recitatives would be of startling dramatic revelation and emotional charge, largely through the subtle, sublime and effortless deployment of harmonic progression. But here, in *Mitridate*, he executed his task with straightforward competence, as was only to be expected from a young composer setting a text in his fourth language, and working essentially in a vacuum, without any direct knowledge yet of the strengths and ranges of his individual singers, nor therefore of the keys in which their arias should best be set – where musically his recitatives were actually going. Once he had completed this narrative framework, and probably also written *Mitridate*'s purely instrumental numbers – the overture, and a march – he at last started to meet his cast, and could begin composing the twenty-three arias, plus one duet and a concluding brief quintet which would make up the substance of his opera.

Leopold meanwhile took it upon himself to supervise his son's regime, keeping him well supplied with everything that he needed (paper, quills, ink, sand) for the process of composition, and no doubt supervising all the copying procedures, as he always did. He also made sure Wolfgang had regular exercise, and tried to keep him from becoming too obsessively solemn: 'Wolfgang is now busy with serious matters and is therefore very serious himself. So I am delighted when he occasionally gets hold of something really funny.'[38] As he settled into a strict discipline of writing to Salzburg every Saturday, Leopold shared regular bulletins on the opera's progress with his wife and daughter. Wolfgang barely contributed to these weekly letters, and seemed to be feeling the pressure of his massive task, as he briefly confided to his mother: 'Mamma, I beg you to pray for me, that my opera may go well'.[39] To his sister his tone was altogether more light-hearted, albeit now in German again, his easiest linguistic option. But his play on the word *müde* ('tired') would also have indicated to Nannerl just how much strain he was feeling: '*ich bin wie allzeit Dein bruder wolfgang Mozart dessen finger von schreiben Müdhe Müdhe Müedes müde sind*'.[40] (I remain always your brother Wolfgang Mozart, whose fingers are tired, tired, tired, tired from writing.)

It was not just the physical process of writing music, for an altogether different level of performer, and a different profile of venue, that was stressful for Wolfgang. There was clearly considerable resistance building up among Milan's musical community to the very notion of a fourteen-year-old Austrian boy receiving such an important operatic commission. As early as 3 November, Leopold referred in his letter home to 'unavoidable annoyances which every Kapellmeister has to face with this canaille of virtuosi';[41] and in due course there were mutinous suggestions to the principal singers that they should simply refuse to sing Wolfgang's arias, and substitute instead those from Gasparini's original setting of the same libretto. But, as Leopold could triumphantly report a week later, this preposterous course of action failed utterly:

> God be praised, we have won the first battle and defeated an enemy, who brought to the prima donna's house all the arias which she was to sing in our opera and tried to persuade her not to sing any of Wolfgang's . . . But she gave that wretch a flat refusal, and she is now beside herself with delight at the arias which Wolfgang has composed to suit her. So also is her accompanist, Signor Lampugnani, who is rehearsing her part with her and who cannot sufficiently praise them.[42]

This prima donna was the twenty-nine-year-old German-born Antonia Bernasconi (she had taken the name of her stepfather and teacher, the composer Andrea Bernasconi). After her debut in Munich at the age of twenty-one, she had sung repeatedly in Vienna, which is where the Mozarts had briefly heard and admired her in 1768, and, noted also for her admirable acting abilities, she was the distinguished creator of Gluck's Alceste, among many other leading roles. She had sung in Wolfgang's final concert – his 'audition' – in Milan the previous March. Now

120

she was to sing the role of Aspasia; and, far from being scornful or dismissive of a teenage composer, she was indeed thrilled with her arias.

As well she should have been. The five numbers that Wolfgang wrote for Bernasconi – three self-contained arias, one duet with Sifare to conclude the second act, and an extraordinary scena for her contemplation of suicide in the third act – are all quite remarkable. This was a completely new way of working for him. Having met his singers, and assessed their vocal strengths, ranges and attributes, he then had to deliver music which showed those characteristics off to the greatest advantage, all in the context of the aria's affect and place in the dramatic narrative. It was practically a collaborative workshop, in which the individual singers, too, evidently had some say. There are two versions, for instance, of Bernasconi's entrance aria, 'Al destin che la minaccia', which expresses her longing to be free of Farnace, and of course, importantly, introduces her to the audience. The first version he wrote, in G major, is certainly arresting and well constructed. But the C major version on which she settled is truly splendid, with energetic coloratura and a wide range (she evidently had a wonderful top C, which Wolfgang happily exploited), and a gentler contrasting middle section. Her second aria, 'Nel sen mi palpita', a tender farewell to Sifare, is shorter, more lyrical and extremely touching. But then Wolfgang had second thoughts again about her third aria, the second-act soliloquy, 'Nel grave tormento', reflecting the anguished conflict between her love for Sifare and her duty to Mitridate. He abandoned his first attempt after forty bars and started again, in a very similar vein, but with much greater confidence and fluency, alternating between adagio and allegro sections. Bernasconi's final aria, her potential suicide scene, is of exceptional maturity, portraying with real emotional authenticity Aspasia's Juliet-like vacillation between resolving to take her poison and fearing its reality. After an agitated accompanied recitative, she sings a (significantly Gluckian) invocation of Elysian shades, again deploying Bernasconi's impressively wide vocal range as well as her sublime lyric gifts; but, as her courage falters, her music moves again into frenzied accompanied recitative, interrupted, inevitably perhaps, by Sifare, who rushes in to dash the poison from her hand. The trouble Wolfgang took for Bernasconi in his various writings and rewritings demonstrates not only his burgeoning musico-dramatic insights, but also his deep respect for a phenomenal artist. Leopold's happy reports that Bernasconi was 'infinitely pleased' with her music confirmed that she considered herself extremely fortunate to have such a genius writing for her.[43] But then, Wolfgang was equally fortunate in having Bernasconi and her stellar gifts available to him. This was a very early example of the kind of two-way osmosis that he developed throughout his life with several first-class performers: they inspired him, and he produced inspirational music for them.

Bernasconi no doubt spread her enthusiasm among her colleagues. If the great prima donna was delighted with her music, how could more subordinate cast members refuse to sing theirs? And so, one by one, the singers came to work with Wolfgang on music that he had written especially for them, and in the main they too were happy. The tenor Guglielmo d'Ettore and the castrato Giuseppe Cicognani, respectively singing Mitridate and Farnace, were both already known to the Mozarts. D'Ettore had met them on the earlier Milan visit and then again in Bologna; and they had heard Cicognani in Cremona, met him again in Milan, and got to know him well in Bologna, when he had sung in Wolfgang's concert at Count Pallavicini's palace and was

122

thereafter described by Leopold as their 'good friend'.[44] Cicognani did indeed seem to be perfectly content with his four arias, though did perhaps suggest to Wolfgang that his third aria, 'Son reo', was too long. In it, Farnace admits his own treachery but declares that his brother is culpable too, for loving Aspasia, and the aria alternates strongly between guilt and blame. It survives in two versions, the second much shorter than the first, and it is therefore likely that Cicognani himself, knowing his own vocal stamina, requested a more concise alternative. Guglielmo d'Ettore, on the other hand, was considerably more demanding, and there was much rewriting in three of his five arias. His first, introduced by a splendid march halfway through the first act, is 'Se di lauri il crine adorno'. Wolfgang had no fewer than five attempts at pleasing d'Ettore with this entrance, eventually settling on an andante which combines strength (wide vocal leaps demonstrating the tenor's impressive range) with a gentle authority. Similarly, for his second aria, 'Quel ribelle e quell'ingrato', a soliloquy in which Mitridate rages against Farnace, Wolfgang made several drafts, each gaining in sophistication. The final result was an excellent combination of his previous attempts, with an accompanied recitative (completely absent in the first version) and an aria which, if lacking his colleagues' coloratura (it seems that d'Ettore's voice was not especially nimble), again certainly exploited the singer's wide range. And Mitridate's final aria, 'Vado incontro al fato', had two versions, the first slightly tame in comparison with the second, which greatly featured d'Ettore's top Cs. Mitridate's two other arias, 'Tu che fedel me sei', a bipartite musical structure showing tenderness to Sifare but hostility to Farnace, and 'Già di pietà mi spoglio', a rage aria promising revenge on all those who have done him wrong, apparently pleased the singer straight away.

123

With the primo uomo, Pietro Benedetti, still engaged elsewhere and therefore absent from Milan, Wolfgang continued
to work with the rest of his cast, all based in the city. The soprano Anna Francesca Varese was to sing Ismene, and, as seconda
donna, would have two arias. For the first of these, 'In faccia
all'oggetto', Varese apparently followed the lead of her colleagues
and negotiated with Wolfgang for something more flashy than
the gentle minuet he originally offered her: the second version
is an altogether more energetic allegro with impressive explosions of coloratura. The two minor roles of Marzio and Arbate
were sung by the tenor Gaspare Bassano and the castrato Pietro
Muschetti, and each was given a single aria. Both of these, and
Ismene's arias too, underline just how good Wolfgang's cast was.
All of them involve demanding coloratura and real vocal stamina.
Wolfgang must have been thrilled at the consistently high quality
of all his artists.

The twenty-five-year-old castrato Pietro Benedetti, known
as 'il Sartorino', arrived at last at the beginning of December, a
whole month after everyone else. Like d'Ettore, Cicognani and
Varese, he had met the Mozarts earlier that year in Milan, and
then subsequently in Rome, where he had sung to them, possibly
so that Wolfgang could already begin to form an impression of his
vocal prowess and therefore consider how best to write for him.
Like Bernasconi, he was to have four arias, plus the duet with her.
And again Wolfgang took infinite trouble to show off his star (for
castrato singers were still operatic idols) to his best advantage.
His first appearance, like that of Bernasconi, and indeed coming
immediately after it, is extremely impressive. 'Soffre il mio cor'
expresses both Sifare's hopes of happiness with Aspasia, and his
dismay at the arrogance of his brother Farnace, and the aria vacil-
lates between tenderness and frustration, also incorporating his

124

wide vocal range and considerable coloratura skills. His second aria,'Parto', declares his faithfulness as a son and brother, and is gentler and shorter. But 'Lungi da te', the most agonized of farewells as he and Aspasia agree that they should part for ever, is the heart of his role, and again Wolfgang took great trouble with it. There are three versions of this aria, each of them improving and developing its predecessor; and the final version actually incorporates an obbligato solo horn, adding extraordinary musical heft to an already persuasive musical argument. Sifare's final aria, 'Se il rigor d'un ingrata sorte', after he has prevented Aspasia from taking her poison and sent her away under military protection, declares his resolve to prove his innocence in battle – again with impressive vocal acrobatics and a forthright C major energy. And the duet for Bernasconi and Benedetti, 'Se viver non degg'io', which closed the second act, was the musical highlight of the whole opera, uniting its two superstars. Wolfgang wrote two versions of it, the first perhaps before Benedetti arrived, and then the second, actually a little shorter, once he had full knowledge of their two voices and how they might best combine. But this version on which they all agreed was altogether richer, with four horns rather than the usual two in the accompaniment, and – significantly perhaps for the fledgling composer – was in the key of A major, which very much became the key of passion and seduction in all Wolfgang's later operas. Both singers had their opportunities to shine separately before their voices combined, and then their dazzling coloratura skills united in a breathtaking allegro section. Bernasconi and Benedetti were especially thrilled with this duet, and so were the audiences, for it regularly brought the house to its feet and had to be encored.

By the time Wolfgang had met and satisfied all his singers, there was not the slightest suggestion of trouble, however much 'calumniators kept on spreading evil reports', as Leopold subsequently reported in detail to Padre Martini.[45] Harmony reigned among the gifted cast, who gave the young composer their fullest possible support: 'The singers are . . . altogether delighted, and especially the prima donna and the primo uomo, who are simply enchanted with their duet. The primo uomo has actually said that if this duet does not go down well, he will let himself be *castrated* again.'[46] Leopold continued to monitor closely the effects of all this on his son, tending to any slight ailment ('Wolfgang has had an abscess in a tooth with a slight inflammation on one side of his face'),[47] and making sure he had distractions. He himself betrayed signs of strain too, snapping at his wife and daughter in his letters, and accusing them – quite wrongly – of slacking in their own epistolary duties. But he and Wolfgang accepted gratefully an invitation from their good friend Herr Troger (Count Firmian's secretary) to spend a weekend in the countryside, where he and his family were building themselves a villa. And the Mozarts also attended a concert at Count Firmian's palace on 26 November, though this was perhaps a mixed blessing, for they found the orchestra to be 'wretched' because the 'good people have gone off to the country with their patrons and it will be eight or twelve days before they return for rehearsals for the opera'.[48]

Formal rehearsals for the full company together began on 5 December with three days of work on the recitatives, which presumably also accounted for the basic staging. A week later Wolfgang met the orchestra, at first just sixteen players to read through the material and 'discover whether the score had been copied correctly', and then, a week after that, the full complement of sixty musicians.[49] As with the singers, the orchestral players were completely won over by the quality of the music

126

in front of them, and from then on there was no trouble at all ('the malevolent are now silent'),[50] and Leopold could allow himself some optimistic perspective as he received encouraging approbation from Milan's top musicians: 'The greatest and most distinguished Kapellmeisters of this town, Fioroni and Sammartini, are our true friends; and so are Lampugnani, Piazza, Colombo and others.' But he was dismayed when he heard that, in Naples, an opera by their recent friend Jommelli had 'failed so miserably that people are even wanting to substitute another; and Jommelli is a most celebrated master, of whom the Italians make a great fuss.'[51] If capricious audiences could cruelly discard the work of a celebrity composer, could they also try to destroy a teenage upstart? Could the performers, even, still turn on their young maestro? Leopold became increasingly protective, ensuring that Wolfgang was 'not hindered and that no malevolent members of the orchestra or disagreeable singers should play him any tricks.'[52] As the first night of *Mitridate* approached, despite all his positive feedback, Leopold was still nervous on behalf of his son: 'We now stand on the brink of this enterprise . . . On St Stephen's Day, a good hour after Ave Maria, picture to yourselves Maestro Don Amadeo seated at the clavier in the orchestra and myself a spectator and a listener in a box up above; and do wish him a successful performance and say a few paternosters for him.'[53]

God be praised, the first performance of the opera took place on the 26th and won general applause; and two things, which have never yet happened in Milan, occurred on that evening. First of all, contrary to the custom of a first night, an aria of

127

the prima donna was repeated, though usually at a first performance the audience never call out 'fuora'. Secondly, after almost all the arias, with the exception of a few at the end, there was extraordinary applause and cries of 'Evviva il Maestro! Evviva il Maestrino!'[54]

Leopold's excitement and relief did not exaggerate Wolfgang's undoubted triumph. Dressed 'in a scarlet suit, trimmed with gold braid and lined with sky-blue satin', Wolfgang directed the performance from the first harpsichord, with his supportive colleague Giovanni Battista Lampugnani at the second.[55] Quite apart from that prolonged applause and Bernasconi's repeated aria, the evening was extended even more by the customary inclusion of some completely irrelevant ballets, composed not by Wolfgang but by Francesco Caselli. The whole performance therefore lasted for six hours. But on the following night the audience was even more enthusiastic, demanding encores now for two of Bernasconi's arias and especially for 'Se viver non degg'io', her duet with Benedetti. At this point the management of the opera had serious thoughts about making cuts, and the ballets at least were shortened. Public acclaim continued to grow. 'How we wished that you and Nannerl could have had the pleasure of seeing the opera!' continued Leopold. 'Within living memory there has never been such eagerness to see the first opera [of the season] as there has been this time'.[56]

Wolfgang conducted the first three performances, and then handed the direction over to Lampugnani, with Melchior Chiesa coming in to play the second harpsichord. Like the rest of the Milan opera company, both these musicians were of the highest quality. Lampugnani, now in his late sixties, had himself had a distinguished career as an opera composer, having even been resident at the King's Theatre in London for the 1743–4 season (where he will surely have heard, at the rival Covent Garden theatre, oratorios by Handel), and having also written operas for Venice and Barcelona. In 1758 he had returned to Milan, his home city, and become a permanent and central figure at the opera, supervising all the musical preparation, coaching the singers, playing the harpsichord and, as now, conducting some performances. Chiesa was well known as a composer of sacred works, but with Lampugnani was also a permanent member of the opera's music staff. Certainly Leopold was enormously impressed by these two generous musicians, writing to Maria Anna: 'If about fifteen or eighteen years ago, when Lampugnani had already composed so much in England and Melchior Chiesa in Italy, and I had heard their operas, arias and symphonies, someone had said to me that these masters would take part in the performance of my son's composition, and, when he left the clavier, would have to sit down and accompany his music, I should have told him he was fit for a lunatic asylum.'[57] The Mozarts basked in Wolfgang's glory, and now attended performances of *Mitridate* as 'listeners and spectators, sometimes in the parterre and sometimes in the boxes or palchi, where everyone is eager to speak to the Signore Maestro and see him at close quarters. During the performance we walk about here and there, wherever we like.'[58]

In the first two weeks of 1771, the intensity of the rehearsal preparation, the excitement of *Mitridate*'s opening and the consequent explosion of adulation and praise, all gradually subsided. Leopold and Wolfgang stayed up late ('going to bed at half past one or even two o'clock in the morning, as we must have something to eat after the performance'),[59] but then allowed themselves to sleep long into the morning, and gently to unwind.

They resumed a social life and visited friends, especially of course their great supporter Count Firmian, at whose palace they gave a small concert; and the Troger family too were as usual extremely welcoming. Leopold Troger's sister Marianne, born like her brother in Salzburg, had come to Italy in 1770 and married Francesco D'Aste, the (considerably older than she) head of Milan's postal service. On 3 January the Mozarts dined with her, and, at Wolfgang's specific request (after over a year away, he was touchingly homesick for Austrian food), she served them sauerkraut and dumplings. And so it continued: Leopold declared they had so many visits to pay that he doubted they could fit everyone in. But these days were entirely pleasurable, and capped by the excellent, if brief and curiously enigmatic, report of the opera in the *Gazzetta di Milano*: 'the young *Maestro di Cappella*, who has not yet reached the age of fifteen, studies the beauty of nature and exhibits it adorned with the rarest of Musical graces'.[60] (As it happens, the music critic of the *Gazzetta* was Giuseppe Parini, who had originally translated Racine's play *Mithridate* into Italian, and who would shortly find himself collaborating with Wolfgang on another project.) There was also news of Wolfgang's becoming accepted, as in Bologna, as a member of the Accademia Filarmonica of Verona. And after weeks of absence from Leopold's letters home to Salzburg, Wolfgang at last managed to write his own postscript to Nannerl on 12 January, offering the most modest apology: 'I have not written for a long time, for I was busy with my opera, but as I now have time, I will be more attentive to my duty.'[61]

While Wolfgang had been absorbed in the composition and preparation of his opera, Leopold had also been considering how they might see some more of Italy before they returned to Salzburg. They wished to visit Turin, to the west of Milan, for

instance, and of course Venice, to the east, at the time of its celebrated Carnival and then for some Lenten concerts. After that
there were options for how they might return to Salzburg, either
by reversing their journey through the Tyrol, or by travelling
a more easterly route through Carinthia. Either way, Leopold
was anticipating difficulties, stressing again to Maria Anna
that it was 'no joke travelling through the mountains in spring,
when the snow is melting.'[62] And so, on 14 January, the Mozarts
temporarily left Milan and travelled to Turin, the main city of
Piedmont, and capital of the Kingdom of Sardinia. They stayed
there, at the Dogana Nuova inn, for two weeks, during which
time they wrote no letters home at all, nor ever described their
seventy-five-mile journeys there and back. Dr Charles Burney
had travelled the same route some six months earlier, and been
revolted by the conditions, which he found to be 'utterly com-
fortless . . . it should seem as if the inhabitants of this renowned
and beautiful country thought that dust, dirt, cobwebs, fleas,
bugs and all manner of filth were necessary mortifications in this
world, in order to entitle us to better treatment in the next.'[63] The
Mozarts were undertaking these challenging conditions, furthermore, in the depth of winter: their fur-lined footbags, purchased
a year earlier in Mantua, would have been gratefully brought
back into service.

For the first time since they had left Naples, back in June,
Leopold resumed his practice of listing in his travel notes those
whom they had met; and this list is the only documentation of
the Turin stay. But, in a city which had a reputation for fine string
playing, and boasted two functioning opera houses, there were
some impressive names. The *maestro di cappella* at Turin's duomo
was none other than Quirino Gasparini, composer of *Mitridate*'s
first incarnation there in 1767. He and Wolfgang will surely

have had notes to compare. Then there was Giovanni Paisiello, the leading composer of *opera buffa*, whom the Mozarts had met in Naples, and whose (gloriously named) *Annibale in Torino* was opening at the Teatro Regio Ducale just as they arrived in Turin, and which they will certainly have seen. Distinguished instrumentalists appear in Leopold's list too, among them the violinist Gaetano Pugnani, whose pupils included Giovanni Battista Viotti and the renowned if eccentric wind-playing brothers Alessandro and Paolo Besozzi, respectively an oboist and bassoonist, whose playing Leopold especially remembered for years to come. (Burney had been intrigued by them: 'Their long and uninterrupted regard for each other is as remarkable as their performance . . . they have ever lived together in the utmost harmony and affection; carrying their similarity of taste to their very dress, which is the same in every particular, even to buttons and buckles.'[64]) Perhaps the Mozarts enjoyed some music-making, if not some concert-giving, with any combination of these fine musicians. And then there were the local dignitaries – ministers, ambassadors and noblemen – to host the visitors and pay them attention. But on all this likely activity Leopold was uncharacteristically reticent, merely dashing off a quick excuse to Maria Anna after their return to Milan at the end of the month: 'you will have gathered that our journey to Turin prevented us from writing. From that very beautiful town, where we saw a magnificent opera, we returned here on January 31st. You will hear everything in due course . . . I have hardly time to write, as I must pack.'[65]

It was indeed time to leave the Milan apartment, after fifteen incredible weeks. But the Mozarts had one final city to visit before they were at last to return home. They could not leave Italy without spending time in Venice, centre of a once glorious republic, whose political clout was thoroughly diminished in the eighteenth century, but whose unique allure to artists, musicians and travellers was as vibrant as ever. Venice's musical reputation rested partly on the magnificent sacred music at the Basilica of San Marco and other huge churches, their architecture and acoustic bestowing on the rest of Europe a tradition of poly-choral brilliance, and partly on its famous conservatories, or music schools, founded as charitable institutions but also (through such dedicated composers as Vivaldi, who worked for thirty years at the Ospedale della Pietà) producers of sophisticated singers and instrumentalists, and therefore of high-quality concerts. But most of all, Venice was the birthplace, and indeed the propagator, of public opera. Following the immediately modest but histori-cally momentous reopening, in 1637, of an old comedy theatre, the Teatro San Cassiano, for the presentation of Francesco Manelli's opera *Andromeda*, new venues had sprung up across the city in virtually every parish. They had often opened and closed quite quickly. All theatres were vulnerable to fire hazards and many burned down, some more than once; others were casualties of economic and financial restraints, or simply of the fickle and fluctuating tastes of audiences. By the eighteenth century, there were fewer of them – merely seven as opposed to the dozen of the previous century – but still a remarkable number for a city as small as Venice, with its finite watery boundaries. Some special-ized in *opera buffa*: the Teatro San Moisè, for instance, reopened in 1741 to present comic operas by Traetta, Paisiello, Piccinni and Cimarosa. The Teatro San Samuele tried to develop a rival to these Neapolitan models, and initiate a specifically Venetian version, based on spoken comedy with musical intermezzos. And the Teatro Sant'Angelo, after many years of presenting Vivaldi's serious operas in the first half of the century, began in the 1740s also to concentrate on *opera buffa*, and to combine the talents of two of Venice's most distinguished masters, the current *maestro di cappella* at San Marco, Baldassare Galuppi, and the great playwright Carlo Goldoni. (Among other composers on its playbills was Lampugnani, Wolfgang's supportive Milanese colleague.) But *opera seria* had been much presented in Venice too, especially at the Teatro San Giovanni Grisostomo, where the twenty-four-year-old Handel's *Agrippina* had caused a sensation in 1709, and where all the great composers (Caldara, Alessandro Scarlatti, Hasse) and singers (Farinelli, Cuzzoni, Faustina, Grimaldi) had appeared. In 1755 its owners, the Grimani family, recognized a decline in its fortunes and boldly countered this by opening yet another theatre, the Teatro San Benedetto, which became the principal operatic venue for the rest of the century, and would host the premieres of over 140 works, including Rossini's *L'italiana in Algeri*. Composers and performers floated freely between all the functioning theatres. So there was much potential for a now fully respected young opera composer. After a remarkably productive year of adulation, in which Italy's great opera houses, not only in Milan but also in Naples and Bologna, were angling for future commissions from Wolfgang, the Mozarts were confident that a Venetian visit too would pay dividends.

On 2 February the Mozarts joined Count Firmian for a farewell dinner in Milan, reflecting no doubt on the gratifying triumph of the past weeks, and formulating plans for a return engagement. It was not quite a year since, on the eve of their first departure from the city, they had likewise dined with Firmian and emerged with the promise of an engagement, for which a contract was subsequently issued and sent after them. Now there must have been similar negotiations, for, sure enough, within a month there was indeed another thrilling contract, for an opera to open the Milan season in 1773. If this date seemed somewhat distant, especially to Leopold, who was always impatient for the reward of future employment, it is extremely likely that there was discussion too of an additional and earlier project for Wolfgang. As everyone in Milan knew, there was to be a spectacular imperial wedding in the city later that very year. For the moment, however, Leopold and Wolfgang were tight-lipped about any specific engagement, and addressed themselves at last to packing up all their possessions. This mammoth task took them more than a day; but, on 4 February, they finally loaded their trunks and themselves into carriages, and embarked on the 175-mile journey to Venice.

Their route, once more across the frigid North Italian Plain, took the Mozarts through the boundary of the Venetian state at Canonica (where, according to Burney, the quality of the roads deteriorated markedly, becoming 'intolerably rough and stony'),[66] to Brescia. There, they went to the opera and met some singers of their acquaintance. Continuing past Lake Garda, they travelled across the familiar territory of Verona, and on to Vicenza and Padua, after which the road ran parallel to the Brenta Canal, with its *burchielli* or barges transporting the Venetian aristocracy to their impressive villas. On 11 February, they arrived at Fusina, the embarcation point for transport by boat to Venice. For the Mozarts, as for all other first-time travellers there, this was a staggering and novel experience. Against a wintry sky, the towers and domes of the 'city wedded to the sea' emerged with an allure both muted and yet breathtaking. Once across the lagoon, passengers and luggage were laboriously dispersed onto smaller gondolas, and thus conveyed, with unique and consummate skill, through narrow canals in a city throbbing with Carnival festivities. Then as now, the sense of disorientated wonder would have been overwhelming. The Mozarts were brought to their arranged lodgings with the Ceseletti family at the Ponte dei Barcaroli, just five minutes' walk from the celebrated Piazza San Marco. They remained there for four weeks, constantly imbibing the richest and rarest of Italian experiences.

The Mozarts' main contact in Venice, certainly for social and domestic concerns, was the family of Johannes Wider, a close business acquaintance of Lorenz Hagenauer. Their home was just across from the Mozarts' lodgings, and effectively became the base for Leopold and Wolfgang, who were warmly welcomed, fed, entertained and cosseted there every day. The Widers had no fewer than six daughters, and Wolfgang was enchanted. He referred to them constantly as his 'pearls', and wrote (in Italian) with blokish exuberance to Hagenauer's son Johannes Nepomuk, who had himself spent time with the Widers in the previous year: 'The particularly splendid pearl and all the other pearls too admire you very greatly. I assure you that they are in love with you and that they hope that like a Turk you will marry them all, and make all six of them happy.'[67] And Leopold too was fulsome in his praise of the family: 'If Johannes is always saying nice things about the Widers, I assure you he can never say enough. I too have had some experience of people in this world, but I have met few, indeed very few, like them. For besides being willing, sincere, absolutely honest and full of human kindness, they are also courteous, they have excellent manners and are not at all puffed up by the kindnesses they perform.'[68]

The day after their arrival was *martedì grasso*, or Shrove Tuesday, and the climax of Carnival. Leopold's timing was perfect, as it had been for Easter in Rome in the previous year. After lunch with the Widers, the Mozarts were taken to the opera (this was already their second visit: they had gone straight to the theatre on arrival on the Monday), where they heard again another great singer, Anna De Amicis, with whom Wolfgang had been particularly impressed in Naples. They returned with the Widers for dinner, and some dancing with the 'pearls', at their house. Then, late at night and through crowded and boisterous squares and streets, they all went to the Ridotto, where they took part in the masked gambling that was such a feature of the Carnival season. The effect of that night on both Mozarts was profound. Leopold was certainly impressed by the unique experience of walking through the city at such a time: 'about eleven or twelve o'clock by German time we were on the Piazza San Marco on our way to the Ridotto. We said to one another that at that moment both of you would probably be with Herr Hagenauer and would be little thinking that we were talking about you on the Piazza San Marco.'[69] But, for his adolescent, genius son, it was all intoxicating and enduring. Carnival was of course celebrated in various forms throughout Europe, before the austere disciplines of Lent. But in Venice its experience was (and indeed is) somehow more intensely individual than it was anywhere else: the masked, costumed merriment and raucous abandonment of moral propriety were conducted, both overtly and covertly, against a background of wide piazzas, narrow calles, and the watery reflection of nocturnal light and shadow. Fifteen years after this visit to Venice, Wolfgang would collaborate with the (significantly Venetian) poet Lorenzo Da Ponte – the most thrilling partner he ever had – and produce his three masterpieces of so-called *opera buffa*: *Le nozze di Figaro*, *Don Giovanni* and *Così fan tutte*. All of them, from wildly differing narrative bases, share elements of false identity, disguise and even masks, adding remarkable texture to an already dense fabric of human interaction. Although Wolfgang never returned to Venice after 1771, the Serenissima had seared itself deeply into his imaginative world, even in his first day.

After Carnival was over, life in Venice returned to a more sedate pace. The Grand Tourists departed, continuing their journeys southwards to Florence and Rome, and the streets and canals were altogether emptier and quieter. The opera houses closed for Lent, but there was early discussion with the Teatro San Benedetto of a possible commission for Wolfgang, for November 1772. Both Leopold and Wolfgang will have been very satisfied that their plan to secure future operatic work was continuing well. Leopold was certainly appreciative of the city itself ('Later on I shall tell you in detail how I like the Arsenal, the churches, the ospedali and other things, in fact Venice as a whole. Meanwhile I shall content myself with saying that beautiful and unusual things are to be seen here.'),[70] and he was deeply impressed by its inhabitants, as he activated his still-bulging portfolio of helpful introductions: 'we have got to know the whole nobility very well; and everywhere, at parties, at table, and in fact in all occasions we are so overwhelmed with honours that our hosts not only send their secretaries to fetch us and convey us home in their gondolas, but often the noble himself accompanies us on our return; and this is true of the greatest of them, for instance, the Cornaro, Grimani, Mocenigo, Dolfino, Valieri and so forth.'[71] His list of patrician families is indeed impressive, the Cornaro, Grimani and Mocenigo between them fielding a dozen doges over the last 400 years, including the current incumbent, Alvise Giovanni Mocenigo. (He was, however, among the last: in 1797, his successor's successor, Doge Ludovico Manin, was forced by Napoleon to abdicate.) They visited the Imperial Ambassador to Venice, Count Giacomo Durazzo, whose own career had included a decade as *Intendant des spectacles* in Vienna, where he had been heavily involved with Gluck's new type of music drama. Durazzo will have looked upon the Mozarts with multi-layered proprietorial perspective. And yet Leopold was not entirely happy with his Venetian experience. He quickly tired of water transport ('We shall soon have had enough of gondolas. During the first days the whole bed rocked in our sleep and the whole time I was thinking that I was in one of them.'),[72] and more to the point found that the reaction of these noble families to Wolfgang's talents was, though polite, decidedly casual. The Mozarts gave one of their concerts in the Palazzo Maffei on 5 March, but there was no report either of its content or of any of the usual acclaim. Giovanni Maria Ortes, the secular priest, political author and wealthy opera lover to whom Hasse had written from Vienna back in 1769, before the Mozarts had set out for Italy, reported back with kindly but perspicacious observations:

> I do not think, however, that [the Mozarts] are very much pleased with this city, where they probably expected that others would seek after them, rather than they after others, as will have happened to them elsewhere. The truth is that it is not much the custom here to go out of one's way to esteem others, however meritorious or estimable they may be, and they tend on the contrary to admire those who go in search of admiration. What a curious thing it is, this unconcern with which the boy notes this difference, whereas the father appears to be somewhat piqued by it.[73]

By the time the Mozarts left Venice on 12 March, Leopold had fully decided that, with its combination of untamed Carnival

behaviour and aristocratic indifference, it was 'the most dangerous place in all Italy'.[74]

Wolfgang, on the other hand, was having the time of his life.
He knew that this was the last stop on his life-changing tour
of the Italian peninsula, the final piece in his jigsaw of operatic
activity. He was assuredly looking forward to seeing his mother
and sister again, and regaling them with tales of his travels. But
for the moment, released at last from any pressure, obligation
or deadline, he was discovering the absolute joy of unalloyed
female company – his Wider 'pearls'. Recently turned fifteen,
he was balanced between childhood and self-aware adulthood,
and experiencing the delights and dangers of awakening feelings.
(Nowhere is that confusion of adolescent exhilaration, embarrassment and fear more potently expressed than in the aria 'Non
sò più cosa son, cosa faccio' that Wolfgang would in due course
write for his enchanting teenager Cherubino, in *Le nozze di
Figaro*.) He revelled in the attention the Wider sisters paid him –
Leopold reported approvingly to Maria Anna that the girls were
'at this moment engaged in washing and mending my lace cuffs.
The elder daughter has presented Wolfgang with a beautiful pair'[75]
– and in the games that they played. He described one of these
to his sister: 'Tell Johannes that Wider's pearls, especially Made-
moiselle Catarina, are always talking about him, and that he must
come back soon to Venice and submit to the *attacco*, that is, have
his bottom spanked when he is lying on the ground, so that he
may become a true Venetian. They tried to do it to me – the seven
women all together – and yet they could not pull me down.'[76]
As Ortes had observed, Wolfgang was quite undismayed by any
apparent indifference to his gifts among the Venetian patricians
whose approval his father so obsessively sought. He preferred
instead to spend time at last with people of his own generation,

who could no doubt introduce him, not just to their arcane pastimes, but to the splendours of their city. 'I am charmed with Venice', he concluded to Johannes Nepomuk Hagenauer.[77]

These intense new friendships continued as the Mozarts finally left Venice on 12 March. Herr Wider, together with his wife and two eldest daughters, Caterina and Rosa, and the Abbate Ortes too, all joined them most pleasurably for the first part of their journey. They opted to travel not by carriage, but via the Brenta Canal, hiring their own *burchiello*, upon which they cooked and ate their meals. On arrival in Padua, they were guests of the Pesaro family, and spent two nights there being shown as much of the city 'as can be seen in a day, as there too we were not left in peace and Wolfgang had to play at two houses.'[78] Among those they met in Padua were Francesco Antonio Vallotti, composer, organist and *maestro di cappella* (for fifty years) at the great Basilica of San Antonio, and, after Padre Martini, one of the most important musical theorists in Italy; and the Marchese Giuseppe Ximenes D'Aragona, an ardent patron of music, and indeed regular correspondent with Martini in Bologna. The Marchese's passion for older, contrapuntal music led him to commission from Wolfgang an oratorio, *Betulia liberata*, to a libretto by Metastasio. No doubt to Wolfgang's great sadness, the Widers and Ortes returned from Padua to Venice, whereupon Johannes Wider wrote charmingly to Maria Anna, reassuring her of her family's health and wellbeing. The Mozarts meanwhile travelled via Vicenza (where they will surely have visited Palladio's sublime Teatro Olimpico) to Verona, staying once more with their old friend Pietro Lugiati. More glad tidings were delivered to them there. They received not only confirmation of an imminent contract from Milan of the opera for 1773, but 'another very pleasant piece of news' which Leopold would not divulge in his letter to Maria Anna.[79]

This was in fact Maria Theresa's commission for a serenata, to be performed during those highly anticipated celebrations, later that year, of the marriage between her son Archduke Ferdinand and the Princess Maria Beatrice d'Este. (For the canny Maria Theresa, this newest dynastic marriage would bring Modena once more under Austrian influence.) So Wolfgang now had two guaranteed, and very high-profile, return trips to Milan. As he and his father finally clambered back into their carriage and reversed their route up to the Brenner Pass, any inevitable weariness and discomfort with challenging conditions (the snows were indeed heavy, as Leopold had predicted) would have been offset by an enormous sense of achievement and satisfaction. Once back on the Austrian side of the Alps, they stayed again in Innsbruck, and finally arrived home in Salzburg on Maundy Thursday, 28 March, just in time for Easter. As always, Leopold's timing and journey-planning had been immaculate.

The fifteen months of Wolfgang's first, exhaustive journey to Italy had been arduous, challenging, at times frantic, and probably coloured too by deep anxiety and even self-doubt. But, in a huge learning curve, his triumphs had far outweighed any sufferings or disappointments. All four major operatic centres – Milan, Naples, Bologna and Venice – were, in various stages of development or confirmation, interested in employing him; and now Padua too wanted an oratorio. He had been honoured by the Pope, and accepted not just by learned masters, but, perhaps most important of all, by the country's foremost musicians and singers, whose working practices had effectively taught him his trade, even as he earned their profound and genuine respect.

The Mozarts must have imagined for themselves a huge future in Italy, perhaps even a permanent settlement there for the entire family. If Leopold, in his persistent quest for attention and preferment, had again ruffled some feathers, Wolfgang had spread nothing but delight and admiration. When Hasse, in Vienna, received his letter from the Abbate Ortes reporting on the Mozarts' demeanour in Venice, he wrote back with similar, and very typical, thoughtfulness:

Young Mozard is certainly marvellous for his age, and I do love him infinitely. The father, as far as I can see, is equally discontented everywhere, since here too he uttered the same lamentations. He idolises his son a little too much, and thus does all he can to spoil him; but I have such a high opinion of the boy's natural good sense that I hope he will not be spoilt in spite of the father's adulation, but will grow into an honest fellow.[80]

5

IMPERIAL SPLENDOUR

'Plenty of ideas!'

Nothing, of course, can be known of the atmosphere in Getreide-gasse after the return of the travellers. There would have been the greatest joy, certainly, and eagerness to hear accounts of all Italian experiences, and an amazed wonder, tinged with pained longing, at the hearing of them. There would have been almost forensic inspection of physical changes in all four members of the Mozart family after their fifteen months of separation. Leopold, now fifty-one, would have returned in a state of some exhaustion, the dramatic scar on his leg a symbol of the strains and heavy responsibilities he had undergone as he piloted his son through triumphs and vicissitudes. His wife, who had turned fifty on the previous Christmas Day, had aged a little, and his daughter was approaching her twentieth birthday: Nannerl had now become an adult member of Salzburg society, receiving suitors and teaching young charges. But their world had effectively stood still within the city's narrow confines, while that of their men-folk had burst open so spectacularly; and, even as they surveyed young Wolfgang – not much taller, but with his deeper voice and, beyond his constantly sunny confidence, a newer authority within him – their happiness at reunion, and voracious desire for detail of all they had missed, could have been coloured too by continuing resentment and fractiousness. The situation, in their tiny home, was not uncomplicated.

What was incontrovertible was that the Getreidegasse apartment was now far too small. With its single bedroom, it was simply no longer possible for them all to huddle down together 'like soldiers . . . Wolfgang is no longer seven years old', as Leopold had written to his wife from Venice on 20 February – just six weeks before their return would really necessitate addressing the problem.[1] He and Wolfgang had frequently shared not merely a room but also a bed on their travels, and so presumably had Maria Anna and Nannerl back at home. It seemed appropriate therefore that this arrangement should somehow continue, and that Leopold and Wolfgang should take a room in another household, although by day the family would of course interact normally in Getreidegasse. Leopold instructed Maria Anna to investigate lodgings with three possible neighbours ('either with Sailerwirt, with Stern or with Saulentzl'), and presumably one of these families obliged. For the moment there was no plan at all to move the whole family to a larger home (this would not happen for another two years), the implication surely being that, with the current excitements in Italy, Leopold was anticipating a relocation for all of them much further away. His own promotion prospects in Salzburg were thoroughly stalled, largely through his constant absences, which gave the musicians who remained in the Archbishop's service more opportunities to satisfy and shine. But even if Leopold had kept his place on the ladder of promotion, he would, like his predecessors, have been at the mercy of its unpredictability; and this awareness, coupled with a growing conviction (shared with his son) of the essential mediocrity of Salzburg music-making, in comparison with the glorious standards in Rome, or Bologna, or Milan, or Venice, would have persuaded him that the whole family would soon benefit from better employment secured elsewhere. That first Italian trip had been enormously successful in preparing the ground, as Wolfgang had garnered his honours and admiration everywhere. The imminent, high-profile engagement for the imperial wedding in Milan would surely deliver some permanent job offer for both Mozarts. So, for now, Getreidegasse would carry on serving as a cramped family base, and the nocturnal separation that Maria Anna had endured for fifteen months would continue. Even if her husband and son were now only a few streets away, a gulf, albeit considerably narrowed, remained.

This new living arrangement was indeed to last only a few months: Wolfgang was due back in Milan by September, to prepare his wedding serenata. As yet, he had no knowledge of the libretto he was to set, for this choice resided ultimately in the hands of Maria Theresa herself, who, although she would not be present at her son's nuptials, was indubitably in control of them. For the main operatic attraction, she was turning to two of its most stalwart and distinguished practitioners, her long-time court poet Pietro Metastasio and the composer Johann Adolph Hasse, resident in Vienna since the coronation of her co-regent son Joseph II in 1764. By now, both these septuagenarian men had effectively retired, but Maria Theresa's imperial command persuaded them to emerge from their seclusion and collaborate once more (it would be their sixth, and last, partnership) on a celebratory opera, *Ruggiero*. (This story of Ruggiero and Alcina, from Ariosto's *Orlando furioso*, had been much mined operatically: among many adaptations, Handel's *Alcina* is based on it, as was the *Ruggiero* by Mazzolà and Guglielmi that Leopold and Wolfgang had seen in Verona in 1770.) Metastasio had begun, but failed to complete, an earlier version of this libretto for the marriage of Maria Theresa's youngest daughter Maria Antonia (Marie Antoinette) to France's Louis XVI in May of the previous year; now, he was instructed by the Empress to finish it properly for her son's wedding. Maria Theresa then made her imaginative decision to supplement the veterans' *Ruggiero* with a smaller work by a teenage composer, albeit one whom she had known for nearly a decade. Hasse's seniority, and therefore superiority, were comfortably guaranteed.

Hasse himself would have to travel to Milan in person, to oversee his opera and direct its performances. But while there may have been some reluctance to undertake this journey in the Hasse household, in Salzburg the Mozarts were all thrilled to learn that Wolfgang would appear alongside the generous and lauded composer they had got to know back in 1768, when Hasse's discreet supervision had been so important in firing Wolfgang's early fascination with *opera seria*. As Leopold proudly reported to their good friend Count Pallavicini in Bologna, 'the oldest Maestro Signor Adolfo Hasse, known as il Sassone, will write the opera, and the youngest Maestro the Serenata'.[2] Years later, in the memoir about her brother compiled for Friedrich Schlichtegroll in 1792, Nannerl made the same point: 'As H: Majesty had appointed Hr: Hasse, the oldest Capellmeister to write the opera, she had chosen the youngest to write the Serenata' – an indication surely of the profound and lasting satisfaction this felicitous juxtaposition had afforded them all.[3]

As Wolfgang awaited news of his serenata text, he had other major projects to fulfil. One was his oratorio *La Betulia liberata* for Padua, to be completed before he left for Milan in order that the score might be delivered in person as he and his father made their way south again. (This would in fact entail a significant detour.) But another large commission was closer to home. The Mozarts' employer, Archbishop Schrattenbach, was due to celebrate not only the anniversary of his consecration, in December, but also, in the following month, fifty years since his ordination. Among multiple festive plans, Wolfgang was commissioned to write *Il sogno di Scipione*, an allegorical '*azione teatrale*', or semi-staged cantata; and, as it would be required immediately after Wolfgang's return from Italy, he would have to set about composing this too before he left. Both these projects had texts by Metastasio, so Wolfgang would have felt on comfortable territory. He could keep his impending operas in focus, and continue to develop his storytelling skills in the respected idiom with which he was currently so preoccupied. But while the gesture and language will have been happily familiar to him, he was no doubt aware that the singers in Padua (an unknown factor) and in Salzburg (certainly known to him) would be of a considerably lesser distinction than those in Milan, and that compromises would have to be made.

So it was with cautious efficiency that, between April and August 1771, Wolfgang set to work on his two big Metastasio projects. The libretto of *Il sogno di Scipione* (K.126) had originally been commissioned by the Empress Elisabeth, in praise of Charles VI, in 1735, and since then, pursuing a tradition of semi-staged works celebrating illustrious patrons or visitors, it had been set several times. Despite its definition as an '*azione teatrale*', it is in fact very static: in a dream, Scipio is instructed to choose either Fortuna or Costanza as his protector. The two rival goddesses lay out their respective virtues, and eventually Scipio opts for Costanza's reliable strength over the fickleness of Fortuna, thus demonstrating his astute judgement as a political leader. The cantata ends with a '*licenza*', a separate and dramatically unrelated movement lauding the dedicatee of the work – so here Wolfgang replaced all textual references to 'Karl' with the first name of his own employer, 'Sigismondo' (the Italian form of Sigismund). The vocal scoring, for the three main characters plus three smaller roles, is very similar to that in earlier works that Wolfgang had written for Salzburg (*Die Schuldigkeit des ersten Gebots*, K.35, for instance), with the clear implication that the same singers, with their individual strengths and, more relevantly, weaknesses, would be employed again. While all the writing for the two goddesses, for example, is of stolid and predictable virtuosity, none of it is at all at the same level as that for his opera singers in Milan. But, as a work of grateful homage to his Prince-Archbishop, it would fit the bill perfectly well; and Wolfgang put his completed score to one side.

Next he wrote his oratorio for Padua, *La Betulia liberata* (K.118), to another Metastasio libretto from approximately the same period (1734). Like *Il sogno di Scipione*, and so many other Metastasio texts, it received over sixty settings in the eighteenth century and was a very suitable choice of subject for a Lenten substitute for opera. Despite some innate violence (it is the story of Judith and Holofernes, from the Apocrypha), most of its action was offstage, and the oratorio's message told of Judith's profound courage and the overarching power of God. Again, Wolfgang seemed to write cautiously and obediently. *La Betulia liberata* has swathes of explanatory recitative, punctuated by simple, homo-phonic choruses – very far from the complex contrapuntal style in which Wolfgang had been tutored, first by his father and then by Padre Martini – and arias of perfectly manageable coloratura for singers with reliable stamina and a decent technique. Unusually, the main role of Giuditta was written in the contralto register, implying that some specific Paduan singer, with a low range and vocal timbre, had already been cast by the Marchese D'Aragona, and perhaps even heard by the Mozarts. But although Wolfgang ticked this completed commission off his list, too, and packed it up ready for transmission to Padua, it would in fact never be performed there. Perhaps it did not arrive on time (certainly the Mozarts themselves did not make the necessary detour to deliver it in person); or perhaps the Marchese simply decided he did not like it. In Advent 1771 another setting of the same libretto, by the local Paduan composer Giuseppe Calegari, was sung instead; and Wolfgang's early foray into the world of oratorio would remain unperformed for two centuries.

Another work written in the cramped space of the Getreide-gasse apartment, in that spring of 1771, between trips to Italy, and one which surely reflects an experience from Italy, was his *Litaniae Lauretanae* (K.109/74e). This was the setting of a medieval text (a series of Marian invocations, all ending with the refrain '*ora pro nobis*') associated with the Convent of Santa Casa in Loreto, which Wolfgang and Leopold had visited the previous summer, on their swelteringly uncomfortable journey between Rome and Bologna. Although Wolfgang was still only fifteen, he did have a nominal court position as an archiepiscopal Konzertmeister, and this composition – the first of two settings of the Loreto text, and of four litanies altogether – was no doubt fulfilling his obligation. But again, the obedient simplicity of this work, certainly in comparison with his second setting of the same text three years later, implies that, as the summer months unfolded, Wolfgang's mind was thoroughly focused on his glittering project in the autumn.

By late July, Leopold was again making travel plans with his customary efficiency. Having considered all possibilities of transportation, he decided on this occasion to travel all the way to Milan in a single carriage, rented exclusively for their sole use. But once again he refused to countenance any notion of his wife and daughter joining him and Wolfgang on this most prestigious of visits. The women's argument for being included would certainly have carried considerable weight. This trip, unlike the constant upheaval and unsettlement of the previous one, had a single destination and was for a very much shorter period. Maria Anna and Nannerl could claim to have known the bridegroom, Archduke Ferdinand, since he and his siblings had entertained the Mozart children at Schönbrunn in 1762, so their presence at his wedding, in which Wolfgang was to play a small but important part, would surely be welcomed. They had many Salzburg friends in Milan, who would take trouble to make them too feel at home. And although the cost of housing and feeding four people would inevitably be more expensive than it was for two, the whole family was accustomed to living together in close quarters, and Maria Anna could herself do the cooking and take care of her family, as she had on countless occasions on their previous travels. But all such reasoned supplications were dismissed, as Leopold determinedly forged ahead with his arrangements for father and son only. Almost certainly there will have been discussion, recrimination and ultimately the return of disappointment, as Maria Anna and Nannerl were made aware that, for the second time, they were to share none of the Milanese experience and excitement.

∾

Wolfgang and his father duly set out from Salzburg on Tuesday, 13 August 1771. Their objective was to arrive in Milan as quickly as possible, and, with long summer days (as opposed to the hazardous winter conditions in which they had first travelled that route, twenty months earlier), and also the more robust stamina now of a fifteen-year-old boy, they were able to cover greater distances each day – often negotiating three stages rather than two. On the first journey, they had lingered, partly for rest, but also for networking, in Innsbruck (for four days) and Rovereto (three days), and then spent two formative weeks in Verona and nine days in Mantua. It had therefore been six weeks before they had arrived in Milan. Now, they achieved this in just eight days, taking an extra night only in Verona, where they stayed again with their loyal friend Pietro Lugiati. From there they did not take the southerly detour to Mantua (and certainly did not go east to Padua for any delivery of an oratorio score), but travelled on the more northerly route to Milan, through Brescia. They had encountered other old friends en route, especially in Rovereto on their fourth day of travel. But they were anxious to move swiftly (they were after all paying for their rented carriage by the day) and were tiresomely delayed only twice, first by slow-moving peasants' carts on the narrow road between Rovereto and Ala, and then, after Verona, by the necessity to replace a wheel, which had collapsed under the strain of tremendous heat (which had dried out the wood) and then torrential rain (which corrupted it). In general, Leopold was delighted with the quality of their journey: 'I must now praise my sedia, which stood the journey very well. For although we rattled along the Venetian roads from Verona and even from Peri at a terrific pace and over the biggest stones, I did not feel the slightest discomfort.'[4]

On arrival in Milan on 21 August, Leopold and Wolfgang based themselves in the same apartment that they had used during the *Mitridate* period, and immediately felt at home. Wolfgang was happy to see again the son of the landlord, with whom he enjoyed communicating in sign language; and he also drew special energy from being close to the theatre, and in a building where several musicians were lodging – and noisily practising: 'Upstairs we have a violinist, downstairs another one, in the next room a singing master who gives lessons, and in the other room opposite ours an oboist. That is good fun when you are composing! It gives you plenty of ideas.'[5] There was further good news to greet them on their arrival: a contract from the Teatro San Benedetto in Venice, for an opera for the 1773 Carnival season – those final discussions on their last trip had certainly borne fruit. In their first few days in Milan, they caught up with friends (the Germani family entertained them almost immediately) and were presented again to the bride-to-be, Princess Maria Beatrice of Modena, who was, as Leopold wrote to Salzburg, 'so gracious that she not only spoke to us for a long time and was most friendly, but, strange to say, rushed up when she saw us, took off her glove, held out her hand and began to talk before we had time to address her.'[6] Leopold was as usual much obsessed by the weather, sending Maria Anna detailed conditions they had encountered on their journey: 'Until we reached Bozen [Bolzano] the weather was mild, but from Bozen to Innsbruck it was rather cold. The sun, which came out now and then, drew up in places mists, which collected and came down in rain, so that during our first night in St Johann

I took my flannel jerkin out of our night-bag and put it on, taking it off again at noon at our first stage outside Bozen, while the horses were being changed. Since then it has been warm.'[7] (As Wolfgang's first biographer, G. N. von Nissen, would point out, Leopold 'always wrote about the weather at great length.'[8]) Now, in Milan, it was extremely hot, and there were frequent and dramatic thunderstorms, which Leopold feared might endanger the upcoming wedding festivities – though these were not due to start until the middle of October. The focus of both father and son, clearly, was on the task they had come to Milan to fulfil.

Disconcertingly, however, there was still no sign of the actual text for this wedding serenata. Although Wolfgang must by now have known its librettist (Giuseppe Parini), its title (*Ascanio in Alba*), and perhaps even its structure too, he could not begin the huge task of setting words to music, either in the recitatives or in the specially tailored arias for specific singers. He could compose his overture ahead of time, and think on the subject matter as he gradually met his cast. If he had been hoping for some of his *Mitridate* singers to reappear, he was disappointed, for none of them was contracted either to his project or to Hasse's *Ruggiero*. The same group of singers would be in both presentations, and, especially after Hasse himself arrived in Milan at the end of August and almost immediately reconnected with his young quasi-protegé ('Hasse arrived yesterday and we are calling on him today'),[9] the two composers could perhaps share their perceptions and experiences of their soon-to-be colleagues. (Again, it is tempting to speculate on the insights into the capabilities of these singers that might have been offered by Hasse's distinguished soprano wife, Faustina Bordoni.) The three main singers for both *Ruggiero* and *Ascanio* were to be the soprano Antonia Maria Girelli-Aguilar, the castrato Giovanni Manzuoli and the tenor Giuseppe Tibaldi. They were all extremely experienced, but perhaps past their prime. Manzuoli, who would sing both title roles, and therefore two vigorous young men, was now fifty-one years old. But his voice and his great sense of style were highly praised by Burney ('the most powerful and voluminous soprano that had been heard on our stage since the time of Farinelli; and his manner of singing was grand and full of taste and dignity'[10]). The Mozarts had known Manzuoli since he had befriended them in London in 1764, when he had been at the height of his vocal powers, and then had met him again in Florence in 1770. At that time Wolfgang was even speculating that he might be cast in *Mitridate*, so, although that had not happened, he would surely have been happy that this generous and highly gifted star would now be in his new opera. Tibaldi, a forty-one-year-old tenor from Bologna, who had studied with Padre Martini and was a member of the Accademia Filarmonica, was also known to Wolfgang: he had heard him singing in Gluck's operas in Vienna in 1767. Tibaldi too would bring starry presence and experience to his cast. The prima donna, Girelli-Aguilar, had actually begun her professional life as a dancer in the 1750s, becoming a singer in 1759. She had appeared in Prague as well as Bologna and Parma, and after her current stint in Milan would travel to London for a season. She and her colleagues Geltrude Falchini and Adamo Solzi, of whom little is known, were all new to Wolfgang, but almost certainly they were familiar to Hasse.

Where Hasse was collaborating with his old colleague Metastasio, with whom there could indeed have been creative dialogue and discussion, Wolfgang's librettist was a total stranger. Giuseppe Parini was a local Lombardian who had studied in Milan from an early age. Despite having somewhat irrelevantly been ordained as a priest (a condition for inheriting a substantial legacy from a great-aunt), he had become an active poet, a teacher of rhetoric at the University, a member of Milan's august Accademia dei Trasformati, and indeed one of the most important figures in Enlightenment Italian literature. He had attracted the attention of Count Firmian, who had appointed him as editor of the *Gazzetta di Milano* – in which capacity Parini had written the short but approving review of *Mitridate* earlier that year – and then recommended him to Maria Theresa in Vienna as librettist for her son's wedding serenata. But any text that he produced had to be scrutinized and approved by the Empress, and possibly by Metastasio too; and it was for this reason that its return to Milan that summer was later than the arrival of its young composer. Even then, Parini had to make some final adjustments to the text, and Wolfgang received it only on 30 August, after nine days of waiting for it. But now at last he could throw all his energies into the project he had been anticipating for so many months.

In a letter written on 7 September, Leopold explained to Maria Anna and Nannerl the late arrival of the text, and Wolfgang's subsequent intense industry: 'At the moment we are up to our eyes in work, for the libretto arrived late and then remained until two days ago in the poet's hands, because this and that passage had to be altered. I hope it will be a success. Wolfgang is now very busy composing'. (He himself was rather more preoccupied with his own digestive health, requesting his wife to send him 'a few boxes of Hansl Spielmann pills which I really need, for I know they do me good when owing to constipation I get my old giddiness. Since I left Salzburg I have had it a good deal, but not so violently as to have to vomit or be obliged to go to bed.'[11] By contrast, Wolfgang was thoroughly enjoying Italian fruit: 'I have already eaten lots of good pears and peaches and melons'.[12]) A week later, Leopold was able to report that Wolfgang had already finished all the recitatives, 'with and without instruments', the choruses and, crucially, the dances.[13] These would assume enormous importance in the visual impact of the wedding serenata, as indeed they would in Hasse's opera, and they were already in rehearsal. Wolfgang had always enjoyed dancing and dancers, and now he readily engaged with the choreographers, for even his overture would involve dance in two of its three movements. Perhaps knowing that Maria Anna and Nannerl too would appreciate this aspect of performance, Leopold reported in meticulous detail the interaction between dancers and chorus that they had approvingly witnessed, particularly admiring 'the hard work of the ballet masters, Pick and Fabier'.[14] Now that the structural framework of choruses and dances was built, and the narrative thrust achieved too in the all-important recitatives, Wolfgang could concentrate on composing the arias for his principal singers. And, as he had done nine months earlier with *Mitridate*, he worked closely with his cast to discover the best way to showcase their individual talents. Although he was physically a little run down ('I have a very heavy cold and a bad cough', he confessed to Nannerl),[15] this was the part of opera composition that he relished, for it was the most challenging, the most educational, and the most rewarding.

For the next twelve days Wolfgang wrote tirelessly. ('I cannot write much, firstly because I have nothing to say, and secondly, because my fingers ache so much from composing', he apologized, again to Nannerl.[16]) His singers spent their precious time with him, and were all thrilled with what he produced, as Leopold related:

On Monday or Tuesday at the latest Wolfgang will have finished his work. Signor Manzuoli often comes to see us, but we have only been to see him once. Signor Tibaldi comes almost every day at about eleven o'clock, and remains seated at the table till about one, while Wolfgang is composing. Everyone is extremely kind and has the greatest respect for Wolfgang. Indeed we have not experienced any unpleasantness whatsoever, for all these famous singers are most excellent and sensible people.[17]

Meanwhile the whole of Milan was becoming feverishly involved in the multifarious preparations for the wedding. Despite his disapproval of the Italian capacity for brinkmanship, Leopold was enormously impressed by the daily industry and achievement:

All Milan is astir, the more so as a great deal, in fact most of the work has been postponed to the last minute. Consequently everyone is now at work. Some are getting the theatre ready, as the whole building requires to be renovated and redecorated. Others are busy preparing for the reception of His Highness, engaging lodgings and rooms, illuminating and adorning the Cathedral, obtaining garments and liveries for the servants, and horses and carriages and so forth for the balls. There are in fact a hundred things to do and I cannot keep them all in my mind. So everyone is frightfully busy! . . . Did you see the rope-dancers when they were in Salzburg? They are now on their way here and ought to arrive very soon. Great work is in progress, for an extraordinarily large hut is being built for them. The Italian plays came to an end two days ago, for the theatre must now be kept free for rehearsals and the painters must not be prevented from working day and night . . . Whoever now comes to Milan to attend these wedding festivities will certainly see some fine things.[18]

On 23 September, just three weeks after Wolfgang had begun setting Parini's text, the composition of *Ascanio* was complete. A team of copyists must have been put into fast action, for the chorus began rehearsing on 27 September, and the orchestra a day later ('the singers . . . are looking forward even more than we are to hearing the serenata performed this evening with all the instruments').[19] Constantly sharing personnel and rehearsal time, *Ascanio* and Hasse's *Ruggiero* were prepared in parallel. On 5 October, Leopold reported: 'The theatre is full from eight o'clock in the morning to eleven o'clock at night, for the dancers are always there', as indeed were the extremely hard-working singers.[20] This alternation between the two operas did allow Wolfgang time to relax a little between his own rehearsals ('we have resumed our walks'), and the now-balmy autumn weather was glorious. This time around, there was a quiet confidence in both father and son that Wolfgang had acquitted himself well, and that once again he would receive justified admiration and praise. Leopold, usually quick to detect, or imagine, negative response to their presence, was almost effusive in his assessment of the current situation: 'You will be pleased to hear that I have good hopes that Wolfgang's work will win great applause: firstly, because both Signor Manzuoli and all the other singers are . . . immensely pleased with their arias . . . and secondly, because I know how good Wolfgang's work is and what an impression it will make, for it is more than certain that his composition is excellently adapted both to the singers and the orchestra.'[21] Meanwhile both he and Wolfgang continued to chart the mounting excitement, and mounting security, in the city, as dignitaries arrived from all over Europe to attend this grandest of weddings:

The Duke of York has already arrived and also a prince of Saxe-Gotha. The Hereditary Princes, that is, the father and the mother of the Princess bride, have also arrived. Count Sauerau [from Salzburg] too is here. The crowds are enormous and people will have to see everything in the greatest discomfort. Admirable regulations have been issued, as, for instance, that commoners may not bear swords or any other arms, that everyone must be identified at the gates and that all householders must hand in to a specially appointed committee a description of their tenants. No one may go about the streets at night without a light. Soldiers and sbirri patrol the town and hussars its outskirts. Everyone must have tickets for the opera, the serenata, the ball, the court banquet and all other festivities and so on.[22]

Leopold was also happy to report that the new Archduchess had been taken to the hearts of the Milanese public: 'some anxiety was felt lest [Ferdinand] should not have been pleased with his bride, because she is not beautiful. On the other hand she is unusually friendly, agreeable and virtuous, and greatly beloved by everyone; and she has completely won over the Archduke, for she has the best heart and the most pleasant manners in the world.'[23]

Like all such imperial nuptials, the marriage between the sixteen-year-old Archduke Ferdinand and his older bride Princess Maria Beatrice (twenty-one) was to be lengthily celebrated, with daily excitements over the course of two weeks. The actual wedding ceremony and benediction took place at the magnificent duomo on 15 October, and was followed by a mighty banquet. Then every day there were processions, as the bridal couple were displayed through all the major streets of the city, sometimes accompanied by masques, or music, or spectacular illuminations;

and there were more huge banquets, often observed by the public. There was also a *cuccagna*, a curious festival tradition borrowed from Naples, where, two years earlier, one had featured at the marriage between the Archduke's sister Maria Carolina and King Ferdinand IV. A fake fortress decorated with the finest foods had been built in front of the royal palace, and, at a signal from the King, a mob of Neapolitan spectators had clambered through a muddy moat to fight over meats and cheeses and other various delicacies, to the imperious delight of the noble wedding guests. So Archduke Ferdinand included one of these, too, at his own celebrations. And then in the evenings there were the operas. Hasse's *Ruggiero* opened on the day after the wedding, 16 October, followed on 17 October by Wolfgang's *Ascanio in Alba*, after which they alternated. Those industrious and elderly singers thus had to perform, after a ferocious rehearsal schedule, almost nightly for two weeks. They should have had a three-day respite between 18 and 20 October, as 20 October was the anniversary of the death of Emperor Charles VI (father of Maria Theresa), and homage to this was customarily observed. But in fact Wolfgang's *Ascanio* caused such a stir that an extra performance was immediately added for the evening of 19 October. If this was challenging news for his weary cast and orchestra, it was simply wonderful for Wolfgang himself. For the second time in ten months, he had taken Milan by storm.

The subject matter of *Ascanio in Alba* had been carefully chosen to flatter both the wedding couple and the Empress. Venus (representing Maria Theresa) descends to tell her son by Aeneas, Ascanio (Ferdinand), to marry the nymph Silvia (Beatrice) and found a new city, Alba. To test Silvia's virtue, Ascanio must conceal his identity. Silvia has already encountered his likeness in a dream, and has no wish to marry anyone else; but she knows she must obey Venus's wishes. So, when she and the disguised Ascanio do meet, she recognizes but rejects him, thus passing the test. Venus descends again and brings the couple together, directing them to rule their new city with love and justice. The two main characters, Ascanio and Silvia, sung by Manzuoli and Girelli, were each given six arias; a sympathetic priest, Acaste (Tibaldi), had three, and Venere (Falchini) and a shepherd, Fauno (Solzi), two each. There were no fewer than eight choral numbers, none of them in any way challenging, but many of them repeated throughout the evening, giving the chorus and their dancing counterparts great structural significance, not least in their contribution to the visual impact of the work. If the somewhat flimsy narrative was essentially static, the whole presentation, with its brilliant entrances for Venus, and extravagant design, costumes, transformations and displays of wondrous lighting effects, represented the height of eighteenth-century stagecraft. Given the flamboyance of the occasion, no expense was spared.

The finest singer in Wolfgang's cast was clearly Girelli as Silvia. She had splendid coloratura, which Wolfgang readily exploited, but she could also convey the greatest tenderness. In two of her arias she did both. 'Spiega il desio' is a vigorous allegro, enriched by four horns, and then a beguiling andante grazioso section before the reprise of the allegro. Conversely, her 'Infelici affetti miei' has slow outer sections, and an agitated allegro at its centre. While none of her music is as spectacular as that which Wolfgang had written for the great Bernasconi in *Mitridate*, it certainly shows that Girelli had a secure technique and an appealing presence. By contrast, the six arias for Manzuoli as Ascanio are all much less showy, for Wolfgang was manifestly aware of vocal gifts no longer at their peak. And yet, with impressive maturity and sympathetic understanding, he produced arias for his friend that still made an impact, largely through vibrant orchestral writing (he even added 'serpenti', or cors anglais, to one aria); and, most significantly, he wrote him several excellent accompanied recitatives, in which Ascanio's every thought and desire are mirrored in the orchestra, and dramatic energy flows. Interestingly, the most dazzling vocal music was written for the secondo uomo, the castrato Adamo Solzi, as the shepherd Fauno. As one of his arias, 'Dal tuo gentil sembiante', shows, Solzi had an astonishing range and stamina, for he is taken to top Ds in his repeated bursts of fast coloratura. Again, this seems to be an area of the voice that excited Wolfgang – and always would. The arias for both Aceste (Tibaldi) and Venere (Falchini) are fine if unremarkable; and the one welcome ensemble, a trio for Silvia, Ascanio and Aceste at the opera's denouement, again shows greater vocal gymnastics for Girelli and Solzi, and a central supporting presence for Manzuoli. Such sensitivity to comparative ability was something to which Wolfgang was increasingly alert; and what he learned here in *Ascanio* would serve him extremely well in later years. If the overall level of arias in *Ascanio in Alba* shows little if any development from those in *Mitridate* – a factor entirely dependent upon those singers' individual abilities – the continuing, voracious even, improvement in accompanied recitative, and the constant energy of the score, indicate the deepening of Wolfgang's facility. In the assault course of his operatic training ground, he easily cleared his hurdles.

∾

As Leopold had predicted, Wolfgang's wedding serenata was another resounding success. The extra performance was instantly slotted in, and everywhere they went, father and son were 'constantly addressed in the street by courtiers and other persons who wish to congratulate the young composer'.[24] The Archduke and his new wife were especially enthusiastic, ordering two copies of the score of *Ascanio* and attending later performances: 'Their Royal Highnesses the Archduke and Archduchess not only caused two arias to be repeated by applauding them, but both during the serenata and afterwards leaned over from their box towards Wolfgang and showed their gracious approval by calling out "*Bravissimo, maestro*" and clapping their hands. Their applause was taken up each time by the courtiers and the whole audience.'[25] Among those many domestic and foreign guests was Count Raimund Saurau, one of Salzburg's cathedral canons, and his excited account of it to the court chancellor, Franz Felix von Mölk, was duly passed on to Archbishop Schrattenbach, no doubt at Leopold's encouragement. As always, Wolfgang was entirely modest about his success, but, knowing of Nannerl's especial interest in singers, he did take the trouble to inform her which of his arias had been encored.

Reading all this would have been both thrilling and painful for Maria Anna and Nannerl. For several weeks Leopold had alternately raised the possibility of their actually joining them in Milan for these celebrations and triumphs, and then cruelly deflated it, arguing that the expense, the earlier heat and now the crowds would all have tested the endurance of his wife and daughter. Then, on 26 October, he found an unexpected trump card to play. The *cuccagna*, which had taken place two days earlier, had ended in disaster. The stand built to accommodate the spectators for this unedifying spectacle of gluttony had collapsed due to overcrowding: three people had died, and more than fifty were seriously injured. Leopold catalogued all this in avid detail ('many broke arms and legs, others their hands, others their feet, others their backs or their ribs'),[26] while adding that it was only by good fortune that he and Wolfgang had arrived at the *cuccagna* after the accident. 'So you see,' he concluded, 'how right I was in my earlier letters to advise you of the dangers here.' Once more, Maria Anna and Nannerl were marooned in Salzburg, where, to add to their misery, there was a virulent outbreak of dysentery with alarming side effects (some people were apparently losing their minds too),[27] and could enjoy Wolfgang's success only vicariously.

After the excitements of the opening performances of *Ascanio*, Wolfgang and Leopold took the opportunity to unwind, and Leopold addressed again his constant obsession with his own health. ('I am staying indoors for a few days, because I have had very bad rheumatism all over me, which I have almost altogether steamed away simply by drinking elderberry tea. Among our medicines we had only one single black powder. Fortunately Signora D'Aste has quantities of them . . . she sent off the prescription . . . to the chemist and procured some more for me.'[28]) This indisposition actually prevented them from attending at least one performance of Hasse's *Ruggiero*, for if Leopold felt unable to go out, then nor could his son – toast of the town and nearly sixteen years old though he was. Wolfgang was graciously accepting of his being gated: after all, he had his own way of enjoying opera from afar. 'Fortunately I know nearly all the arias by heart and so I can see and hear [*Ruggiero*] at home in my head.'[29]

By the end of October, both the wedding festivities and *Ascanio in Alba* were over. *Ruggiero* continued for another week, despite being deemed the weaker of the two operatic offerings. ('It really distresses me greatly,' wrote Leopold, not entirely convincingly, 'but Wolfgang's serenata has killed Hasse's opera more than I can say in detail.'[30]) The newlyweds Ferdinand and Beatrice disappeared to a castle in Varese, a medieval city at the foot of the Sacro Monte di Varese, which was one of the homes of the Duke of Modena, Beatrice's father. But the Archduke was clearly taken with the achievements of his childhood friend Wolfgang, and was seriously contemplating taking him into his service. He wrote to his mother, the Empress, and asked her advice on the matter.

After the departure of Ferdinand and Beatrice and all their wedding guests, grateful farewells began. On 8 November the redoubtable Count Firmian gave a lunch party for Hasse and Wolfgang, both of whom received generous gifts: 'Apart from the money they have got, Hasse has been given a snuff-box and Wolfgang a watch set in diamonds.'[31] Leopold was planning to leave Milan and begin their return to Salzburg on 18 October, but he then got word that the Archduke wished to see them when he got back from the mountains. This was exactly the sort of news he had wanted: surely there was now a distinct possibility of one if not both of them becoming employed in Milan. Leopold's own job security in Salzburg was still threatened by his continuing and prolonged absences; and he was anxious too about Wolfgang's prospects there ('I very much doubt that, if a paid appointment is vacant, His Grace will remember Wolfgang.').[32] He really could imagine a happy future for the whole family in Milan. So the Mozarts sat tight, and waited.

Wolfgang became a little restless. Now that the pressure was off him, he indulged in some uncharacteristically snide gossip about Giovanni Manzuoli, no less, who was in a not unreasonable, but retrospective (and therefore surely hopeless) dispute with the Milan opera authorities over payment for his recent performances as Ruggiero and Ascanio. As Wolfgang relayed to Nannerl:

> Manzuoli, who up to the present has been looked upon as the most sensible of the castrati, has in his old age given the world a sample of his stupidity and conceit. He was engaged for the opera at a salary of five hundred cigliati, but, as the contract did not mention the serenata, he demanded another five hundred for that, that is one thousand cigliati in all. The court only gave him seven hundred and a fine gold snuff-box (quite enough, I think). But he like a true castrato returned both the seven hundred cigliati and the snuff-box and went off without anything. I do not know how it will end – badly, I expect.[33]

He also took a macabre delight in witnessing four hanged corpses in the Piazza del Duomo, and blithely reported this too to his sister. But he certainly continued to compose, producing in these waiting days a symphony (K.112 in F), another work made up of two movements from the *Ascanio* overture plus a new finale (K.120/111a), and a divertimento in E flat (K.113). Very much influenced by the sort of instrumental music he had been hearing from contemporary Italian composers, Wolfgang here seemed to abandon all his contrapuntal leanings, so precisely sharpened a year earlier under the tutelage of Padre Martini, and turn instead to a more lyrical, even operatic hinterland. The divertimento is remarkable too for being scored for clarinets as well as strings and horns. This was the first time he had composed for the relatively new instrument, which would greatly excite him in later years, both as an orchestral colour and in solo and chamber music.

There was much socializing too, while Wolfgang and Leopold waited. They saw their friends the Trogers and the d'Astes often, and spent 'several hours' making music in the home of Albert Michael von Mayr, son of Maria Theresa's court treasurer, and now himself personal treasurer to Archduke Ferdinand.[34] The Czech composer Josef Mysliveček, whom the Mozarts had met in Bologna in the previous year, arrived in Milan for his opera *Il gran Tamerlano*, which would open the new season in December, and he too immediately spent time with the Mozarts. Every weekend Leopold wrote to Maria Anna announcing yet another delay ('I never thought that at the end of November I should still be in Milan, but circumstances have detained me.').[35] And then at last Ferdinand returned, and granted them an audience. While he was generous and appreciative, he was completely silent about any sort of appointment (he was still awaiting guidance from his mother). So Leopold, disappointed, finally packed up their possessions after fifteen weeks in Milan. They left on 5 December, retracing the steps of their summer journey, but at the mercy now of the winter conditions: 'the days are short and the roads are bad', he wrote from Bressanone.[36] They finally arrived back in Salzburg on 15 December, secure anyway in the knowledge that, at the very latest, they would be returning to Milan within a year, for Wolfgang had his contract to open the 1772–3 season. And Leopold still held out hope that they might yet receive news of an appointment. 'The question which you asked me,' he had written to Maria Anna from Ala on 8 December, '. . . I shall answer when we meet. All I can say now is that the affair is not quite hopeless.'[37]

But it was. Even as Leopold and Wolfgang were making their way back across the Alps, the Empress Maria Theresa was responding to her son. 'You ask me to take the young Salzburger into your service', she wrote on 12 December. 'I do not know why, not believing you have any need of a composer or of useless people. If however it gives you pleasure, I have no wish to hinder you. What I say is only to prevent your burdening yourself with useless people and giving titles to people of that sort. If they are in your service it degrades that service when these people go about the world like beggars. Besides, he has a large family.'[38] Clearly, Maria Theresa still had searing memories of the tiresome persistence with which Leopold had demanded an audience from her, back in 1768, when she was still mourning her husband and dealing with the consequences of the smallpox epidemic. Although she had later softened her attitude, and granted young Wolfgang a concert at the Waisenhaus church, which indeed she had attended, her abiding impression now of the Mozart family (which she somehow remembered as being larger than it was) was of an irrelevant nuisance. There would be no permanent move to Milan for the Mozarts.

6

COMING OF AGE

'Reason to hope for the greatest success'

Once more, any joyful domestic reunion in Getreidegasse, in December 1771, would have been tempered with undercurrents of unease. Maria Anna and Nannerl certainly had ambivalent feelings about Wolfgang's latest Italian triumph, proud though they were of his achievement and the waves of approval it had generated. Leopold cannot have been unaware of their hurt, but he had his own concerns, for his Salzburg salary had been stopped in his four-month absence, and for some weeks he had been angling to get it not only reinstated, but actually backdated to include the period of his absence. Here he had enlisted the help of Count Saurau, the Salzburg cathedral canon who had visited Milan and reported so enthusiastically on *Ascanio in Alba*. On his return to work, Leopold heard that his October and November emoluments had indeed been restored. And Wolfgang, while happy to describe his recent experiences to his mother and sister, was looking ahead to his next obligations and challenges. Among the first of these would be the imminent anniversary celebrations for

Archbishop Schrattenbach, and the performance therefore of his own *Il sogno di Scipione*, neatly prepared several months earlier.

But on 16 December 1771, the day after the Mozarts' return, everything changed. Archbishop Schrattenbach died, at the age of seventy-three. All planned celebrations, musical or otherwise, were of course cancelled; Salzburg went into mourning; and the cathedral chapter initiated elaborate procedures to select his successor. Among the candidates put forward were two internal ones: Count Saurau himself, and the cathedral's dean, Count Ferdinand Christoph Waldburg-Zeil. A third strong contender was Count Hieronymus Colloredo, who ten years earlier had been appointed by Schrattenbach as Prince-Bishop of Gurk. Two voting sessions failed to deliver a winner between these three close competitors, at which point Count Zeil withdrew his candidacy and pledged his support for Colloredo. At a third ballot, on 14 March 1772, the forty-year-old Colloredo was elected the new Prince-Archbishop of Salzburg. He would remain in post for thirty years, until he fled from the city at the approach of Napoleonic troops in 1801; and although he was still nominally ecclesiastical head of the archdiocese, he never returned. But in his thirty years he oversaw many modernizing reforms, sorting out Salzburg's finances, improving its education system and promoting the sciences as well as the arts. In church services everything was simplified, especially musical settings of the Mass, upon which new restrictions were imposed. While his achievements were generally lauded across Europe, they were largely resented by the Salzburgers themselves, who never warmed to him.

Colloredo's autocratic personality was displayed immediately on taking office. Far from showing gratitude to Count Zeil, whose selfless support had secured him his election, he removed him

14. 'Vesuvius is smoking furiously today', wrote Wolfgang to his sister from Naples in June 1770. Pierre-Jacques Volaire painted this eruption in the following year.

Sig: nedi schmid... inglese di 15 añi
Sig: appollonia Marchetti . seconda Doña
Sig: Jomelli . Maestro di Capelle
item . Sig: Caffaro
item: cicio el giusepe de maio. ✝
item: Sig: matta.
item: Sig: paesiello.
item: Sig: tarantina.
Sig: barbella . professore di violino.
Sig : agretta . bravo Musico soprano.

15. Wolfgang loved to keep lists, here of the musicians he met in Naples.

16. Padre Martini, celebrated teacher in
Bologna, who became Wolfgang's mentor,
instructor and admirer.

17. The so-called 'Bologna Mozart' portrait, originally commissioned by Padre Martini for his private collection, in 1772. Wolfgang is fifteen years old, and wearing his Order of the Golden Spur.

PERSONAGGI.

MITRIDATE, Rè di Ponto, e d'altri Regni, amante d'Aspasia.
Sig. Cavaliere Guglielmo D'Ettore Virtuoso di Camera di S. A. S. Elettorale di Baviera.
ASPASIA, promessa sposa di Mitridate, e già dichiarata Regina,
Signora Antonia Bernasconi.
SIFARE, figliuolo di Mitridate, e di Stratonica, amante d'Aspasia,
Sig. Pietro Benedetti, detto Sartorino.
FARNACE, primo figliuolo di Mitridate, amante della medesima,
Sig. Giuseppe Cicognani.
ISMENE, figlia del Re de' Parti, amante di Farnace,
Signora Anna Francesca Varese.
MARZIO, Tribuno Romano, amico di Farnace.
Sig. Gaspare Bassano.
ARBATE, Governatore di Ninfea,
Sig. Pietro Muschietti.

Compositore della Musica.

Il Sig. Cavaliere Amadeo Wolfgango Mozart, Accademico Filarmonico di Bologna, e Maestro della Musica di Camera di S. A. Rma il Principe, ed Arcivescovo di Salisburgo.

ATTO

18. The printed libretto of *Mitridate, re di Ponto* gives the names of the cast, and an effusive description of its young composer.

19. Canaletto's view of eighteenth-century Venice,
as the Mozarts would have seen it.

20 and 21. Pietro Longhi's depictions of gambling at the Ridotto, and dancing in a private home, represent activities enjoyed by Wolfgang in Venice in 1770.

22. The plaque commemorating Wolfgang's stay in Venice touchingly refers to the 'Salzburg boy, in whom the grace of musical genius, and eighteenth-century elegance, were combined in the purest poetry'.

IN QVESTA CASA OSPITE DI AMICI
IL QVINDICENNE

WOLFGANG AMADEVS MOZART

SOGGIORNO' FESTEVOLMENTE
DVRANTE IL CARNEVALE 1771

LA CITTA' DI VIVALDI E DI GOLDONI
VVOLE QVI RICORDATO
IL FANCIVLLO SALISBVRGHESE
NEL QVALE LA GRAZIA DEL GENIO MVSICALE
E IL GARBO SETTECENTESCO
SI FVSERO IN VNA PVRISSIMA POESIA

NEL SECONDO CENTENARIO

IL COMVNE DI VENEZIA
E L'AZIENDA AVTONOMA SOGGIORNO E TVRISMO

1971

23. After composing *Lucio Silla* in December 1772, Wolfgang was coping with a rehearsal period of unforeseen crisis. This nonsensical letter to his sister Nannerl perhaps indicates his need to unwind.

24. Wolfgang's autograph score of the
Act I finale of *Così fan tutte* (1790), set in Naples.

from the chapter by appointing him Bishop of Chiemsee, a post regarded as a demotion. Colloredo was similarly ruthless with his court musicians, dismissing the current Kapellmeister, Giuseppe Francesco Lolli, who was over seventy. If Vice-Kapellmeister Leopold saw an opportunity here for his own promotion, it was quickly dashed, for Colloredo appointed instead an outsider, the Neapolitan composer Domenico Fischietti, who had worked in Venice, Prague, Dresden and Vienna. At forty-six, Fischietti was six years younger than Leopold, who deeply resented having been passed over. Clearly there would be no clean start for him and his family in their dealings with the court. Although Leopold meekly resumed his duties with seeming acceptance of his position, and outwardly maintained proper deference to his employer, neither he nor Wolfgang ever came to admire, let alone trust, Colloredo. And Leopold's resentment naturally embraced his Italian colleagues and superiors too. Despite the fact that he was still planning on finding substantial employment in Italy, the fundamental dislike he had long harboured for some Italians and their practices swelled into a malign and ungenerous mistrust of all its people, which lasted for the rest of his life.

Wolfgang's own position on the ladder of Salzburg's court musicians was stabilized in July of 1772, when Colloredo appointed him as a Konzertmeister – in this instance, a violinist with some composition responsibilities too. He was to be paid 150 gulden a year, about a third of what his father was earning. Wolfgang was only sixteen, and in formally adding him to his roster Colloredo certainly acknowledged his remarkable gifts, even if the post was relatively menial. The new Archbishop would have been thoroughly aware of Wolfgang's impending third visit to Milan, to open its winter opera season, and in the circumstances his handling of this gifted teenager seems entirely reasonable. If Wolfgang himself was disgruntled, it was more because the two major works he had written a year earlier, *Betulia liberata* and *Il sogno di Scipione*, both remained unperformed. (This would have had unfortunate echoes of the debacle over *La finta semplice*.) Thinking that Salzburg might yet use *Il sogno di Scipione* in some official celebration to welcome Colloredo, he changed the name of the dedicatee for a second time: in the final *licenza*, 'Sigismondo' (itself a substitution for the original 'Karl') became 'Girolamo', for Hieronymus Colloredo. But again there is no evidence that *Il sogno di Scipione* was ever performed for his new employer, and having two large Metastasio–based scores languishing on the shelf must have been irksome in the extreme.

Wolfgang nevertheless did continue to compose at a furious rate. Pursuing the direction in which he had been heading when he left Milan, and perhaps reflecting too his new position in the orchestra, he produced no fewer than eight new symphonies (no. 14 in A, K.114; no. 15 in G, K.124; no. 16 in C, K.128; no. 17 in G, K.129; no. 18 in F, K.130; no. 19 in E flat, K.132; no. 20 in D, K.133 and no. 21 in A, K.134) in just a few months, based on the multi-movement model of the Italian overture in which he had now been steeped for two years. Also composed in 1772 between Italian visits were the three exquisite little string masterpieces, the divertimentos in D, B flat and F (K.136–8), and two pieces of sacred music for Eastertide. His second litany setting, the impressive *Litaniae de venerabili altaris Sacramento* (K.125), was written for use in the forty-hour prayer vigil starting on Palm Sunday, and closely followed the model of a similar sacramental litany by Leopold. The Marian antiphon 'Regina coeli' (K.127) had a prominent, if not particularly demanding, solo soprano part that would have been sung by Salzburg's most accomplished singer, Maria Magdalena Lipp, the wife of Michael

Haydn. (Perhaps she shared her husband's fondness for their daily, and generous, allowance of alcohol: the coloratura, even in the concluding 'Alleluia', is decidedly subdued, suggesting a possible concern not to overtax.) And, almost after the manner of a pianist starting the day by playing scales, Wolfgang wrote several canons, as if keeping his hand in with the contrapuntal techniques and styles that he had studied with Padre Martini.

But, once more, Wolfgang's main focus would have been on his next opera for Milan. He knew the subject, for he had been sent a first draft of the libretto by Giovanni De Gamerra, the resident poet at Milan's Teatro Regio Ducale. *Lucio Silla* was also being sent to Vienna, for approval by Metastasio. Wolfgang was instructed to produce recitatives by October; arias, as always, would be composed once he had been introduced to his cast, as they assembled with him in Milan. After the mythological subject matter of *Ascanio in Alba*, he would have been relieved to find himself once more in the realm of classical history, and in a context therefore to which he could now indeed relate. *Lucio Silla* is set in ancient Rome, whose magnificent ruins were etched in his recent memory. Furthermore, Lucius Sulla (102–78 BC) was a military hero whose foes had included none other than Mithridates, King of Pontus. The coincidental connection to Wolfgang's earlier operatic triumph was not unpleasing.

∾

With Wolfgang's recitatives duly prepared, he and his father packed their trunks for a third time, and set out for Milan on 24 October 1772. But, yet again, Maria Anna and Nannerl were left behind. By now they would have become wearily accustomed to Leopold's refusal to countenance their joining them in the country they so longed to see; but missing out on this trip, so much less sensational than the last (a regular-season opera, rather than a magnificent imperial wedding), was perhaps easier to bear. Leopold and Wolfgang spent twelve days on the very familiar road, as opposed to the speedy eight of the previous year's journey. Although the October days were certainly shorter than those of August, on occasion the Mozarts still managed to achieve three stages, again reflecting the more robust stamina of the sixteen-year-old Wolfgang. But they did schedule more time in some towns on the way, in order to see friends. They spent two nights in Innsbruck, and visited Count Firmian's sister-in-law, the Countess Lodron, at her convent in Hall in Tirol, where Wolfgang played the organ. Once through the Brenner Pass, they had an unplanned delay: driving rain forced them to wait in Bozen (Bolzano), a town they both loathed (Leopold called it a 'wretched town';[1] Wolfgang 'a pigsty'[2]). As so often, Wolfgang escaped from his frustration and discomfort by writing a string quartet (possibly K.155 in D). Further along their resumed journey, they stayed for two nights in Rovereto, and two more with Pietro Lugiati in Verona, where of course they went to the opera. They arrived in Milan on 4 October.

The Mozarts had different accommodation on this third operatic visit: an apartment closer to the theatre than the last, prettier and better appointed. Furthermore, it was only fifty yards from their attentive friends the D'Astes, who had perhaps found it for them. They had certainly helped to furnish it, for Leopold praised not just its bigger beds, but also their softer pillows, crediting Signora D'Aste with having supplied them.[3] As Wolfgang reported to his mother on 7 November, most of their good friends were out of town when they arrived, apart from Mysliveček, and the D'Astes, from whose home he was indeed writing, while Leopold ('too lazy to write') chatted happily to their hosts.[4] And perhaps, as she had done on their first lengthy stay in Milan for *Mitridate*, Marianne D'Aste could again provide them with sauerkraut, dumplings and other Austrian foods when they craved them.

By now Wolfgang had been told who was to sing in his opera; and the cast was both more distinguished and, thankfully, younger than his *Ascanio in Alba* team. To his certain delight, the biggest name on his roster was the prima donna Anna Lucia De Amicis. The brilliant career of this Naples-born soprano had already taken her to the European capitals of Paris, Dublin, Brussels and London, as well as all the important opera houses in Italy. Now approaching her fortieth birthday, she had recently married a Florentine physician and had a child; but, even with a toddler in tow, she continued to be greatly in demand. Wolfgang had first heard her in Mainz, in 1763, when, though he was merely seven years old at the time, she had made an enormous impression on him. Then, on the first Italian trip with his father, in 1770, they had encountered her again in Naples, where they had not only heard her sing ('amazingly well'[5]) in Jommelli's *Armida abbandonata*, but also enjoyed her company in social gatherings. At the time, Wolfgang had hoped she might be in *Mitridate* ('I should like her and Manzuoli to take the parts', he had written to his sister from Rome).[6] That had not been possible in 1770, but now, two years later, she was contracted for Milan. Both Wolfgang and his father were impatient to see her again: 'Signora De Amicis is to leave Venice today and will therefore be here in a few days; then the work will be really enjoyable', wrote Leopold on 28 November.[7]

Partnering De Amicis in *Lucio Silla* would be the primo uomo Venanzio Rauzzini. The Mozarts had heard him sing in Hasse's

Partenope in Vienna in 1767, when Leopold had judged him –
along with the rest of the cast – as 'nothing out of the ordinary'.[8]
At that time Rauzzini was only twenty-one, and just embarking
on his career. But now, five years on, he was clearly hitting his
peak. Charles Burney had recently met him in Munich: 'The
first singer in the serious opera here is Signor Rauzzini, a young
Roman performer of singular merit, who has been six years in
the service of this court; but is engaged to sing in an opera composed by young Mozart, at the next carnival in Milan'.[9] Over the
next few days he had again heard Rauzzini sing, often in duet
with the veteran castrato Gaetano Guadagni, whom Burney had
known twenty years earlier, singing with Handel in London, and
who had in 1762 created the title role in Gluck's *Orfeo ed Eurid-
ice*, with which he was ever after associated. Although the two
castrati were of different generations and completely different
experiences (Guadagni was eighteen years older than Rauzzini),
they had blended well both musically and socially, to Burney's
sage approval. But above all it was Rauzzini's charm and all-
round musicianship that had impressed Burney: 'his taste is quite
modern and delicate; the tone of his voice sweet and clear; his
execution of passages of the most difficult intonation amazingly
neat, rapid and free: and his knowledge of harmony is far beyond
that of any stage-singer I ever knew: he has likewise a very good
person, and, I am told, is an excellent actor.'[10] All of those attributes will have been key, too, to Wolfgang.

The third important cast member for *Lucio Silla*, and por-
trayer of its title role, was to be the tenor Arcangelo Cortoni.
Like De Amicis he came from Naples, and sang with her there
at the Teatro San Carlo. The Mozarts had heard them both in
Jommelli's *Armida abbandonata* in 1770, and they were together
again in the following season too, establishing a familiar theatrical

178

chemistry which was attractive to promoters and audiences alike. The three other cast members were to be the sopranos Felicità Suardi and Daniela Mienci, and the tenor Giuseppe d'Onofrio, all now confined to obscurity. But, after the slightly disappointing level of casting for *Ascanio in Alba*, Wolfgang's new team was once more headed by some formidable singers, in the same league as the great Bernasconi.

Unfortunately, none of these top-billing singers was yet in Milan when the Mozarts arrived, so Wolfgang could still not begin his main compositional process with them. But, surprisingly, he did have to rework some of his recitatives. Metastasio, having read Giovanni De Gamerra's libretto, had sent it back to Milan with some extensive alterations, including the addition of a whole new scene in the second act. This did not seem to bother Wolfgang, who, according to Leopold, 'got much amusement' from these revisions, and from writing three choruses as well.[11] Together with the three-movement overture – written in Salzburg before they had travelled, and very much in the mould of those latest symphonies – the completion of the revisions meant he had now done all he could without the presence of his cast.

Leopold meanwhile became somewhat pensive, and was still dwelling on his recent personal disappointment: 'now that I have been here for almost a fortnight, some trifling disorders have begun to plague me again; indeed I drop into thinking about Salzburg and, without noticing it, I go on brooding for some time.'[12] But in a rare exhibition of tenderness towards his wife, he noted on 21 November that it was their twenty-fifth wedding anniversary: 'It was twenty-five years ago, I think, that we had the sensible idea of getting married, one which we had cherished, it is true, for many years. All good things take time!'[13] A week later, in one of his reports of his own health ('As for my headache, I do

JANE GLOVER

not get it very often and it is only occasionally that I am seized for a few moments by my old giddiness'), he revealed something too of their austere nutritional regime: 'we only eat once a day, at two o'clock in the afternoon. In the evening we have an apple and a slice of bread and we drink a small glass of wine.'[14] The constant rain depressed him, and would indeed have consequences for the arrival of the singers if roads became flooded and impassable. But, by the last week in November, Suardi, Mienci, d'Onofrio and then Rauzzini had all made it to Milan, and Rauzzini had begun what would become a vibrant collaboration with Wolfgang. Leopold reported that the first fruit of this, the aria 'Il tenero momento', was 'superlatively beautiful and he sings it like an angel'.[15] This was a highly promising start.

Exactly a month after the Mozarts settled in Milan, Anna De Amicis finally arrived from Venice. She had had a terrible journey, lasting a whole week: even with a six-horse mail-coach, the fastest means of travel, muddy roads and appalling conditions had made her progress slow and miserable. (And throughout that ordeal she had had the added responsibility of looking after her small daughter.) But, true professional that she was, she instantly engaged with her young composer, working with him to identify her voice's particular glories and strengths, and inspiring him therefore to produce the most thrilling arias he had yet composed. She herself was 'very well satisfied' with the process and the result.[16] She became a close friend of both Wolfgang and his father, and also sent her greetings to Maria Anna and Nannerl, whom she apparently remembered from that first meeting in Mainz, nine years earlier.

But there was very bad news about the final cast member, the tenor Arcangelo Cortoni, who was ill and could not now come at all. Leopold described Milan's panic measures, as they

180

desperately sought in all directions to find a replacement singer for the title role, just three weeks before the opera's premiere: 'the Secretary to the Theatre has been sent off by special post-chaise to Turin and a courier has been despatched to Bologna to find some other good tenor, who, as he has to play the part of Lucio Silla, must not only sing well, but be a first-rate actor and have a handsome presence.'[17] It was indeed a tall order, and a solution was not found for over a week. Eventually they settled on one Bassano Morgnoni, 'a church singer from Lodi who has never before acted upon such a big stage'.[18] He arrived barely a week before the opening, and Wolfgang had to make radical adjustments to the title role. He reduced his arias from four to two, stayed up late to compose more straightforward music for his floundering newcomer, and then coached him assiduously in it. But throughout this eleventh-hour emergency, which particularly agitated Leopold ('these blessed theatrical people leave everything to the last minute'[19]), Wolfgang seems to have remained calm and in control. His release from pressure, as so often, was to write almost nonsensically to his sister. On 18 December, with just a week to go before the premiere, his usual postscript to Leopold's letter home became increasingly wild and fantastical. He began with a comic (if incomprehensible) drawing, and proceeded to write every other line upside down. As the letter progressed, there were recurring phrases and motifs – variations on 'my dear sister' or 'my child', inane questions and answers, and references to various body parts:

So, my child, I beg you not to mention it to anyone, my child, otherwise too many people will come running in, my child. That reminds me. Have you heard what happened here? I will tell you. We left Count Firmian's today to go home and when we reached our street, we opened the hall door and what do you think we did? Why, we went in. Farewell, my little lung. I kiss you my liver, and remain always, my stomach, your unworthy fraterbrother[20]

This absurd rigmarole is surely indicative of high-spirited exhaustion, even as the glare of the operatic spotlight increased its intensity on him. On the day after he wrote this, his rehearsal schedule became its most concentrated and demanding, with stage-orchestra sessions on 19, 20 and 22 December. And, in addition to these, Wolfgang was required to attend, and perform at, three huge parties given by Count Firmian on 21, 22 and 23 December, as reported by Leopold:

> there were great parties in Count Firmian's house, at which all the nobles were present. On each day they went on from five in the evening until eleven with continuous vocal and instrumental music. We were among those invited and Wolfgang performed each evening. On the third day in particular, Wolfgang was called upon to perform, at the request of Their Royal Highnesses, immediately after their arrival. Both of them spoke to us for a long time.[21]

The day of that final Firmian extravaganza was also the day of the dress rehearsal. After that there would be no further rehearsal while Milan celebrated Christmas. But despite all these physical strains, the succession of availability problems and the wild disparities between the vocal gifts of Wolfgang's individual singers, the dress rehearsal actually went very well – 'so well,' reported Leopold with palpable relief, on 26 December, 'as to give us reason to hope for the greatest success.' He added, 'De Amicis is our best friend. She sings and acts like an angel and is extremely pleased because Wolfgang has served her extraordinarily well.'[22] So Wolfgang and Leopold finally relaxed over Christmas, and enjoyed all the seasonal fun that the town had to offer: 'the greatest houses of the town were illuminated with enormous torches, the bells of the churches near Count Firmian's house played melodies like the carillons in the Netherlands, and in the street there was music with trumpets and drums'.[23] As they were warmly welcomed into the houses of their greatest Milanese friends, first Fernando Germani and his family on Christmas Eve, and then Signora D'Aste on 26 December, just hours before the first performance, they were feeling gratefully confident.

The story of *Lucio Silla* was taken by De Gamerra from Plutarch's *Lives of the Noble Greeks and Romans*: fifty biographies of notable historical figures living in the first two centuries AD. In these, Plutarch explored his subjects' moral character by examining their behaviour at key moments in their lives, and he was particularly concerned with stoicism, heroism, and the relationship between the individual and the state. (Shakespeare had drawn on Plutarch in his preparation for *Julius Caesar*.) Lucius Sulla was one of the more colourful of these 'Noble Romans', for he was a brilliant commander in war, who ultimately became a ruthless and tyrannical dictator. De Gamerra's libretto certainly begins in the context of his ruthlessness, but, with the Enlightenment twist so much favoured by the eighteenth-century opera libretto, Sulla is given a wholly unexpected change of heart in the final scene, when he pardons everyone and becomes a model of benevolence and magnanimity.

The narrative of the libretto begins with Cecilio (sung by Rauzzini), a Roman senator banished by Lucio Silla, returning in secret to meet his friend Cinna (Suardi), and learning that Silla (Morgnoni) has taken his own bride Giunia (De Amicis) for himself. Silla is being counselled by his sister Celia (Mienci) to be gentle, but by a Roman tribune Aufidio (d'Onofrio) to be brutal. Giunia spurns Silla's advances, and goes to pray for release from his tyranny at the tomb of her father in the cemetery; and there she finds the hidden Cecilio. In the second act, Cinna advises Giunia to marry Silla and then kill him, but she cannot bring herself to agree to this. On the Capitol, Silla publicly demands Giunia's hand as a way to end civil strife, at which point Cecilio appears to defend her. He is arrested. In the final act, after various troubled interlocutions, Silla undergoes his volte-face, pardons everyone and abdicates. Giunia and Cecilio are reunited.

Despite *Lucio Silla*'s title, its narrative and emotional thrust are very much centred on the relationship between Giunia and Cecilio, and the musical balance reflects this. Lucio Silla himself should have had a much greater musical presence. But once Bassano Morgnoni's aria quota had of necessity been reduced in the panic of the final fortnight, his focus, both musical and dramatic, faded, leaving the centre of the stage, literally, to De Amicis and Rauzzini. Purely in terms of quantity, therefore, the musical numbers are dominated by arias or ensembles for the two of them; and the quality too of these superlative singers is the thrilling factor that inspired Wolfgang to lift his game and produce his greatest operatic music yet. De Amicis had nine arias or ensembles, four of them preceded by accompanied recitatives – ever more sophisticated as Wolfgang developed what was becoming one of his most significant operatic specialities. Rauzzini had seven arias or ensembles, and no fewer than six accompanied recitatives. Above all, the scene that they sang together – the tense, furtive, emotional meeting in the cemetery at the end of the first act – was Wolfgang's most extraordinary achievement in the whole opera, and a thrilling precursor of what he would do in the next two decades.

Both De Amicis and Rauzzini dazzled on their first appearances. Rauzzini, as Cecilio, opened the opera with his unhappy conversation with Cinna, and then had a long soliloquy of reflection. An accompanied recitative, in which his various moods of excitement, tenderness and anxiety are severally reflected in, and enhanced by, the orchestral accompaniment (there are five different tempo indications in twenty-nine bars), leads into that first aria, 'Il tenero momento', where all Rauzzini's impressive vocal armoury is displayed. He evidently had an enormous range, and could leap from one end of it to the other with great facility; his coloratura was phenomenal, and so too was his breath control, for Wolfgang gave him exceptionally long and tricky phrases to navigate. And yet, throughout all this resplendent technical accomplishment, there is an emotional authenticity, too, which shines through. Described by Leopold as 'superlatively beautiful', this was a sensational first aria for Rauzzini.[24]

In the following scene, after a gentle aria for Celia and much explicatory recitative for Aufidio and Lucio Silla, Giunia gets her own equally brilliant musical entrance. 'Dalla sponda tenebrosa' is almost two arias in one: a slow invocation to her dead father, marked andante ma adagio, and punctuated with ringing and funereal horn chords, alternates with fiery (allegro) disdain for Lucio Silla. De Amicis's equally astonishing technique is similarly exploited, and at the same time she too was allowed to show her lyrical and emotional gifts. Subsequent individual arias for these two stellar singers continue to impress, especially

Cecilio's 'Quest'improvviso tremito', with its fortifying trumpets and timpani, and Giunia's 'Ah se il crudel periglio', demanding truly vertiginous coloratura. (Wolfgang would later hand this aria to other singers, to challenge their abilities in a yardstick test.) But the apex of Wolfgang's writing and his stars' singing was the cemetery scene at the end of act one. It begins with a brief and atmospheric orchestral interlude (just nine bars, classily accompanying a scene change), which leads into an accompanied recitative of sombre thoughts on death from the distressed Cecilio. He hides as he sees Giunia approaching with a crowd of Roman nobles, who come to invoke their dead forebears at their graves. A solemn chorus is followed by Giunia again summoning the spirit of her own late father, before the Romans express their anger at the tyrannical regime of Lucio Silla, and their desire for his removal. At this point Cecilio darts out of his hiding place, to Giunia's terrified shock, which gradually calms (through accompanied recitative) to expressions of the greatest tenderness; and the two unite in a sophisticated, protracted and glorious duet, 'D'Elisio in sen m'attendi'. The whole scene – approximately twenty minutes of music – is handled masterfully by Wolfgang. It has momentum, contrast, drama and passion. The two matchless voices, both of them in the soprano register, blend equally, with their individual gifts (her wide-leaping range, his great breath control) fully and democratically exploited; and their shared expertise in delivering coloratura brings the scene, and the first act, to its brilliant conclusion. For Wolfgang this was a significant step up in his operatic development, and one that was thoroughly enabled by the distinction of his colleagues.

With the exception of poor Bassano Morgnoni, the cast members were accomplished singers with good techniques, and they were all rewarded with fine music. Playing the male role of Cinna, the female soprano Felicità Suardi was continuing a tradition not uncommon in the eighteenth century, but for Wolfgang this was his first experience of gender-fluid casting (apart from a boy treble singing the female role of Melia in *Apollo et Hyacinthus*, back in 1767), and as such a precursor of the role of Cherubino in his much later *Le nozze di Figaro*. Suardi had three arias, one of them ('Nel fortunato istante') placed immediately and unenviably after Giunia's great 'Ah se il crudel periglio'; but here, as elsewhere, Wolfgang supplied her with her own decent showcase in expressions of energetic vengeance. Similarly, Daniela Mienci as the sympathetic Celia, and Giuseppe d'Onofrio as the basically unsympathetic Aufidio, had their chances to shine. After his eleventh-hour arrival, Morgnoni probably spent the short amount of remaining rehearsal time learning his recitatives. His two surviving arias certainly reveal his limitations as a singer, for they are relatively brief (approximately two minutes in length, as opposed to eight for De Amicis or Rauzzini), and undemanding in vocal dexterity and range. But Wolfgang handled this crisis with expert sensitivity and practicality. The orchestral accompaniments to Silla's arias are arresting and vibrant, and even his one accompanied recitative, syllabic and straightforward though it is, is carried by the colour and dynamism of the instruments. Lucio Silla is included in the trio at the end of the second act, where De Amicis and Rauzzini have coloratura but he does not, but the trio works perfectly nonetheless. As with the writing for the chorus, which is also uncomplicated, Wolfgang found a way of delivering atmosphere or dramatic involvement (menace, sorrow, relief) through the colours in, and the deployment of, the instruments in his orchestra.

∿

'The opera was a great success, although on the first evening several very distressing incidents took place', wrote Leopold, a week after *Lucio Silla*'s highly anticipated premiere. Having come through the traumas of the rehearsal period, and arrived at the end of the dress rehearsal with a finished and classy product, the opening night was riven with absurd mishaps, which dashed all the confidence of the opera's leading protagonists. The performance was scheduled for approximately half past five in the evening ('one hour after the Angelus'); but, as Leopold continued bitterly in his report to Salzburg, 'It was only just before the Angelus that the Archduke rose from his midday meal and then he had to go to write with his own hand five letters of New Year greetings to Their Majesties the Emperor and Empress; and, I ought to mention, he writes very slowly.' The opera could not begin without the Archduke's presence, so 'for three hours singers, orchestra and audience (many of the latter standing) had to wait impatiently in the overheated atmosphere'. By the time it could start, at about eight o'clock, the already nervous singers were understandably exhausted. Even the experienced De Amicis was unsettled by the three-hour delay, and she was then further unnerved by a somewhat ungenerous ruse on the part of Rauzzini. In the first scene, he had engineered for himself an enthusiastic welcome from the Archduchess, who had been told that he was crippled with nerves, and so clapped heartily when he appeared. No such round of applause greeted De Amicis, for she was known to be a stalwart and infallible performer. Then matters continued to deteriorate. Bassano Morgnoni was by now a complete wreck, and in his inexperience he managed unwittingly to sabotage De Amicis's brilliant first aria, 'Dalla sponda tenebrosa': 'At the point where . . . the prima donna expected from him an angry gesture, he exaggerated his anger so much that he looked as if he was about to box her ears and strike her on the nose with his fist. This made the audience laugh. Signora De Amicis . . . did not realize why they were laughing, and, being thus taken aback, did not sing well for the rest of the evening.' On the following day, their Royal Highnesses acted swiftly to placate their injured diva, summoning her to their presence and graciously entertaining her for an hour. 'Only then did the opera begin to go well.'[25]

It had certainly been an inauspicious premiere for *Lucio Silla*, but its run was by no means affected. It was performed no fewer than twenty-six times, with extra outings added in late January, causing the opening of the second opera of the season, Paisiello's *Il Sosmano del Mogol*, to be delayed by a week. As usual, and according to the terms of his contract, Wolfgang directed his first three performances, and then made way for colleagues at the Teatro Regio Ducale to take over. Once more he could relax and enjoy the company of friends. He would write gaily to his sister about their mutual acquaintances, as he had done ever since he left Salzburg in October. Some of them – the Milan-based Salzburg-ers, the Trogers and D'Astes, together with Fernando Germani and his wife – were all about to visit Salzburg, and, as Leopold assured Maria Anna, 'they all long to meet you'.[26] Wolfgang joined in the mutual exchange of greetings ('Signor and Signora D'Aste, Signor and Signora Germani, Signor Mysliwecek and Signora De Amicis have asked me to send you their compliments and regards'[27]); and there were also arcane references to girls he admired in Salzburg ('I hope you have been to see the lady – you know who. If you see her, please give her my compliments'[28]). As always, he was keen to share with his sister his fanatical following of operatic traffic, of which he so longed to be a part: 'Signora Teiber is now at Bologna. She is singing in Turin during the coming carnival and the following year she will go and sing at Naples.'[29] And, with his father, he was keen to encourage their good friend Joseph Leutgeb to visit them in Milan. Leutgeb was an outstanding horn player, who knew Haydn well, having worked with him in Esterházy (Haydn's wife was godmother to Leutgeb's daughter), and who had joined the Salzburg roster in 1763. The then seven-year-old Wolfgang had been drawn first to the warmth of his personality and then to his musical expertise, and Leutgeb had become close to the whole Mozart family. In due course, in Vienna in the 1780s, Wolfgang would write major horn concertos for him. Their manuscript scores are littered with verbal in-jokes and scribal eccentricities (in one of them he used multi-coloured inks), but their epic musical content has ensured that these concertos have remained at the heart of the horn repertoire. So Wolfgang was anxious to see Leutgeb in Milan – perhaps even to have him actually play in *Lucio Silla* – and he was disappointed when Leutgeb missed the opera altogether ('I am vexed that Leutgeb left Salzburg too late to see a performance of my opera; and perhaps he will miss us too, unless we meet on the way'[30]).

For, even from the back of the auditorium, Wolfgang was still largely concerned with *Lucio Silla*, and with the rest of Milan's operatic activity. He attended rehearsals of Paisiello's *Sosmano*: 'The first orchestral rehearsal of the second opera took place yesterday evening . . . I like the music, but I do not know whether the public will like it'.[31] He was impressed by, if also nervous of, its enormous forces deployed for maximum visual effect: 'In this opera there are to be twenty-four horses and a great crowd of people on the stage, so it will be a miracle if some accident does not happen.' But his chief reason for continuing to frequent the theatre and its rehearsal rooms was that his two leading singers were now true friends. Anna De Amicis and her little daughter

Giuseppina regularly sent warm wishes to Maria Anna and Nannerl. And Rauzzini, as if singing those twenty-six performances of *Lucio Silla* in five weeks was not enough, was also the recipient of Wolfgang's incomparable Latin motet, 'Exsultate, jubilate', K.165, written for him in that same month. Again adopting the hilarious but nonsensical (in this case word-jumbled) writing style that seemed to follow a spate of remarkable creativity, Wolfgang informed his sister of his latest composition: 'I for have the primo a uomo motet compose which to tomorrow at Church the Theatine performed be will.'[32] On 17 January he and Rauzzini duly gave its premiere in Sant'Antonio Abate, the church of the Theatine order. This joyous cantata of three movements, with interlinking recitative, celebrates the Nativity, with exuberant and bravura outer movements, and a central cavatina ('Tu virginum corona') of serene reverence. All Rauzzini's vocal distinctions – his impressive technique, especially in coloratura, his great range (the final 'Alleluia' invites a top C) and his lyrical expressiveness – are here arrayed. Written just days before Wolfgang's seventeenth birthday, 'Exsultate, jubilate' is perhaps the first work of his output thus far to have acquired the status of immortal masterpiece.

Leopold, meanwhile, had resumed his campaign of the previous year, and was trying to find good employment for Wolfgang or himself, or preferably both of them, here in Italy. Even Nannerl was part of Leopold's imagined plan, as an earlier letter reveals: 'I send greetings to Nannerl and a message urging her to practise hard,' he had written on 12 December. 'I know well that she herself will benefit if she accustoms herself to teaching someone else very thoroughly and patiently. I am not writing this without a motive.'[33] After the still-rankling disappointment of having been passed over in Salzburg, he had to renew his search with ever greater intensity, and ever more complex strategy. Accepting that there could be nothing permanent for them in Milan with the Archduke, who had certainly heeded his mother's stern advice, Leopold now set his sights on the Grand Duke Leopold, the Archduke's brother, in Tuscany. On their first journey in Italy, the Mozarts had been graciously received and entertained by him in Florence – a city Leopold knew his entire family would adore. So he wrote to the Grand Duke and sat tight, awaiting a reply. To justify their staying on in Milan after the conclusion of Wolfgang's contract, rather than returning to take up their duties in Salzburg, he began to invent some serious medical issues, and remained melodramatically housebound. He certainly did suffer from rheumatism, but he exaggerated his symptoms in graphic detail, no doubt instructing Wolfgang to broadcast these throughout Milan, just as he enumerated them for Salzburg in letters to his wife. On 23 January he wrote:

I am writing in bed, for during the last week I have been plagued with acute rheumatism and have had to lie up. The pain began in the joint of the left thigh, moved down after a few days to the left knee and has now settled in the right knee. The only remedy I have tried is root burr tea, three or four large glasses of which I drink every day. I have to lie on the mattress, for the room is often even colder than the street outside. The most distressing circumstance is that I have to cover these painful thighs with cloaks, furs and so forth in order to keep warm and perspire, because I have only been given one or two single blankets. So I am lying wrapped in my dressing-gown and furs in order to keep warm, and you can imagine how heavy they are on my feet, and how uncomfortable it is for me when I want to move.[34]

But a week later, in the code he adopted for information that was for Maria Anna's eyes only, he added, 'What I wrote about my illness is all quite untrue. I was in bed for a few days, but now I am well and am off to the opera this evening. You must however spread the news everywhere that I am ill. You should cut off this scrap of paper so that it may not fall into the hands of others.'[35] (Clearly, she did not obey this final instruction.) But, even as he kept up the pretence of dismal ill health, he was also conveying weekly updates on their Florentine prospects. On 9 January, his coded postscript had read, 'I hear from Florence that the Grand Duke has received my letter, is giving it sympathetic consideration and will let me know the result. We still live in hope.'[36] A week later, he was getting anxious because he had had no reply, and his colleagues were advising him not to build hopes: 'Up to the present no reply has come from the Grand Duke, but we know from the Count's letter to Troger that there is very little likelihood of our getting work in Florence. Yet I still trust that at least he will recommend us.'[37] And at this point he urged Maria Anna to save money, 'for we must have means, if we want to undertake a journey', adding angrily, 'I regret every farthing which we spend in Salzburg.' In the course of the following week Leopold tried another tactic, and sent the Grand Duke a score of *Lucio Silla*. But this too elicited no response, and the gloomy bulletins continued: 'I have received no further reply from the Grand Duke in Florence', on 30 January;[38] 'I cannot start on my journey, as I must await the arrival of a courier from Florence', a week later;[39] and the ominous silence reigned throughout the month of February. (Perhaps the Grand Duke had consulted his mother, and on her counsel decided, like his brother, to steer clear of the Mozarts.)

Wolfgang seemed to corroborate details of Leopold's 'illness', if a little half-heartedly: 'I hope that my father will be able to get out tomorrow'.[40] But, with no obligation or deadline to meet, he was again somewhat restless in Milan. According to Leopold, he wrote another string quartet,[41] but, after the astonishingly adult achievements of *Lucio Silla* and 'Exsultate, jubilate', he seemed on occasion to resort to rather childish behaviour ('Wolfgang is well, and at this very moment, as I write, he is turning one somersault after another'[42]). He was cheered by the arrival at last of Joseph Leutgeb, who immediately charmed the Milanese. Leutgeb was given free lodging with the court painter Martin Knoller; a concert was arranged for him at court and the Archduke himself summoned him to his presence. Leopold noted, a little bitterly, 'he has arranged his affairs pretty well and he will make quite a fortune here, for he is extraordinarily popular. If the concert takes place which the courtiers want to arrange for him, I wager he will get one hundred cigliati just like that.'[43] The spotlight had moved on.

By the end of February, Leopold decided to throw in the towel: 'As to the affair you know of there is nothing to be done. I shall tell you all when we meet. God has probably some other plan for us.'[44] Once again, he packed up their possessions after their nineteen-week stay, and he and Wolfgang set off on their return journey at the beginning of March, fully two months after Wolfgang's contract had ended. Travelling as usual through Verona, Ala, Trento, Bressanone and Innsbruck, often through heavy and hazardous snow, but again staying wherever possible with friends en route, they finally reached Salzburg on 13 March. 'I find it hard to leave Italy', Leopold had written before they left.[45] Neither he nor Wolfgang would ever return.

7

COROLLARY

*'I should dearly love to show what I can do
in an Italian opera'*

By the time the Mozarts crossed the Brenner Pass from south to
north, in early March 1773, Leopold's regret at leaving Italy had
almost certainly developed into an instinctive realization that,
for him at least, this would be the last time. Now fifty-four, he
had been organizing and meticulously planning lengthy periods
of travel, almost without pause, for over ten years, and he was
tired. The three-and-a-half-year tour of northern Europe, from
June 1763 to November 1766, had brought the greatest attention,
adulation and reward, but little if any long-term opportunity.
Now Italy, after thorough assaults on all its main centres, and
three separate, increasingly anxious attempts to break into its
Habsburg artistic fabric, had similarly failed to deliver. Like his
son, Leopold had drawn immense inspiration from the whole
Italian peninsula, and built up a vast reservoir of triumphant and
glorious memory. But, constantly hovering over all the exhilarating achievement, there was the ultimate pall of disappointment.

Although for him there would be future journeys out of Salzburg, they were relatively short: just the ninety miles to Munich, or the 185 miles to Vienna. In terms of exhausting, long-haul travel, Leopold had had enough.

Wolfgang, on the other hand, surely had no sense of his business in Italy being finished. After his three operas in three years, at the very heart of the opera world, he must have felt he could do anything. He had been completely happy in a theatrical community, and stimulated by every section of it, from singers and dancers, to instrumentalists and coaches, to builders and painters; and he could not wait to be part of it all again. Furthermore, Italy had felt right for him. He had experienced its multifarious and profound Mediterranean beauty; he had in general enjoyed good health (this was rare for him); and he had met an incredible cross section of people, from popes, princes and archdukes, to learned teachers and academics, to the highest-quality musicians, to people of his own age, and especially (for a teenage boy) those of the opposite sex. Of course there had been pressures and sufferings and disasters, but none had floored him. He had risen to the challenge every time, and surmounted it. Although his immediate contacts had somewhat cooled (Milan was seeking new composers after three years; the Venice contract had clashed with *Lucio Silla*, and the Teatro San Benedetto had similarly moved on), he knew he had made excellent connections in Italy, where he would be fondly remembered.

∾

It was not until 1778 that Wolfgang got even close to returning to Italy. Until then, he spent four long years effectively grounded in Salzburg, assuming once more his position as Konzertmeister, playing, teaching, composing – mainly symphonies and chamber music, and some church music – but still yearning to be part of an opera company again. In that time, he made just two short journeys out of the city, still in the company of his father, before planning a much longer one in 1777 with, surprisingly, his mother. The first of those trips was to Vienna, just four months after the return from Italy in 1773, when Leopold learned that the current Hofkapellmeister, Florian Leopold Gassmann, was unwell, and that possibilities of prestigious and lucrative employment might therefore be opening up there. From mid-July to late September (during which summer season there was of course no opera), Leopold and Wolfgang gave concerts and made extensive social rounds, and they did achieve a cool audience with Maria Theresa ('Her Majesty the Empress was very gracious to us, but that was all').[1] Wolfgang wrote a second set of six string quartets, and demonstrated his usual keyboard skills at every opportunity; but fundamentally he was kicking his heels in Vienna ('Little Wolfgang has no time to write, for he has nothing to do', he wrote ironically to his mother. 'He is walking up and down the room like a dog with fleas').[2] When Gassmann recovered in September and returned to work – only temporarily, as it happened, for he died four months later – the Mozarts returned home, again empty handed.

At this point it seems that Leopold finally ran out of energy and perhaps even desire to seek employment elsewhere. He accepted the reality that there would be no major relocation for the entire family, and that he, certainly, was destined to remain in Salzburg. So at last they moved out of their small home in Getreidegasse, and upgraded to a splendid eight-room apartment on the first floor of a dwelling known as the Tanzmeisterhaus, in Hannibal-Platz (now Makart-Platz), on the opposite side of the river. Once owned by a French dancing-master, it had one very large room in which balls had indeed taken place, and where the Mozarts could give their own concerts and recitals; and beyond that there was ample and airy space for each member of the family to have independence, comfort and privacy. Leopold and Nannerl could teach their students, and Wolfgang could compose. There was also a small garden, where they could all enjoy their pastimes of target shooting and skittles. Their new situation in a generally quieter and more affluent area of the town did mark a distinct improvement in the lifestyle of the whole family.

But still Wolfgang's feet itched for the opera house. So an invitation in 1774 to write an *opera buffa* for the winter Carnival season in Munich was extremely welcome. He was sent a libretto (by an unknown writer), *La finta giardiniera*, which concerned the intertwining relationships of seven characters, and which had been set in the previous year in Rome by Pasquale Anfossi. At the beginning of December Wolfgang and his father travelled to Munich (merely two days on the road), and stayed there for three months. To her great excitement, Nannerl, now twenty-six and allowed at last to travel on her own, would join them for three weeks, early in the new year. But writing *opera buffa* for Munich was a very different experience from writing *opera seria* for Milan, where the first production of the season played for as many times as there were audiences to see it (twenty-six, in the case of *Lucio Silla*), and was then succeeded by the second opera. Leopold explained the Munich system in a letter to his wife: 'An opera [in Munich], for which the public has to pay, cannot be performed here more than twice in succession, for otherwise the attendance would be poor. So for two or three weeks other operas have to be performed and then the first one may be trotted out again, just as is done in the case of plays and ballets. Thus the singers know the parts of at least twenty operas which are performed in turn, and at the same time they study a new one.'[3] So the singers who were engaged for such a frenetic and unpredictable schedule, possessed though they had to be of phenomenal energy and stamina, were inevitably not of the same vocal calibre as those to whom Wolfgang had become so luxuriously accustomed in Milan. But nor did they need to be. *Opera buffa* required syllabic singing (one note per syllable) rather than melismatic singing (several expressive notes to one syllable); arias in general were shorter, the dramatic action was swifter, and there was greater interplay between the protagonists.

Wolfgang duly wrote a thoroughly entertaining comic opera, with neatly characterized arias, and extremely assured finales to the first two acts (the third act ends with a tame chorus), alert as always to the building and releasing of drama through the balancing of contrasts and textures. His handling of the orchestra throughout was masterly, and he certainly sharpened his comedic and ensemble skills. But he cannot have enjoyed any meaningful or collaborative creative process with any of the singers, who were so laden with operatic responsibilities in so many other directions. Furthermore, the whole system of preparation and rehearsal was patchy and drawn out, and often dictated by the health, and therefore the availability, of the cast. Although it was planned that *La finta giardiniera* should open on 29 December, everything was delayed, partly through illness in the cast (Wolfgang too was ill for a week in mid-December, but nothing would stop him attending his rehearsals), and also by the infuriating but unsurprising fact that the singers were not properly prepared. On 28 December, Leopold reported to Maria Anna: 'the first performance has been postponed until January 5th in order that the singers may learn their parts more thoroughly and thus, knowing the music perfectly, may act with greater confidence and not spoil the opera. To have got it ready by December 29th would have been a fearful rush.'[4] In the event, the opening night was postponed again to 13 January, when finally, according to Wolfgang, it was 'such a success that it is impossible for me to describe the applause to Mamma. In the first place, the whole theatre was so packed that a great many people were turned away. Then after each aria there was a terrific noise, clapping of hands and cries of "Viva Maestro".'[5] But after its opening, *La finta giardiniera* had just two more outings, on 2 February and 2 March. With such extraordinarily long gaps between them, these two later performances must themselves have felt worryingly unfamiliar to the singers. Wolfgang could not countenance their putting on his opera without him, and explained to his mother, left alone at home for weeks on end, precisely why they could not yet return to Salzburg: 'One very urgent and necessary reason for our absence is that . . . my opera is being performed again and it is most essential that I should be present. Otherwise my work would be quite unrecognizable – for very strange things happen here.'[6] So, although he and his father, and eventually his sister too, had an enjoyable time in Munich, attending masked balls, going to other operas and plays, and even performing some sacred music for the Elector, the operatic experience was very far from that in which he had been immersed, and for which he still pined, in Italy.

Almost immediately upon their return home, however, there was an interesting operatic commission. Maria Theresa's youngest son, the Archduke Maximilian, with whom Wolfgang had played as a child, was due to visit Salzburg on his way to Italy. Archbishop Colloredo took the opportunity to commission two serenatas to entertain his important guest, one from

Kapellmeister Fischietti, who had had early operatic experience working with Goldoni in Venice in the 1750s, and the other from Wolfgang. These serenatas were to be given on consecutive evenings, and they would both have texts by Metastasio. Wolfgang's libretto was *Il re pastore*, which he would have considered to be of excellent pedigree, for it had already been set over twenty times by, among others, several of his early operatic mentors: Hasse (in 1755), Gluck (1756), Piccinni (1760) and Jommelli (1770). Wolfgang however was to produce a shortened version of it, with the customary three acts compressed to two. There were five characters, headed by the eponymous king who is believed to be a shepherd; and while the action mixed elements of both comic and serious opera, it was essentially an allegorical tale about a benevolent ruler. Wolfgang threw himself into this project immediately upon his return from Munich. He knew that its occasion was highly prestigious and that the Archbishop, keen therefore to make the best impression on his important visitor, might be generous with his budget. So he requested a castrato soprano – essential for all Italian opera, but of which Salzburg had none – for the title role, and Colloredo agreed to pay for one to be imported. In due course Tommaso Consoli, who had sung Ramiro in *La finta giardiniera*, arrived from Munich, together with a brilliant flute player, Johann Baptist Becke. With at least one good singer, therefore, together with competent members of Salzburg's own establishment, Wolfgang created another delightful opera, with longer arias once again, and vibrant involvement of orchestral colour. Two arias had prominent instrumental parts: Becke's flute featured in 'Se vincendo, vi rendo felici' for Alessandro, and there was a solo violin (could Wolfgang have played this himself, for this was part of his official position?) in Tommaso Consoli's charming rondeau, 'L'amerò, saro costante'. But

Il re pastore was put together very quickly – Consoli arrived only four days before the single performance – and it was presented not in an opera house, for Salzburg did not have one, but was semi-staged in the beautiful Prunkräume (State Rooms) in the Archbishop's palace. Again, Wolfgang's operatic cravings were fed, but ultimately not satisfied.

After the excitement of the Archduke's visit, there were no further opportunities for any kind of opera in Salzburg. Wolfgang slunk back into his Konzertmeister position, and became increasingly sullen. His father too, who had to assume more responsibility at court when Kapellmeister Fischietti left later that year, but for which he received no pay rise at all, deeply resented their situation, which he now seemed powerless to improve. Archbishop Colloredo continued to reform his establishment, simplifying the liturgy and closing the university theatre, and both Mozarts felt increasingly stifled. Eventually, in September 1776, their combined frustration found an outlet – in Italy. They wrote to their great mentor and adviser, Padre Martini, in Bologna. Together they concocted a long letter to him, ostensibly to pay him the courtesy of sending him a motet ('Misericordias Domini', K.222) which Wolfgang had composed and performed in Munich, and to invite him to comment on it. The letter is signed by Wolfgang, but is in Leopold's hand, and there is little doubt that they both wished to air individual grievances. Leopold's situation as an apparently overlooked and undervalued employee is thoroughly set out: 'My father . . . has already served this court for thirty-six years and as he knows that the present Archbishop cannot and will not have anything to do with people who are getting on in years, he no longer puts his whole heart into his work, but has taken up literature, which was always a favourite study of his.' But Wolfgang's chief complaint is the absence of good singers, and of any opportunity for opera: 'Oh how often I have longed to be near you, most Reverend Father, so that I might be able to talk and have discussion with you. For I live in a country where music leads a struggling existence . . . As for the theatre, we are in a bad way for lack of singers. We have no castrati, and we never shall have them, because they insist on being handsomely paid; and generosity is not one of our faults.' They explained their shared frustration at Colloredo's shackling of music in the context of the Mass: 'Our church music is very different from that of Italy, since a Mass . . . must not last longer than three quarters of an hour. This applies even to the most solemn Mass said by the Archbishop himself . . . At the same time, the Mass must have all the instruments – trumpets, drums and so forth.' And this diatribe concluded with a very personal *cri du coeur*:

> Alas, that we are so far apart, my very dear Signor Padre Maestro! If we were together, I should have so many things to tell you! I send my devoted remembrances to all the members of the Accademia Filarmonica. I long to win your favour and I never cease to grieve that I am far away from the one person in the world whom I love, revere and esteem most of all and whose humble servant, most Reverend Father, I shall always be.[7]

Quite what Leopold or Wolfgang hoped to achieve by sending this letter is unclear. It was now three years since their last visit to Italy, and five since they had actually been in the company of the great man. Perhaps Wolfgang entertained some wild hope that Padre Martini, or one of his fellow members of the Accademia Filarmonica to whom he carefully sent his 'devoted remembrances', thus apprised of his compositional progress, and of his being no longer a prodigious child but a young man of twenty with boundless talent, might discover or create an opening for him in Bologna. If that was the aim, it too misfired. Three months later, in December 1776, Padre Martini's reply was careful, dignified and sympathetic, but ultimately dismissive:

> Together with your most kind letter, which reached me by way of Trento, I received the Motet . . . It was with pleasure that I studied it from beginning to end, and I can tell you in all sincerity that I was singularly pleased with it, finding in it all that is required of Modern Music: good harmony, mature modulation, a moderate pace in the violins, a natural connexion of the parts and good taste. I am delighted with it, and rejoice that since I had the pleasure of hearing you in Bologna on the harpsichord you have made great strides in composition, which must be pursued ever more by practice, for Music is of such a nature as to call for great exercise and study as long as one lives.[8]

Starved therefore of opera, Wolfgang poured his creativity into instrumental music: symphonies, divertimentos, serenades, his major violin concertos, and piano concertos – a genre he would develop most spectacularly within a few years. His interest in the opposite sex, awakened in his first year in Italy, had since developed somewhat passively. Like so many teenage boys, he had always been self-conscious about his appearance, and in his case especially about his small stature. Now out of his teens, his physical needs seemed to be as arrested as his operatic ones. Throughout his life, he was most infatuated with girls and women who were highly gifted musicians, perhaps because this gave him a platform on which to meet them on equal terms. And in this period of intense frustration in Salzburg, some of his finest music was now written for women. The piano concerto in C, K.246, for instance, was written for Archbishop Colloredo's niece, the Countess Lutzow; and his concerto for three pianos, K.242, was for the Countess Lodron and her two teenage daughters, on whom Wolfgang's eye surely fell. There was also, as a result of his having met the French-Swiss dancing-master Jean-Georges Noverre in Milan in 1771, around the time of *Ascanio in Alba*, a commission for another piano concerto for Noverre's daughter, Victoire Jenamy, and here Wolfgang produced his first truly superlative work in the genre, the piano concerto in E flat, K.271, known as the 'Jeunehomme', or 'Genomai' after its gifted dedicatee. And one other glorious work from this professionally fallow time came about through the arrival in Salzburg – at last – of another exceptional singer. A young Czech soprano, Josefa Duschek, the young wife of the Bohemian composer Franz Duschek, and distantly related to the Mozarts' friend and ex-landlord, Johann Lorenz Hagenauer, came to visit her family in the summer of 1777. Wolfgang was thrilled to meet once more someone with vocal experience and expertise beyond those of the Salzburg singers, and immediately wrote her an operatic scena in Italian, 'Ah, lo previdi', K.272, with a text taken from *Andromeda* by Cigna-Santi, the librettist of *Mitridate*. Combining dramatic accompanied recitative and highly contrasted arias, one with a beguiling solo oboe, this startlingly effective scena simultaneously honoured the gifts of a superior artist, and indulged his own longing for Italian opera and a theatrical environment. Nine years later, he and Josefa Duschek would meet again in Vienna, and then again a year after that when Wolfgang was in Prague for *Don Giovanni* and he stayed with the Duscheks. Despite the huge responsibilities and pressures he was then navigating, she persuaded him to write her another magnificent scena, 'Bella mia fiamma', K.528. This happy connection between them had been nurtured in Salzburg in 1777, giving the greatest happiness and release to Wolfgang – if perhaps not to the approval of Leopold. Never one to be overgenerous with his praise, or even his appreciation, of singers, Leopold wrote to Nannerl, having heard Duschek sing in Vienna in 1786, that she 'shrieked . . . with exaggerated expression'.[9] The scena that Wolfgang wrote for her in Prague a year later – by turns dramatic and lyrical, and of breathtaking harmonic challenge – surely proves that Leopold's judgement of her was far from that of his son.

But aside from these very fleeting brushes with the world of Italian opera that Wolfgang so craved, the horizon was as empty as ever, and he increasingly felt a desperate need to get away from Salzburg. By the summer of 1777, even Leopold agreed that his son should undertake another job-seeking trip, and together they concocted a petition to Archbishop Colloredo for leave of absence. Like the letter to Padre Martini, this document is signed by Wolfgang but in Leopold's hand, and the tone of it is very much that of the elder Mozart. By turns petulant, bossy, self-pitying, rebellious, recriminatory, and always seeking to inhabit the higher ground of moral superiority over his archiepiscopal employer, this was no humble, or concise, request. Colloredo was infuriated, and his patience snapped. On 1 September he decreed that 'father and son shall have permission to seek their fortune elsewhere'.[10] While Wolfgang was of course delighted at finally being freed from his Salzburg shackles, Leopold was appalled that he too was being dismissed. The family simply could not survive without at least one court salary, so he quickly managed to reinstate himself on the Archbishop's roster. But it was he who decided and planned the journey that Wolfgang should undertake. Believing that at twenty-one his son was still incapable of travelling on his own, he now instructed Maria Anna to go with him. And he decreed that they should head not south again to Italy, but west, to the important musical centres of Munich, Mannheim and Paris: one of these, surely, would welcome Wolfgang, and then possibly Leopold too, into their employ. As always, he planned their route in meticulous detail; and he would continue to issue micro-managing instructions to them in his copious letters, after they had gone.

On 24 September 1777, Wolfgang and his mother left Salzburg in the greatest of spirits (unlike Leopold and Nannerl, both of whom took to their sickbeds for several days). First they spent five weeks in Munich, knocking on doors, reviving old acquaintances (the first person they literally ran into on arrival was Tommaso Consoli, Wolfgang's recent colleague from *La finta giardiniera* and *Il re pastore*), playing concerts and generally announcing Wolfgang's presence as a gifted, adult musician who would considerably adorn the court of the Elector of Bavaria. From his remote command post, Leopold advised using his Italian credentials, and name-dropping his two greatest supporters in Italy: 'you may state quite frankly both to the Elector and to Count Seeau that in regard to your knowledge of counterpoint His Highness need only consult Padre Maestro Martini of Bologna and Herr Hasse in Venice and hear what they think. If you really must have them, I will send you your two diplomas which state that when you were only fourteen you were appointed maestro di cappella of the Academies of Bologna and Verona.'[11]

(Leopold might perhaps have thought of this before his son left Salzburg.) Count Seeau was Munich's Privy Councillor, and controller of operatic and dramatic performances at court; like many others, he had excellent memories of *La finta giardiniera*, and was prepared to plead Wolfgang's cause with the Elector. But, after his initial overtures there, he was obliged to report to the Mozarts that it did not look promising, and that the Elector had declared that Wolfgang 'ought to go off, travel to Italy and make a name for himself'.[12] When Wolfgang did get his audience with the Elector, he sought immediately to correct him, declaring, 'I have been three times to Italy already, I have written three operas, I am a member of the Bologna Academy, where I had to pass a test, at which many maestri have laboured and sweated for four or five hours, but which I finished in an hour. Let that be proof that I am competent to serve in any Court.'[13] But the Elector's reply, as reported by Wolfgang to his father, had chilling echoes of Maria Theresa's attitude towards him: 'Yes my dear boy, but I have no vacancy. I am sorry.' Nevertheless, Wolfgang and his mother lingered in Munich for another fortnight, not least because his old colleague from Milan, Josef Mysliveček, was in the city (actually in hospital at the time), and also fighting his corner. Mysliveček had written to Leopold, saying he was trying to get Wolfgang a contract to appear, like him, in Naples. Leopold was utterly dismissive of this: 'The journey to Naples is too far and too expensive, especially if you decide to go beyond Munich. Our object is now quite a different one'.[14] In the event, Mysliveček's generous endeavour on Wolfgang's behalf came to nothing, but contact was restored between these two composers with similar passions. Against the stern advice of Leopold, who presumed that Mysliveček's illness was the consequence of disreputable sexual liaisons ('Where does the blame lie, but on himself and on the horrible life he has led? What a disgrace he is before the whole world! Everybody must fly from him and loathe him. It is a real calamity, which he has brought on himself')[15] and therefore he should be avoided, both Wolfgang and his mother visited Mysliveček in the hospital, with warm gratitude and genuine affection. 'He is a true friend to Wolfgang and has said the kindest things about him,' wrote Maria Anna to her husband. 'Everyone has told us so.'[16]

Wolfgang was fired again by Mysliveček's Italian proposal: 'When I think it over carefully,' he wrote to his father, 'I have to admit that in no country have I received so many honours, nowhere have I been so esteemed as in Italy; and certainly it is a real distinction to have written operas for Italy, especially for Naples.' And he added, 'I have an inexpressible longing to write another opera.'[17] As always, he neglected no opportunity to hear operas of all kinds, and he critically assessed every singer he heard:

The leading soprano is called Mlle Kaiser. She is the daughter of a cook by a count here and is a very attractive girl; pretty on the stage, that is . . . She has a beautiful voice, not powerful but by no means weak, very pure and her intonation is good . . . When she sustains her voice for a few bars, I have been astonished at the beauty of her *crescendo* and *decrescendo*. She still takes her trills slowly and I am very glad . . . People here are delighted with her – and I am delighted with them.[18]

(Perhaps, as Leopold immediately surmised, Wolfgang also entertained feelings other than of operatic appreciation for this young soprano.) But he and his mother finally had to accept the

Elector's firm refusal to offer any hope of employment, and to move on to their second destination, Mannheim.

Their journey took them through Augsburg, where Leopold had been born, and where many members of his family still lived. His brother Franz Alois continued their father's bookbinding business, and Franz's daughter Maria Anna Thekla was just eighteen months younger than her cousin Wolfgang. In the two weeks that Wolfgang and his mother stayed in Augsburg, he and his Bäsle (little cousin), as he called her, became inseparable. He wrote carefully to his father: 'our little cousin is beautiful, intelligent, charming, clever and gay; and that is because she has mixed with people a great deal, and also spent some time in Munich. Indeed we two get on extremely well, for, like myself, she is a bit of a scamp.'[19] In fact, their activities seem to have been of untrammelled hilarity and vivacity, and these attitudes continued, to startling effect, in the subsequent train of letters that they exchanged after Wolfgang's departure. Their relationship, which unquestionably gave him the greatest pleasure, had, it seems, been intimately physical, and there was subsequently no bodily function to which he did not allude.

The court of Mannheim was ruled by the Elector Karl Theodor, a passionate supporter of the arts and sciences, and particularly of music – he himself played the flute and cello. Largely because of his enthusiasm, musical activity was particularly strong at his court. It was headed by the composer Christian Cannabich, who had inherited a fine tradition established by the founding father of the so-called Mannheim school, Johann Stamitz, and its roster boasted many superb instrumentalists. Its orchestra was therefore of an excellence unsurpassed in Europe, renowned for its depth of talent, for the technical brilliance of its individual players and for their combined ensemble precision. Dr Burney, who had spent time there in 1772, wrote that 'it is an army of generals'.[20] Opera too thrived in Mannheim, under the direction of the composer Ignaz Holzbauer. Johann Christian Bach's setting of *Lucio Silla* had been performed there in 1775 (two years after Wolfgang's for Milan, therefore), but Mannheim most frequently welcomed Italian composers, including Piccinni, Paisiello and Anfossi. And Europe's best singers came to work there, on short or long contracts; some local ones, having trained there, went on to make big careers elsewhere. All in all, Mannheim was highly promising territory for a young composer with prodigious gifts and a passion for Italian opera.

Wolfgang and his mother arrived in Mannheim on 30 October 1777. It was in fact their second visit: they had been there fourteen years earlier on their big European tour, and the then seven-year-old Wolfgang had played, together with his sister, at the Elector's summer residence in Schwetzingen. Now an adult, Wolfgang immediately felt at home among first-rate musicians, and for two happily busy months he hovered at their periphery, composing, performing and teaching. The Cannabich family was particularly welcoming and generous to both Wolfgang and Maria Anna, and their thirteen-year-old daughter Rosa, a very gifted pianist, became his pupil – he wrote his piano sonata in C, K.309, for her. Other fine musicians whose company, both musical and social, Wolfgang sought and enjoyed were the oboist Friedrich Ramm and the flautist Johann Baptist Wendling, whose wife, daughter and sister-in-law were all sopranos. While enjoying as always the company of singers too, Wolfgang was more critical of Mannheim's standards at the opera. He was particularly damning about its most distinguished participant, the tenor Anton Raaff, who, after having sung in his early twenties for the Empress Maria Theresa's wedding in 1738, had had a vibrant international career in Vienna, London, Madrid (with Farinelli) and Naples. Now sixty-three, here in Mannheim he was clearly past his best; Wolfgang, minutely perceptive as ever of singers' strengths and weaknesses, was brutal in his criticism: 'I thought to myself, "If I didn't know that this was Raaff, I should double up laughing." As it is, I just pull out my handkerchief and hide a smile. Moreover, he has never been, so people tell me here, anything of an actor; you'd only have to hear him, without even looking at him; nor has he by any means a good presence.'[21] Despite these unkind (however true) observations, Raaff became another good friend to Wolfgang and his mother, and three years later, in 1781, Wolfgang would write for him the best role he ever had: Idomeneo.

During those first two months in Mannheim, relations between Wolfgang and his father strained considerably. Leopold worried, with some reason, about Wolfgang's lack of strategic organization and financial acumen, accusing his son of 'having a holiday' and losing opportunities.[22] Wolfgang retaliated crossly, and lengthily. As winter increased its grip, immediate onward travel became inadvisable, especially with Maria Anna's well-being to consider. (She was fifty-seven, but Leopold repeatedly described her as being 'old'.) Various plans were aired: perhaps Wolfgang should proceed to Paris in the company of two Mannheim instrumentalists, his friends Ramm and Wendling, who were also heading there, and Maria Anna should return – somehow – to Salzburg. But then, as difficult exchanges continued between father and son, two events had seismic effects on Wolfgang and his future, both personal and indeed operatic. The first was the death in

Munich, on 30 December 1777, of the Elector, Maximilian III. His successor was Mannheim's Karl Theodor, who immediately travelled to Munich; and of course all artistic activity, in both cities, ceased. 'There are no operas (for which I am truly sorry),' wrote Maria Anna, 'all plays, balls, concerts, sleigh-drives, music, everything has been stopped.'[23] In the long term, the transposition of Karl Theodor's court to Munich would in fact have significant artistic outcome, for he brought over his entire musical establishment, and standards there soared. And just three years later Wolfgang would again be part of this vibrant, brilliant group of musicians when he was invited to Munich for his mighty *opera seria* – and arguably the greatest ever opera in that genre – *Idomeneo, re di Creta*.

The second event that had profound consequences in Wolfgang's life was his encounter, early in the new year, with another family of gifted musicians, the Webers. Fridolin, the father, was a court singer, and also a professional music copyist. When Wolfgang had occasion to call on his services to copy some of his arias, which he was to take on a visit to the Princess of Orange at nearby Kirchheim-Bolanden, he met his four daughters, Josefa, Aloysia, Constanze and Sophie, ranging in age from nineteen to fifteen. All of these girls, severally and together, would become deeply involved in Wolfgang's life; but in January 1778 it was the second of them, the seventeen-year-old Aloysia, who completely captivated him. Quite apart from her beauty and her vivacious personality, she was already a singer of extraordinary accomplishment, and Wolfgang could hardly believe his luck. He immediately gave her some of his own arias to sing, two of them written in Milan for his most stellar soprano, Anna De Amicis (ever his yardstick of vocal magnificence), and was astonished at her instant mastery of them: 'She sings most excellently my aria written for De Amicis with those horribly difficult passages'.[24] Like Wolfgang, Aloysia and her father were also summoned to Kirchheim-Bolanden; and during those few days of performing together for the Princess, far from parental scrutiny and in a state therefore of emotional truancy and freedom, Wolfgang and Aloysia completely fell for one another. Wolfgang was fired with the same all-consuming energy with which he had frolicked with his naughty cousin in Augsburg, but elevated now with the ecstasy of making music to a vocal standard he had not encountered since he had left Italy. By the time they returned to Mannheim, Wolfgang was hatching the grandest of plans. He should return straight away to Italy – and he should take Aloysia with him.

Wolfgang was understandably nervous of how Leopold might react to this complete change of plan. He began the letter in which he was to break his news by describing at length his trip to Kirchheim-Bolanden, with only passing references to Aloysia ('Mlle Weber sang three arias. I say nothing about her singing – only one word, excellent!'[25]), and making a protracted complaint about the disappointing remuneration they had received there. He then changed tack, and having outlined his (utterly fabricated) sudden misgivings about the suitability of Wendling as a potential travelling companion, expressed his complete trust in Herr Weber: 'When I am with him, it is as if I were travelling with you. The very reason why I am so fond of him is . . . he is just like you and has exactly your character and way of thinking.' And finally he arrived at his bombshell:

I have become so fond of this unfortunate family that my dearest wish is to make them happy; and perhaps I may be able to do so. My advice is that they should go to Italy. So now I should like you to write to our good friend [Pietro] Lugiati, and the sooner the better, and enquire what are the highest terms given to a prima donna in Verona – the more the better, one can always climb down – perhaps too it might be possible to obtain [a contract for] the [festival of the] Ascensa in Venice. As far as her singing is concerned, I would wager my life that she will bring me renown . . . She sings superbly the arias that I wrote for De Amicis, both the bravura aria and 'Parto, m'affretto' and 'Dalla sponda tenebrosa'. I beg you to do your best to get us to Italy. You know my greatest desire is – to write operas.

And later, truly from the heart, he reiterated: 'Do not forget how much I desire to write operas. I envy anyone who is composing one. I could really weep for vexation when I hear or see an aria. But Italian, not German; *seriosa*, not *buffa*.'[26]

Two days after dispatching this letter, and therefore before Leopold could possibly have received it, Wolfgang wrote again. He began with another lengthy defence of his determination not to travel to Paris with Wendling, and then returned to his proposals for Italy: 'Please do not forget about Italy. I commend this poor, but excellent Mlle Weber to your interest with all my heart, *caldamente*, as the Italians say. I have given her three of De Amicis's arias, the scena I wrote for Madame Duschek (to whom I shall be writing soon) and four arias from "Il Rè pastore". I have also promised her to have some arias sent from home. I hope you will be kind enough to send them to me, but send them *gratis* I beg you, and you will really be doing a good work!'[27] Meanwhile, on the sidelines, Maria Anna was apparently a little bewildered by her son's new plans, but accepted them ('You will have seen . . . that when Wolfgang makes new acquaintances, he immediately wants to give his life and property for them'),[28] and

215

was perfectly calm about travelling back to Salzburg on her own, once the weather had warmed up ('I am not at all nervous about the journey on to Salzburg').[29]

Inevitably, Leopold was appalled by Wolfgang's proposal. He took to his sleepless bed for two days, and then roared off a veritable pamphlet of a reply (over 3,000 words). Point by brutal point, he dismantled Wolfgang's arguments. There is a touch of hysteria underlying his responses ('it depends solely on your good sense and your way of life whether you die as an ordinary musician, utterly forgotten by the world, or as a famous Kapellmeister, of whom posterity will read, – whether, captured by some woman, you die bedded on straw in an attic full of starving children, or whether, after a Christian life spent in contentment, honour and renown, you leave this world with your family well provided for and your name respected by all'), but the overall effect of this vast document is chilling. Specifically regarding their shared Italian experiences and acquaintances, he wrote:

You are thinking of taking her to Italy as a prima donna. Tell me, do you know of any prima donna who, without having first appeared many times in Germany, has walked on the stage as a prima donna? In how many operas did not Signora Bernasconi sing in Vienna, and operas too of the most passionate type, produced under the very severe criticism of Gluck and Calza-bigi? In how many operas did not Mlle Teiber sing in Vienna under Hasse's direction . . . ? How many times did not Mlle Schindler appear in Italian opera in Vienna, after making her debut . . . under the direction of Hasse and Tesi and Metastasio? Did any of these people dare to throw themselves at the head of the Italian public?[30]

There was no question of anything other than Wolfgang returning to his (Leopold's) original plan, and moving on to Paris: '*Off
with you to Paris!* And that soon! Find your place among great
people. *Aut Caesar aut nihil.*' By the time Leopold had finished
this diatribe, he had convinced himself that Wolfgang would obey
him: 'Though half-dead, I have managed to think out and arrange
everything connected with your journey to Paris.' And then, in
an afterthought scrawled onto the covering of the letter, he
decreed that poor Maria Anna, who had been so looking forward
to returning home to Salzburg, should continue to accompany
and monitor her son, who simply could not be trusted to do the
right thing: 'Mamma is to go to Paris with Wolfgang, so you had
better make the necessary arrangements.'

Still in (slightly nervous) ignorance of the devastating epistolary tsunami that was approaching him, Wolfgang continued to
write cheerfully to Salzburg. He asked his father to send more of
his arias and cadenzas for Aloysia, describing his coaching of and
performing with her, and repeated his request for help getting
them both to Italy. But then he received Leopold's apocalyptic
letter. Severely startled, he immediately climbed down: 'I always
thought you would disapprove of my undertaking a journey with
the Webers, but I never had any such intention'. But while he
back-pedalled furiously, and did agree to proceed to Paris, he
defended himself against most of Leopold's accusations, and
continued staunchly in his support of Aloysia, whom Leopold
had so roundly dismissed for inexperience. Wolfgang brought to
his argument his still encyclopaedic knowledge of singers, resid-
ing in the mental database that he had compiled over many years
since his earliest days in Italy. His citing of Caterina Gabrielli,
for instance, with whom he had never even worked, shows just

how thoroughly alert was his passion for Italian opera and all its practitioners:

> Everything you say about Mlle Weber is true, except one thing – that 'she sings like a Gabrielli'; for I should not at all like her to sing in that style. Those who have heard Gabrielli are forced to admit that she was adept only at runs and roulades; she adopted however such an unusual interpretation that she won admiration; but it never survived the fourth time of hearing. In the long run she could not please, for people soon get tired of coloratura passages . . . in short she sang with skill but no understanding. Mlle Weber's singing, on the other hand, goes to the heart, and she prefers to sing cantabile. Lately I have made her practise the passages in my grand aria, because if she goes to Italy she will have to sing bravura arias. Undoubtedly she will never forget how to sing cantabile, for that is her natural bent. Raaff himself (who is certainly no flatterer), when asked to give his candid opinion, said 'She sang, not like a student, but like a master'. So now you know all. I still commend her to your interest with all my heart.[31]

The encounter in Mannheim with Aloysia especially, but also with the Wendling sopranos and even the elderly tenor Raaff, had once more unleashed Wolfgang's energies for writing for singers. His final weeks in the city, where he wrote nothing at all for its distinguished orchestra, were consumed with producing Italian arias and scenas for all of them; and again he adjusted his musical instincts to fit the capabilities of his performers – exactly as he had as a teenager in Milan. His account of writing 'Se al labbro mio non credi', K.295, for Raaff, for instance, shows just how sensitively he could make these adjustments:

I asked him to tell me candidly if he did not like it or if it did not suit his voice, adding that I would alter it if he wished or even compose another. 'God forbid,' he said, 'the aria must remain as it is, for nothing could be finer. But please shorten it a little, for I am no longer able to sustain my notes.' 'Most gladly,' I replied, 'as much as you like. I made it a little long on purpose, for it is always easy to cut down, but not so easy to lengthen.' After he had sung the second part, he took off his spectacles, and looking at me with wide-open eyes, said 'Beautiful! Beautiful! That is a charming *seconda parte*.' And he sang it three times. When I took leave of him he thanked me most cordially, while I assured him that I would arrange the aria in such a way that it would give him pleasure to sing it. For I like an aria to fit a singer as perfectly as a well-made suit of clothes.[32]

But those days among first-rate singers (if a little faded now) in Mannheim were effectively to be Wolfgang's last for several years in the genre of Italian opera. Any thought of returning to Italy itself was now off the agenda. What followed was a veritable catalogue of discomfort, frustration, disappointment, despair, isolation and – worst of all – bereavement.

Wolfgang and his mother did proceed to Paris, where Maria Anna, having not fared well on a miserable, nine-and-a-half-day journey from Mannheim in the biting wintry conditions of March, fell ill immediately on arrival. While Wolfgang scurried about the city, presenting letters of introduction and seeking employment, she languished all day in a cold lodging, mostly without company. After almost four months of suffering, she died on 3 July 1788, aged fifty-seven. For the first time in his life, Wolfgang was truly alone. First he had to break the shattering news from so far away to his father and sister, and then to take responsibility for his mother's funeral arrangements and the transportation of her belongings back to Salzburg. Up to this point he had barely even had to order a meal for himself, let alone make complicated travel plans, and although he attempted to put a brave face on all of it, for the benefit of Leopold and Nannerl, he was in truth broken and lost. His Mannheim friends Ramm and Wendling, and especially Anton Raaff, who had also been solicitous to his mother in her final weeks, did supply some support, as did other Parisian acquaintances, all of whom were deeply shocked at his predicament. But there was still no sign of any employment or substantial remuneration, and eventually Wolfgang crept away from Paris, never to return there, just as he would never return to Italy.

His route back to Salzburg was by no means direct. Naturally he sought the presence, both comforting and exhilarating, of Aloysia, and he travelled to Mannheim, only to find she had, with most of her colleagues, been summoned to Karl Theodor's court now in Munich. So he followed her. But there too he found that, in another sense, Aloysia had moved on. She had no interest now in a small, excitable musician with no immediate prospects: her career was about to explode in Munich and then Vienna, and she saw no part in it for Wolfgang. His heart was broken, and his devastation complete. 'I really cannot write – my heart is too full of tears', he wrote to his father on 29 December.[33] With any hopes for Italy now utterly abandoned, he returned to Salzburg at the beginning of 1779, and for two years composed virtually no vocal music at all, nor indeed any kind of music associated with Italian opera. Traumatized and desolate, he sought refuge in writing what was required of him – church music, chamber music, some symphonies. His only flirtations with theatrical music were in the context of altogether different, and German, traditions. He began, but did not finish, *Zaide*, K.344, a *Singspiel* where, in addition to arias and the occasional ensemble, there was spoken text, sometimes enhanced by orchestral comment – like accompanied recitative but without any singing. And he wrote some excellent incidental music for the play *Thamos, König in Ägypten*, K.345. His inner compositional energies did continue to flourish and develop; his vision, however, was blinkered, and his mood fundamentally melancholic.

But if Wolfgang was never to return to Italy, the country which had taught him so much at the most receptive time of his life, he would certainly bring Italy with him whenever he did write for an opera house, or for exceptional singers. And the new decade brought new opportunities, with untold riches, and untold fulfilment at last of all his Italian experience. First, in 1780, he received an invitation from Munich: the Elector Karl Theodor had by no means forgotten him, and nor had his distinguished roster of musicians (transplanted from Mannheim). So, in 1781, Wolfgang wrote *Idomeneo, re di Creta*, K.366. Once more he was energized by an Italian *opera seria* libretto (in this case written by Giambattista Varesco, one of Archbishop Colloredo's chaplains), a close-knit company of outstanding and convivial operatic talent, and, as it happened, the finest orchestra in Europe. *Idomeneo*, truly the first fruit of his Italian training with *Mitridate* and *Lucio Silla* a decade earlier, had three of his now close friends in leading roles, and he wrote spectacularly for all of them. The two sopranos were both from the Wendling family, and their music (their 'clothes', as Wolfgang himself liked to think of it) shows just how accomplished they were: Elisabeth as Elettra – fiery, dramatic and with formidable coloratura – and Dorothea as Ilia – tender, lyrical and profoundly moving. In the title role, Wolfgang would have been both delighted and appalled to discover his old (in every sense: he was sixty-seven) friend Anton Raaff. Even three years earlier, in Mannheim, Raaff had been experiencing vocal difficulties, mainly concerned with fraying stamina. Now his role was the veritable heart of the whole opera, both music-ally and dramatically. Wolfgang handled the situation – as he had with Bassano Morgnoni in *Lucio Silla*, ten years earlier – with sensitivity and practicality. He certainly wrote the role as he wished it to be, with an eye surely on performances in different venues and later years, and spent hours coaching Raaff to dis-cover what he could or could not do. Idomeneo's central aria, 'Fuor del mar', of tempestuous and electrifying rage against the god Neptune, was clearly beyond him; so Wolfgang shortened and simplified it, barely weakening its impact while rendering it manageable to his friend and colleague. And his allies in the orchestra, too, were superbly served with outstanding writing, especially for the flute of Johann Baptist Wendling and the oboe of Friedrich Ramm, who, with Raaff, had been so supportive to him and his late mother during his recent Parisian apocalypse.

Idomeneo, in 1781, was a happy event, shared too with Leopold and Nannerl, who both came to Munich to see it. Afterwards Wolfgang was recalled to the service of his Archbishop, but not actually in Salzburg, for Colloredo was temporarily in Vienna. And it was here that Wolfgang, now an adult, fully appreciated the huge potential for him in a city awash with music-making at the highest level, in all disciplines. But his movement around Vienna was restricted: in Colloredo's service he was treated as a servant, expected to toe lines. After a series of insolent exchanges between himself and his superiors, Wolfgang was – literally – kicked out and left to his own devices, to his defiant exhilaration. Back in Salzburg, Leopold was horrified, and doubly so when Wolfgang took lodgings in the home of none other than the Weber family, who welcomed him warmly. This inevitably brought him back into the orbit not just of Aloysia, now married to an actor, Joseph Lange, and her musical sisters Josefa, Constanze and Sophie, but of opera too. Aloysia was employed by the Burgtheater, home of comic opera in German with spoken dialogue, currently under the stewardship of a playwright and librettist, Johann Gottlieb Stephanie. And it was through his connection with Aloysia that Wolfgang was commissioned to write the work that would be his breakthrough introduction to Vienna, *Die Entführung aus dem Serail*, K.384. Not only did he, with Stephanie, bring profound seriousness to a comic genre (fundamentally it concerns Enlightenment forgiveness and reconciliation), he rejoiced again at last in a cast of consistently superb singers, headed by a soprano born in Vienna but of Italian descent, Caterina Cavalieri. For her he wrote the central role of Constanze, of breathtaking coloratura and lyricism. And through her he proved, with impeccable theatrical instinct, that coloratura per se, impressive though it undoubtedly was, could also be imbued with pathos, and therefore become a vehicle for the deepest emotion. 'People soon get tired of coloratura passages', Wolfgang had written to his father from Mannheim in 1778.[34] Now, four years later, in Vienna, with an Italian soprano singing a German opera, he discovered the way to enhance and justify those passages. It was a hugely important step for him.

By now Wolfgang had found, literally, his own Constanze. He transferred all his ardent passions to Aloysia's younger sister, and married her on 4 August 1782 – in determined disregard for the virulent objections of Leopold in Salzburg. Through Constanze, for the sisters were close, he made his peace with Aloysia. Like her friend and rival, Caterina Cavalieri, Aloysia was now enjoying brilliant success, as Wolfgang had confidently predicted that she would; and, with his equilibrium restored by Constanze, he was able to repair his relationship with her sister and renew his musical partnership with her. He wrote new arias and scenas for her, just as he had in Mannheim, and she sang the role of Constanze in subsequent revivals of *Die Entführung*. And this highly charged artistic liaison might well have continued in the same vein at the Burgtheater, had not the whole nature of opera in Vienna changed significantly in 1783. The Emperor Joseph II, influenced partly perhaps by the culture enjoyed by his siblings in Milan, Parma, Florence and Naples, but also by his own court composer, the Italian Antonio Salieri, arranged for a number of singers to be brought from Italy to Vienna. And so an Italian company with strong imperial support became established in the capital. And, while Aloysia and the other local stars were anxious about this Italian invasion, Wolfgang was thrilled, and longed to be part of it. At last he could bring his own experience and credentials to bear.

Wolfgang's infiltration of Vienna's Italian operatic community was by no means swift. Three stalwart Italian composers, Cimarosa, Paisiello, and the director of Italian opera at court, the powerful Antonio Salieri, were all dominating Viennese operatic output, prolifically producing polished and enchanting entertainments. Without any position at court himself, Wolfgang had no clear path into its hallowed halls. For three years, during which he actually had great success in putting on his own concerts centred around miraculous new piano concertos, he tried to find himself a suitable libretto – something that had moved on from the strictly defined types of *opera seria* and *opera buffa*, as he had; but he found none. 'I have looked through at least a hundred libretti and more, but I have found hardly a single one with which I am satisfied', he wrote to his father in May 1783.[35] He started writing two operas, *L'oca del Cairo*, K.422, and *Lo sposo deluso*, K.424a, but did not complete either of them. Instead he watched from the sidelines as the now two opera companies in Vienna, one German and one Italian, developed a hearty rivalry.

Someone else observing this rivalry with lofty amusement was the Emperor, Joseph II. And in early 1786 – a year that would prove to be of inestimable significance for Wolfgang – he devised an evening, in the Orangerie of his palace at Schönbrunn, that would actually expose and exploit it. Ostensibly to accompany the banquet celebrating the visit of his sister Maria Christina (Maria Theresa's fifth child) and her husband Prince Albert of Saxe-Teschen, who were his co-regents in the Netherlands, he presented an elaborate postprandial entertainment. First, a one-act comedy in German, by Wolfgang and Stephanie, *Der Schauspieldirektor*, K.486, was performed with singers from the Burgtheater at one end of the Orangerie; and then, at the other, there was *Prima la musica e poi le parole* by Salieri (to a libretto by Giambattista Casti), with singers from the Italian company. Both pieces effectively sent up the whole business of putting on operas, by mocking it, and both worked spectacularly because the extremely game singers took it all with immense seriousness, as they poked fun at themselves and each other.

On Wolfgang's team were both his brilliant sopranos, Aloysia Lange and Caterina Cavalieri, working together in a spirit of great harmony to play rival divas (Mesdames Herz and Silberklang – their very names, Heart and Silvertone, already hinting at the comic business to follow). They quarrel over billing, mimic each other's vocal characteristics, and finally, with an exasperated the-atre manager (played by the tenor Johann Valentin Adamberger, Cavalieri's partner in *Die Entführing*), reach an uneasy truce. On Salieri's Italian team were two stalwart basses, Stefano Mandini and Francesco Benucci, and two sopranos, Celeste Coltellini and the half-Italian, half-English Nancy Storace; and their *Prima la musica* similarly (though, it has to be said, with considerably less comedic brilliance) analysed the whole business of opera by debating the relative importance of words and music. Joseph II certainly created for his sister one of the society events of the year, and a truly splendid evening was enjoyed by all present – especially the participants. And for Wolfgang it was a prelude to his own collaboration with singers from both ends of the Orang-erie, and to an artistic partnership that was to define, realize, consummate and perfect his entire operatic experience to date, and would therefore change the whole nature of opera, for ever.

Among the Italians imported by Joseph II in 1783, there was also a poet, and he immediately caught Wolfgang's attention. 'Our poet here is now a certain Abbate Da Ponte,' he wrote to his father. 'He has an enormous amount to do in revising pieces for the theatre and he has to write *per obbligo* an entirely new libretto for Salieri, which will take him two months. He has promised after that to write a new libretto for me . . . I should dearly love to show what I can do in an Italian opera!'[36] Lorenzo Da Ponte, who was born Jewish but converted to Christianity and indeed took holy orders, had resided in Venice from 1773 (just two years after Wolfgang had visited the city), and there became a friend of Casanova. Like Casanova, he had many adulterous affairs, and was therefore drummed out of Venice and forbidden to work any-where in its republic. He had since travelled widely, acquiring, in almost equal measure, both artistic approval (from Metastasio, among others) and social opprobrium. So, in Vienna in 1783, like Wolfgang, he was something of an outsider, with a huge experience of life and an ability to stand apart from it and to describe it; and, again like Wolfgang, he was a minute observer of human behaviour. When these two geniuses did finally collaborate, they merged as like-minded equals, taking risks and showering their product with daring innovation. The three immortal masterpieces they wrote together each broke new ground in a multitude of ways, and represent the pinnacle of Italian opera in the eighteenth century.

Le nozze di Figaro, K.492, *Don Giovanni*, K.527, and *Così fan tutte*, K.588, were, in every sense, astonishingly modern operas. No longer were their stories those of ancient heroes from remote civilizations, or slapstick comedies deriving ultimately from the world of *commedia dell'arte*. Though they were all billed as comedies (*Figaro* as '*opera buffa*', *Don Giovanni* and *Così fan tutte* as '*dramma giocoso*'), and do indeed contain scenes and dramatic strands of extremely well-crafted hilarity, they are all profoundly serious too, with penetrating comments on the human condition: betrayal, loss, bereavement, physical violence – murder, indeed, as well as manipulative domestic violence – are all boldly presented and analysed. And the stories are completely contemporary. The first of them, *Figaro*, was based on Beaumarchais's *Le Mariage de Figaro* ('a very tiresome play', in the opinion of Leopold),[37] in which the appalling behaviour of a prominent member of the aristocracy is exposed by the machinations of his own servants. It had been banned in both Paris and Vienna as being politically subversive, but, in adapting it for operatic treatment, Da Ponte blithely convinced the Viennese authorities that it would be perfectly acceptable as *opera buffa*. *Don Giovanni*, his own reworking of the popular story of Don Juan, begins with a scandalous seduction and a murder, and proceeds through later scenes of mental and physical violence to a cataclysmic denouement. Da Ponte wrote *Così fan tutte* himself, and after the shocking events of *Don Giovanni* its narrative at face value seems innocuous, even silly. But its stripping bare of human conduct, revealing frailty and failure through deceit, counterfeit, betrayal and submission, is no less brutal in its condemnation of the very people at whom it is aimed – its audience. All three operas involve characters in disguise, in order that they may behave differently (a true legacy of masked Carnival activity, especially in Venice); and in all of them the lives of all participants are changed for ever.

Both in overall concept, therefore, and in every detail of his actual texts – line after brilliant line – Da Ponte burst through every possible operatic barrier; and Wolfgang was right there beside him. He relished these stories, the vibrancy of each character, however large or small the role (as with Shakespeare, there are no small roles in the Mozart–Da Ponte operas), and the reality and authenticity of their emotional habitat. Using all his Italian training, he too – while retaining the obvious conventions of aria, recitative, accompanied recitative and ensemble – ignored or changed the rules; and his music, built upon Da Ponte's game-changing texts, rendered them even more completely eloquent, as only the addition of great music can. With profound paradox, even the most shocking and upsetting incidents in Da Ponte's librettos could, in Wolfgang's hands, be presented in the most exquisite music, affording utmost pleasure without in any way diminishing the impact of brutality – rather as can a Raphael painting of the Crucifixion. And all three of the Da Ponte operas, with their very different contexts of production and performance (*Don Giovanni* was premiered in Prague), had completely stellar singers, as their music – their 'clothes' – so strikingly reveals.

More than that, they were fine actors too, able fully to inhabit their every physical and emotional situation, and to communicate it.

The Italian singers who made up this utterly distinguished corps of Mozart–Da Ponte interpreters included, from *Prima la musica*, those two basses, Mandini and Benucci, and the soprano Nancy Storace. Benucci, whom Wolfgang had spotted as soon as they had all arrived, back in 1783 ('The buffo is particularly good – his name is Benucci'),[38] in fact became the bass singer most important to him, for he sang, consecutively, Figaro, Leporello in *Don Giovanni*, and Guglielmo in *Così fan tutte*. Nancy Storace, half English, actually returned to London shortly after *Figaro*'s first season, but her impact on Wolfgang, and therefore on the central, sublime role of Susanna, which she created, was incalculable. Wolfgang adored her, not just for her immense musical and theatrical gifts, but also for the warmth of her personality. He would have noted with pleasure that her first teacher in London, when she was not much more than a child, was none other than Venanzio Rauzzini, his Milanese colleague from *Lucio Silla* and 'Exsultate, jubilate' – and indeed that Michael Kelly, the Irish tenor who was close to Nancy Storace in Italy and Vienna and then created the roles of Basilio and Curzio in *Figaro*, had also been taught by Rauzzini. When Nancy did decide to go home (for all her phenomenal success in Europe, she had had a turbulent marriage in Vienna, which had left her vulnerable and somewhat homesick), Wolfgang wrote for her a concert scena (much in the mould of those he had written for Aloysia, only this time with a prominent part too in the orchestral accompaniment for a solo piano, which he himself would play), 'Ch'io mi scordi di te' (I will never forget you), K.505. When *Figaro* was performed in Prague, a year after its Viennese premiere in 1786, the role of the Count was taken by Luigi Bassi; and it was for him and his fiery, physical energy that Wolfgang wrote the title role of *Don Giovanni*. Joining Bassi to create this mighty new work were three remarkable sopranos based in Prague: Teresa Saporiti (Donna Anna), Katherina Micelli (Donna Elvira) and Caterina Bondini (Zerlina). But when *Don Giovanni* was then performed in Vienna, Aloysia Lange and Caterina Cavalieri respectively sang Donna Anna and Donna Elvira – for the German opera company at the Burgtheater was being disbanded, and they were both now in the Italian company. Perhaps Wolfgang had always had their voices in his ears. None of his singers, whether from the German or Italian teams, disappointed him, not even the twelve-year-old Anna Gottlieb who sang the role of Barbarina in *Figaro*, and who would sing for him again, still only a teenager, within a few years. And, as Wolfgang had so thoroughly learned from his first encounters in 1771 with Antonia Bernasconi in Milan, when his vocal material was sublime and distinguished, it enabled him to deliver his own most sublime and distinguished music.

By the time *Così fan tutte*, and therefore Wolfgang's collaboration with Da Ponte, was finished, in 1790, he – shockingly – had only one year to live. He had endured unimaginable bouts of depression, anxiety (largely about money, as he consistently failed to achieve any lasting employment in Vienna) and personal tragedy. One particular event, the death of his father in 1788, had affected him profoundly. Leopold had continued to be one of the most potent influences on his life, even after his move to Vienna, his happy marriage to Constanze and the intermittent passages of huge success that he had enjoyed in the 1780s. Losing Leopold's passionate love and tireless support, and even his autocratic insistence on correct procedure, and his interminable rants when he believed that procedure to have been disobeyed or abused, was like removing the foundation of his being. He and Leopold had shared so much, especially in his childhood and teenage years; and their journeys together in Italy – truly the period of the greatest enjoyment and fulfilment for them both – were among Wolfgang's happiest, most treasured memories of his father. In the immediate aftermath of Leopold's death, he was seriously destabilized.

Wolfgang and Constanze had other tragedies to endure too. Although they had one healthy child, Karl, who had been born in 1784, their baby daughter, Theresia, born early in 1788, died in June of that year. And Wolfgang and Constanze themselves were often in poor health, Constanze primarily through continual pregnancy, miscarriage and childbirth, though she also contracted a pernicious and ulcerated infection in her foot, which affected her for eighteen months. In 1789 she lost another baby girl, just an hour after it was born. Medical treatment for Constanze and their children, including spa cures in nearby Baden, were expensive, and Wolfgang was compounding his financial problems by borrowing money. And yet in those final years of the 1780s he produced some of his truly greatest music: in addition to the Da Ponte trilogy, his greatest symphonies, concertos and chamber music all flowed from him. Whatever his immediate circumstances, he could always – as he had done on those long and tedious carriage journeys with his father in Italy, all those years ago – retreat into his alternative world of creation, where the horrors of the real one did not impinge. And, as he entered 1791, the final year of his life, matters did at last seem to be improving. He received no fewer than four large commissions, and he retrieved a sense of greater security, and therefore some decided fulfilment, even some optimism.

The four commissions included two operas. One was an indirect consequence of the death in 1790 of the Emperor, Joseph II. He was succeeded by his younger brother Leopold, whom Wolfgang had known not only as a child in Schönbrunn, but later in Florence when, as the Grand Duke of Tuscany, Archduke Leopold had bestowed gracious hospitality on him. Celebrations of the new Emperor's coronation took place in various cities, and Prague – whose musicians and promoters were devoted to Wolfgang and his music – invited him to write an opera for the occasion. The result of this would be *La clemenza di Tito*, K.621. But, closer to home, Wolfgang had another operatic commission too. The multi-talented writer, manager, actor and singer, Emmanuel Schikaneder, whom Wolfgang had got to know in Salzburg when his theatre troupe was briefly in residence, was now running a commercial theatre company in the Freihaus-Theater – a self-contained complex of buildings, including apartments and shops as well as a theatre, on the outskirts of the city. Schikaneder asked Wolfgang to collaborate with him in producing a work for his company, which he himself would write, direct and perform. This would be the miraculous, unclassifiable, hybrid masterpiece, *Die Zauberflöte*, K.620. And, besides these two huge operatic commissions, Wolfgang was writing a clarinet concerto for his good friend Anton Stadler, a superb instrumentalist very much in the class of those he had known in Mannheim, and – the strangest commission of them all – a Requiem Mass for a mysterious count, who had lost his wife and wished to perform a requiem for her that he could pass off as his own. All these commissions, with their promise of generous reward, Wolfgang readily accepted. But while they certainly restored his confidence, and to an extent also his financial stability, the very weight of this workload unquestionably contributed to a serious decline in his own health. As he worked at all hours to fulfil his obligations, he actually failed to complete two of them: for *La clemenza* he had no time to write the recitatives, and his student Franz Xavier Süssmayr had to compose them instead (rendering this work, sadly, uneven); and his requiem lay unfinished on his deathbed in December 1791. Again it fell to others, including Süssmayr, to attempt desperately to complete the work so that it might be performed, and the commission fee delivered.

But, in a sense, in those two operas of Wolfgang's final year his whole operatic circle, begun in Italy twenty years earlier, became full. *La clemenza di Tito* is an *opera seria*, carefully chosen for the occasion: it depicts a benevolent, ancient ruler, in the tradition of the operas he had written in Milan as a boy, but it was now imbued with all the experience of his years in theatre, in singing, and in life. And, with *Die Zauberflöte* for Schikaneder, Wolfgang found himself once more in a company of like-minded, superb musicians of considerable talent. Among them was his sister-in-law, Josefa Hofer (née Weber), who shared with her sisters Aloysia and Constanze a phenomenal technique for coloratura. For her, as the Queen of the Night, Wolfgang wrote the most celebrated coloratura in the entire operatic repertoire – a hang-over, for sure, from his first experiences in Italy, but, as with the arias in *Die Entführung*, bejewelled now with genuine emotions, and the ability therefore to move as well as to impress. Other members of Schikaneder's company, and of Wolfgang's cast, were the tenor Benedikt Schack, who, in addition to being a composer himself, was a superb flautist – he was splendidly cast as the flute-playing Tamino; the bass Franz Xavier Gerl had sung as a boy chorister in Salzburg, and almost certainly had been taught by

Leopold Mozart – he would play the priest Sarastro; and a now fifteen-year-old Anna Gottlieb, Wolfgang's prodigiously talented Barbarina in *Figaro* in 1786, would sing the hugely important role of Pamina. And that quality continued throughout the cast. While he was composing *Die Zauberflöte*, Wolfgang spent much time with them all, even living with them occasionally, and, as he had found in Milan when surrounded by musicians adjacent to the theatre where they were all working, such physical concentration of talent, and sounds, gave him 'plenty of ideas'. He was blissfully happy among them all, as he had been in Milan. And what he produced with and for Schikaneder – a totally brilliant amalgam of German theatre and Italian opera, with affecting arias of all types, ensembles, accompanied recitative (the crucial scene between Tamino and the *Sprecher*), mighty choruses, a solemn chorale prelude that could belong in a cathedral, spoken dialogue, bewitchingly impressive visual effects and a constant undertow of Masonic allegory – amounted to an utterly unique masterpiece which had no business at all to work as theatrical entertainment, but, without question, does.

On the cusp of Romanticism, Wolfgang was almost single-handedly exploding conventions. For him, the austerity of Enlightenment thought – which had been so illuminating and defining for his father – was no longer enough. In which directions, indeed, might he have gone had he lived into the nineteenth century? It is the mark of a genius, at whatever age, that he or she does not just observe and copy what else is going on: a genius takes inspiration from wherever it is offered, and then raises its level to the extraordinary. Wolfgang did so in every genre of music he composed, but especially in opera. Even adhering to the stifling format of *opera seria* (where the drama is arrested and goes back on itself, in da capo arias), he could infuse it with unprecedented sophistication. In *Idomeneo*, Elettra's literally insane aria 'Tutto nel cor me sento' has a da capo in quite the wrong key, a truly shocking moment which allows insights into the turmoil of Elettra's fractured mind. Wolfgang learned to tame coloratura to his own commands, fill them with emotion and make the swirls of notes crucial to the expression of the moment. All Constanze's arias in *Die Entführung*, and Donna Anna's in *Don Giovanni*, and even the Queen of the Night's in *Die Zauberflöte* amply demonstrate this. But above all, Wolfgang was never afraid to make profound statements with the greatest simplicity. Barbarina's 'L'hò perduto' and Susanna's 'Deh, vieni e non tardar', Don Giovanni's 'Là ci darem la mano' and Pamina's 'Ach, ich fühl's' are all moments of sublime dramatic stasis, and therefore the greatest sovereignty. And the roots of all these were in his Italian experience. Indeed, amongst the superfluity of perfectly decent, highly entertaining but ultimately unremarkable operas – both *seria* and *buffa* – created in eighteenth-century Italy, where it flourished, prospered and grew wild, nothing compares with the four towering Italian masterpieces (*Idomeneo*, *Le nozze di Figaro*, *Don Giovanni* and *Così fan tutte*) created subsequently by Wolfgang Amadeus Mozart. After the manner of Caesar, he came to Italy, he saw (and heard) it, and he conquered it.

Notes

———— ༄ ————

Deutsch = Deutsch, O. E. (ed.), *Mozart. Die Documente seines Lebens*, trans. E. Blom, P. Branscome and J. Noble: *Mozart: A Documentary Biography*, London 1966

L = *The Letters of Mozart and his Family*, ed. Anderson, E., London 1938; revised 3rd edition, Sadie, S., and Smart, F., London 1985

MBA = Mozart: *Briefe und Aufzeichnungen*, ed. Bauer, W. A., Deutsch, O. E. and Eibl, J. H., Kassel 1962–75

WAM = Wolfgang Amadeus Mozart
LM = Leopold Mozart
MAM = Maria Anna Mozart
NM = Nannerl Mozart

CHAPTER 1

1   Deutsch, p. 455.
2   LM to Hagenauer, Linz, 3 October 1762; L1, MBA32.
3   LM to Hagenauer, Vienna, 16 October 1762; L2, MBA34.
4   LM to Hagenauer, Vienna, 30 October 1762; L4, MBA36.
5   LM to Hagenauer, Vienna, 29 September 1767; L48, MBA117.
6   LM to Hagenauer, Vienna, 14 October 1767; L49, MBA119.
7   Deutsch, p. 92.
8   Deutsch, p. 88.
9   Deutsch, p. 94.
10 Ibid.

CHAPTER 2

1   LM to MAM, Wörgl, 14 December 1769; L71, MBA147.

2   WAM to MAM, Wörgl, 14 December 1769; L71a, MBA147.

3   Deutsch, p. 101.

4   LM to MAM, Innsbruck, 15 December 1769; L72, MBA148.

5   Goethe, *Italian Journey*, p. 30.

6   LM to MAM, Bozen (Bolzano), 22 December 1769; L74, MBA150.

7   Goethe, p. 38.

8   LM to MAM, Verona, 7 January 1770; L75, MBA152.

9   LM to MAM, Bozen (Bolzano), 22 December 1769; MBA150, not in *Letters*.

10 LM to MAM, Verona, 7 January 1770; L75, MBA152.

11 Ibid.

12 LM to MAM, Bozen (Bolzano), 22 December 1769; MBA150, not in *Letters*.

13 LM to MAM, Verona, 7 January 1770; L75, MBA152.

14 WAM to NM, Verona, 7 January 1770; L75a, MBA153.

15 Deutsch, p. 105.

16 LM to MAM, Mantua, 11 January 1770; L76, MBA155.

17 LM to MAM, Verona, 7 January 1770; L75, MBA152.

18 Goethe, p. 52.

19 LM to MAM, Mantua, 11 January 1770; L76, MBA155.

20 LM to MAM, Verona, 7 January 1770; MBA152, not in *Letters*.

21 LM to MAM, Verona, 7 January 1770; L75, MBA152.

22 WAM to NM, Milan, 26 January 1770; L77a, MBA158.

23 WAM to LM, Vienna, 9 June 1781; L409, MBA604.

24 Deutsch, p. 107.

25 LM to MAM, Milan, 26 January 1770; L77, MBA157.

26 LM to MAM, Mantua, 11 January 1770; L76, MBA155.

27 Ibid.

28 LM to MAM, Milan, 3 March 1770; L82, MBA163.

29 Deutsch, p. 109.

30 WAM to NM, Milan, 26 January 1770; L77a, MBA158.

31 See Elliott Golub and Duane Rosengard, *Paolo Diana 'detto Spagnoletti' (1773–1834)*, privately published, East Greenwich 2018.

32 Burney, *Present State*, p. 79.

33 Ibid.

34 LM to MAM, Milan, 26 January 1770; L77, MBA157.

35 Ibid.

36 LM to MAM, Milan, 26 January 1770; MBA 157, not in *Letters*.

37 WAM to NM, Milan, 26 January 1770; L77a, MBA158.

38 LM to MAM, Milan, 3 February 1770; L78, MBA159.

39 WAM to NM, Milan, 3 March 1770; L82a, MBA164.

40 LM to MAM, Milan, 3 February 1770; L78, MBA159.

41 Burney, *Present State*, p. 76.

42 LM to MAM, Milan, 10 February 1770; L79, MBA160.

43 LM to MAM, Milan, 27 February 1770; L81, MBA162.

44 WAM to NM, Milan, 27 February 1770; L81a, MBA162.

45 WAM to NM, Milan, 3 March 1770; L82a, MBA164.

46 LM to MAM, Milan, 3 March 1770; L82, MBA164.

47 LM to MAM, Milan, 17 February 1770; L80, MBA161.

48 LM to MAM, Milan, 10 February 1771; L79, MBA160.

49 LM to MAM, Milan, 27 February 1770; L81, MBA162.

50 LM to MAM, Milan, 17 February 1770; L80, MBA161.

51 LM to MAM, Milan, 13 March 1770; L83, MBA165.

52 Ibid.

53 LM to MAM, Bologna, 24 March 1770; L84, MBA168.

54 WAM to NM, Rome, 21 April 1770; L88a, MBA177.

CHAPTER 3

1 Medici and Hughes, *Mozart Pilgrimage*, p. 78.

2 WAM to NM, Bologna, 24 March 1770; L84a, MBA168.

3 LM to MAM, Bologna, 24 March 1770; L84, MBA170.

4 Ibid.

5 Deutsch, p. 110.

6 LM to MAM, Bologna, 27 March 1770; L85, MBA171.

7   WAM to NM, Milan, 26 January 1770; L77a, MBA158.

8   LM to MAM, Bologna, 27 March 1770; L85, MBA171.

9   LM to MAM, Verona, 7 January 1770, MBA152 (not in *Letters*).

10   Burney, *Present State*, p. 146.

11   LM to MAM, Bologna, 27 March 1770; L85, MBA171.

12   LM to MAM, Verona, 7 January 1770, MBA152 (not in *Letters*).

13   Ibid.

14   Deutsch, p. 114.

15   LM to MAM, Bologna, 27 March 1770; L85, MBA171.

16   Hester Piozzi, *Observations and reflections made in the course of
     a journey through France, Italy and Germany, 1785*, ed. Herbert
     Barrows, Ann Arbor, 1967.

17   LM to MAM, Florence, 3 April 1770; L86, MBA173.

18   Burney, *Present State*, p. 167.

19   Goethe, p. 116.

20   LM to MAM, Florence, 3 April 1770; L86, MBA173.

21   Ibid.

22   LM to Hagenauer, Ludwigsburg, 11 July 1763; L12, MBA53.

23   Burney, *Present State*, p. 188.

24   Burney, *Present State*, p. 184.

25   LM to MAM, Rome, 21 April 1770; L88, MBA177.

26   LM to MAM, Florence, 3 April 1770; L86, MBA173.

27   LM to MAM, Rome, 14 April 1770; L87, MBA176.

28   Burney, *Present State*, p. 199.

29   LM to MAM, Rome, 14 April 1770; L87, MBA176.

30   Deutsch, p. 459.

31   LM to MAM, Naples, 19 May 1770; L92, MBA184.

32   LM to MAM, Rome, 14 April 1770; L87, MBA176.

33   Ibid.

34   Ibid.

35   WAM to MAM and NM, Rome, 14 April 1770; L87a, MBA176.

36   LM to MAM, Naples, 24 May 1770; MBA188; not in *Letters*.

37   WAM to MAM and NM, Rome, 14 April 1770; L87a, MBA176.

38   LM to MAM, Rome, 14 April 1770; L87, MBA176.

39   LM and WAM travel notes; MBA183.

40   LM to MAM, Rome, 28 April 1770; L90, MBA181.

41   Deutsch, p. 117.

42   Deutsch, p. 118.

43   WAM to NM, Rome, 21 April 1770; L88a, MBA177.

44   Ibid.

45   WM to NM, Rome, 25 April 1770; L89, MBA179.

46   LM to Hagenauer, London, 25 April 1764; L26, MBA86.

47   LM to MAM, Naples, 19 May 1770; L92, MBA184.

48   LM to MAM, Rome, 21 April 1770; L88, MBA177.

49   LM to MAM, Rome, 2 May 1770; L91, MBA182.

50   LM to MAM, Rome, 28 April 1770; L90, MBA181.

51   Burney, *Present State*, p. 238.

52   Burney, *Present State*, p. 239.

53   LM to MAM, Naples, 19 May 1770; L92, MBA184.

54   Burney, *Present State*, p. 240.

55   Deutsch, p. 122.

56   LM to MAM, Naples, 22 May 1770; L93, MBA185.

57   LM to MAM, Naples 26 May 1770; L94, MBA186.

58   LM to MAM, Naples, 5 June 1770; L96, MBA189.

59   LM to MAM, Naples, 19 May 1770; L92, MBA184.

60   LM to MAM, Naples, 5 June 1770; L96, MBA189.

61   WAM to NM, Naples, 19 May 1770; L92a, MBA184.

62   LM to Hagenauer, Ludwigsburg, 11 July 1763; L12, MBA53.

63   WAM to NM, Naples, 29 May 1770; L95a, MBA188.

64   WAM to NM, Naples, 6 June 1770; L96a, MBA189.

65   Burney, *General History*, Vol. IV, p. 479.

66   WAM to NM, Naples, 19 May 1770; L92a, MBA184.

67   LM to MAM, Naples, 22 May 1770; L93, MBA185.

68   LM to MAM, Rome, 30 June 1770; L100, MBA194.

69   LM to MAM, Naples, 5 June 1770; L96, MBA189.

70   LM to MAM, Naples, 22 May 1770; L93, MBA185.

71   LM to MAM, Naples, 16 June 1770; L98, MBA191.

72   LM to MAM, Naples 9 June 1770; L97, MBA190.

73   LM to MAM, Naples, 16 June 1770; L98, MBA191.

74   WAM to NM, Naples, 16 June 1770; L98a, MBA191.

CHAPTER 4

1   LM to MAM, Rome, 27 June 1770; L99, MBA193.

2   LM to MAM, Rome, 30 June 1770; L100, MBA194.

3   Deutsch, p. 123.

4   LM to MAM, Rome, 4 July 1770; L101, MBA195.

5   LM to MAM, Rome, 7 July 1770; L102, MBA197.

6   WAM to NM, Rome, 7 July 1770; L102a, MBA197.

7   LM to MAM, Rome, 30 June 1770; L100, MBA193.

8   LM to MAM, Bologna, 21 July 1770; MBA 199, this section not in *Letters*.

9   Ibid.

10 LM to MAM, Bologna, 28 July 1770; L105, MBA200.

11 LM to MAM, outside Bologna, 11 August 1770; L107, MBA203.

12 LM to MAM, Bologna, 21 July 1770; MBA 199, this section not in *Letters*.

13 WAM to NM, Bologna, 4 August 1770; L106a, MBA202.

14 Ibid.

15 LM to MAM, Bologna, 28 July 1770; L105, MBA200.

16 LM to MAM, Bologna, 4 August 1770; L106, MBA202.

17 LM to MAM, outside Bologna, 11 August 1770; L107, MBA203.

18 LM to MAM, Bologna, 1 September 1770; L110, MBA206.

19 LM to MAM, outside Bologna, 11 August 1770; L107, MBA203.

20 Ibid.

21 LM to MAM, Bologna, 25 August 1770; L109, MBA205.

22 Ibid.

23 WAM to NM, Bologna, 29 September 1770; L115a, MBA211.

24 Burney, *Present State*, p. 162.

25 Ibid.

26 WAM to NM, Bologna, 6 October 1770; L116a, MBA213.

27 LM to MAM, Bologna, 6 October 1770; L116, MBA213.

28 Ibid.

29 LM to MAM, Milan, 20 October 1770; L117, MBA214.

30 Deutsch, p. 126.

31 LM to MAM, Milan, 20 October 1770; L117, MBA214.

32 Deutsch, p. 127.

33   LM to MAM, Milan, 20 October 1770; L117, MBA214.

34   LM to MAM, Milan, 27 October 1770; L118, MBA216.

35   WAM to NM, Milan, 27 October 1770; L118a, MBA216.

36   LM to MAM, Bologna, 24 March 1770; L84, MBA170.

37   WAM to MAM, Milan, 20 October 1770; L117a, MBA214.

38   LM to MAM, Milan, 10 November 1770; L120, MBA218.

39   WAM to MAM, Milan, 20 October 1770; L117a, MBA214.

40   WAM to NM, Milan, 3 November 1770; L119a, MBA217.

41   LM to MAM, Milan, 3 November 1770; L119, MBA217.

42   LM to MAM, Milan, 10 November 1770; L120, MBA218.

43   LM to MAM, Milan, 17 November 1770; L121, MBA219.

44   LM to MAM, Bologna, 28 July 1770; L105, MBA200.

45   LM to Padre Martini, Milan, 2 January 1771; L128, MBA226.

46   LM to MAM, Milan, 15 December 1770; L125, MBA223.

47   LM to MAM, Milan, 17 November 1770; L121, MBA219.

48   LM to MAM, Milan, 1 December 1770; L123, MBA221.

49   LM to MAM, Milan, 15 December 1770; L125, MBA223.

50   LM to MAM, Milan, 22 December 1770; L126, MBA224.

51   Ibid.

52   LM to MAM, Milan, 29 December 1770; L127, MBA225.

53   LM to MAM, Milan, 15 December 1770; L125, MBA223.

54   LM to MAM, Milan, 29 December 1770; L127, MBA225.

55   LM to MAM, Milan, 22 December 1770; L126, MBA224.

56   LM to MAM, Milan, 29 December 1770; L127, MBA225.

57   LM to MAM, Milan, 5 January 1771; L129, MBA227.

58   Ibid.

59   Ibid.

60   Deutsch, p. 130.

61   WAM to NM, Milan, 12 January 1771; L130a, MBA228.

62   LM to MAM, Milan, 27 October 1770; L118, MBA216.

63   Burney, *Present State*, p. 63.

64   Burney, *Present State*, p. 57.

65   LM to MAM, Milan, 2 February 1771; L131, MBA230.

66   Burney, *Present State*, p. 87.

67   WAM to J. N. Hagenauer, Venice, 13 February 1771; L132b, MBA231.

68   LM to MAM, Venice, 20 February 1771; L133, MBA232.

69 LM to MAM, Venice, 13 February 1771; L132, MBA231.
70 LM to MAM, Venice, 1 March 1771; L134, MBA233.
71 LM to MAM, Venice, 6 March 1771; L135, MBA234.
72 LM to MAM, Venice, 20 February 1771; L133, MBA232.
73 Deutsch, p. 132.
74 LM to MAM, Vicenza, 14 March 1771; L136, MBA236.
75 LM to MAM, Venice, 20 February 1771; L133, MBA232.
76 WAM to NM, Venice, 20 February 1771; L133a, MBA232.
77 WAM to J. N. Hagenauer, Venice, 13 February 1771; L132b, MBA231.
78 LM to MAM, Vicenza, 14 March 1771; L136, MBA236.
79 Ibid.
80 Deutsch, p. 134.

CHAPTER 5

1 LM to MAM, Venice, 20 February 1771; MBA232, this section not in *Letters*.
2 LM to Count G. L. Pallavicini, Salzburg, 19 July 1771; MBA239, not in *Letters*.
3 Deutsch, p. 460.
4 LM to MAM, Milan, 31 August 1771; L141, MBA243.
5 WAM to NM, Milan, 24 August 1771; L140a, MBA242.
6 LM to MAM, Milan, 31 August 1771; L141, MBA243.
7 Ibid.
8 Nissen, p. 259.
9 WAM to NM, Milan, 31 August 1771; L141a, MBA243.
10 Burney, *General History*, Vol. IV, p. 485.
11 LM to MAM, Milan, 7 September 1771; L142, MBA244.
12 WAM to NM, Milan, 31 August 1771; L141a, MBA243.
13 LM to MAM, Milan, 13 September 1771; L143, MBA245.
14 Ibid.
15 WAM to NM, Milan, 13 September 1771; L143a, MBA245.
16 WAM to NM, Milan, 21 September 1771; L144a, MBA246.
17 LM to MAM, Milan, 21 September 1771; L144, MBA246.

NOTES

18 Ibid.
19 LM to MAM, Milan, 28 September 1771; L145, MBA247.
20 LM to MAM, Milan, 5 October 1771; L146, MBA248.
21 LM to MAM, Milan, 28 September 1771; L145, MBA247.
22 LM to MAM, Milan, 12 October 1771; L147, MBA249.
23 LM to MAM, Milan, 26 October 1771; L149, MBA251.
24 LM to MAM, Milan, 19 October 1771; L148, MBA250.
25 LM to MAM, Milan, 26 October 1771; L149, MBA251.
26 LM to MAM, Milan, 26 October 1771; MBA251, this section not
    in *Letters*.
27 WAM to NM, Milan, 21 September 1771; L144a, MBA246.
28 LM to MAM, Milan, 2 November 1771; L150, MBA254.
29 WAM to NM, Milan, 2 November 1771; L150a, MBA 254.
30 LM to MAM, Milan, 19 October 1771; L148, MBA250.
31 LM to MAM, Milan, 9 November 1771; L151, MBA255.
32 LM to MAM, Milan, 16 November 1771; L152, MBA256.
33 WAM to NM, Milan, 24 November 1771; L153a, MBA257.
34 LM to MAM, Milan, 24 November 1771; L153, MBA257.
35 LM to MAM, Milan, 30 November 1771; L154, MBA258.
36 LM to MAM, Brixen, 11 December 1771; L156, MBA260.
37 LM to MAM, Ala, 8 December 1771; L155, MBA259.
38 Deutsch, p. 138.

CHAPTER 6

1 LM to MAM, Bozen, 28 October 1772; L159, MBA264.
2 WAM to NM, Bozen, 28 October 1772; L159a, MBA264.
3 LM to MAM, Milan, 21 November 1772; MBA267, this section
   not in *Letters*.
4 WAM to MAM, Milan, 7 November 1772; L160, MBA265.
5 WAM to NM, Naples, 5 June 1770; L96a, MBA189.
6 WAM to NM, Rome, 21 April 1770; L88a, MBA177.
7 LM to MAM, Milan, 28 November 1772; L163, MBA268.
8 LM to L. Hagenauer, Vienna, 29 September 1767; L48, MBA117.
9 Burney, *General History*, Vol. II, p. 46.

10   Burney, *General History*, Vol. II, p. 54.

11   LM to MAM, Milan, 14 November 1772; L161, MBA266.

12   Ibid.

13   LM to MAM, Milan, 21 November 1772; L162, MBA267.

14   LM to MAM, Milan, 28 November 1772; L163, MBA268.

15   Ibid.

16   LM to MAM, Milan, 5 December 1772; L164, MBA269.

17   Ibid.

18   LM to MAM, Milan, 2 January 1773; L168, MBA275.

19   LM to MAM, Milan, 12 December 1772; L165, MBA270.

20   WAM to NM, Milan, 18 December 1772; L166a, MBA271.

21   LM to MAM, Milan, 26 December 1772; L167, MBA272.

22   Ibid.

23   Ibid.

24   LM to MAM, Milan, 28 November 1772; L163, MBA268.

25   LM to MAM, Milan, 2 January 1773; L168, MBA 275.

26   LM to MAM, Milan, 9 January 1773; L169, MBA277.

27   WAM to NM, Milan, 23 January 1773; L171a, MBA281.

28   WAM to NM, Milan, 7 November 1772; L160a, MBA265.

29   WAM to NM, Milan, 23 January 1773; L171a, MBA281.

30   Ibid.

31   Ibid.

32   WAM to NM, Milan, 16 January 1773; L170a, MBA279.

33   LM to MAM, Milan, 12 December 1772; L165, MBA270.

34   LM to MAM, Milan, 23 January 1773; L171, MBA281.

35   LM to MAM, Milan, 30 January 1773; L172, MBA282.

36   LM to MAM, Milan, 9 January 1773; L169, MBA277.

37   LM to MAM, Milan, 16 January 1773; L170. MBA279.

38   LM to MAM, Milan, 23 January 1773; L172, MBA282.

39   LM to MAM, Milan, 6 February 1773; L173, MBA283.

40   WAM to NM, Milan, 23 January 1773; L171a, MBA281.

41   LM to MAM, Milan, 6 February 1773; L173, MBA283.

42   LM to MAM, Milan, 30 January 1773; L172, MBA282.

43   LM to MAM, Milan, 13 February 1773; L174, MBA284.

44   LM to MAM, Milan, 27 February 1773; L176, MBA287.

45   Ibid.

CHAPTER 7

1   LM to MAM, Vienna, 12 August 1773; L178, MBA289.
2   WAM to MAM, Vienna, 8 September 1773; L184a, MBA295.
3   LM to MAM, Munich, 14 December 1774; L190, MBA301.
4   LM to MAM, Munich, 28 December 1774; L193, MBA306.
5   WAM to MAM, Munich, 14 January 1775; L197, MBA311.
6   Ibid.
7   WAM to Padre Martini, Salzburg, 4 September 1778; L205, MBA323.
8   Deutsch, p. 158.
9   LM to NM, Vienna, 21 April 1786; MBA950, not in *Letters*.
10 Deutsch, p. 164.
11 LM to MAM and WAM, Salzburg, 29 September 1777; L211, MBA337.
12 WAM to LM, Munich, 29–30 September 1777; L212a, MBA339.
13 WAM to LM, Munich, 29–30 September 1777; L212c, MBA339.
14 LM to WAM, Salzburg, 30 September 1777; L213, MBA340.
15 Ibid.
16 MAM to LM, Munich, 11 October 1777; L219a, MBA347.
17 WAM to LM, Munich, 11 October 1777; L219, MBA347.
18 WAM to LM, Munich, 2 October 1777; L214, MBA342.
19 WAM to LM, Augsburg, 16 October 1777; L224, MBA351.
20 Burney, *Present State*.
21 WAM to LM, Mannheim, 14 November 1777; L243a, MBA373.
22 LM to WAM, Salzburg, 24 November 1777; L248, MBA378.
23 MAM to LM, Mannheim, 3 January 1778; L269, MBA400.
24 WAM to LM, Mannheim, 17 January 1778; L273a, MBA405.
25 WAM to LM, Mannheim, 4 February 1778; L281, MBA416.
26 Ibid.
27 WAM to LM, Mannheim, 7 February 1778; L283a, MBA419.
28 MAM to LM, Mannheim, 5 February 1778; L281a, MBA416.
29 MAM to LM, Mannheim, 13 February 1778; L286, MBA423.
30 LM to WAM, Salzburg, 12 February 1778; L285, MBA422.
31 WAM to LM, Mannheim, 19 February 1778; L288, MBA426.
32 WAM to LM, Mannheim, 28 February 1778; L292, MBA431.

33   WAM to LM, Munich, 29 December 1778; L348, MBA513.
34   WAM to LM, Mannheim, 19 February 1778; L288, MBA426.
35   WAM to LM, Vienna, 7 May 1783; L489, MBA745.
36   Ibid.
37   LM to NM, Salzburg, 11 November 1785; L532, MBA897.
38   WAM to LM, Vienna, 7 May 1783; L489, MBA745.

Bibliography

Anderson, E. (ed.), *The Letters of Mozart and his Family*, London 1938; revised 3rd edition, S. Sadie and F. Smart, London 1985

Bauer, W. A., Deutsch, O. E. and Eibl, J. H. (eds), *Mozart: Briefe und Aufzeichnungen* (four volumes), Kassel 1962–75

Deutsch, O. E. (ed.), *Mozart. Die Documente seines Lebens*, trans. E. Blom, P. Branscome and J. Noble, *Mozart: A Documentary Biography*, London 1966

Eisen, C., *New Mozart Documents*, London 1991

Burney, Charles, *A General History of Music* (four volumes), London 1776–89; Cambridge 2010

—, *The Present State of Music in France and Italy*, London 1773; Cambridge 2014

Goethe, Johann Wolfgang von, *Italienische Reise*, 1813–1817; trans. W. H. Auden and E. Mayer, *Italian Journey*, London 1962

Angermüller, R., *I viaggi di Mozart in Italia*, Milan 2006

Barzini, L., *The Italians*, London 1964

Black, J., *The Grand Tour in the Eighteenth Century*, London 2009

Cappelletto, S., *Mozart: Scene dai viaggi in Italia*, Milan 2010

Crankshaw, E., *Maria Theresa*, London 1969

Eisen, C. and Keefe, S. (eds), *The Cambridge Mozart Companion*, Cambridge 2006

Gianturco, C., *Mozart's Early Operas*, London 1981

Medici, N. and Hughes, R., *A Mozart Pilgrimage: The Travel Diaries of Vincent and Mary Novello in the Year 1829*, London 1955

BIBLIOGRAPHY

Nissen, G., *Biographie W.A. Mozarts*, Leipzig 1828; latest publication with foreword by R. Angermüller, Hildesheim, 1991

Sadie, S., *Mozart, the Early Years 1756–1781*, Oxford 2006

— and Eisen, C., *The New Grove Mozart*, revised London 2001

Tyson, A., *Mozart: Studies of the Autographed Scores*, London 1987

Wheatcroft, A., *The Habsburgs*, London 1995

Wilson, P. (ed.), *A Companion to Eighteenth Century Europe*, London 2014

Index

INDEX